Understanding OSI

Dedication

This book is dedicated to my two nine-year-old twin children Sarah-Jayne and James Larmouth, in the hope that one day they will read it!

Understanding OSI

John Larmouth

INTERNATIONAL THOMSON COMPUTER PRESS
I⬤P An International Thomson Publishing Company

London • Bonn • Boston • Johannesburg • Madrid • Melbourne • Mexico City • New York • Paris
Singapore • Tokyo • Toronto • Albany, NY • Belmont, CA • Cincinnati, OH • Detroit, MI

Understanding OSI

I ⓣ P A division of International Thomson Publishing Inc.
The ITP logo is a trademark under licence

British Library Cataloguing-in-Publication Data
A catalogue record for this book is available from the British Library

Library of Congress Cataloging-in-Publication Data
A catalog record for this book is available from the Library of Congress

First printed 1996

Commissioning Editor Liz Israel Oppedijk
Editorial Assistant Nikki Vaughan
Typeset in the UK by Keyword Typesetting Services Ltd
Printed in the UK by Cambridge University Press

ISBN 1-85032-176-0

International Thomson Computer Press
Berkshire House
High Holborn
London WC1V 7AA
UK

International Thomson Computer Press
20 Park Plaza
14th Floor
Boston MA 02116
USA

http://www.thomson.com/itcp.html

Imprints of International Thomson Publishing

Contents

Preface

This text aims to provide an intelligent near-beginner (as far as OSI is concerned) with an understanding of Open Systems Interconnection (OSI). Some previous acquaintance with data communications as presented in the many textbooks on that broad subject would be useful. The book is aimed at the reader who is curious enough to ask: 'Why is it that way? What advantages does that approach give? Might there be other or better ways?'

This text is not an exposition of the technical detail of the OSI Standards. Rather it aims to explain why OSI is the shape it is, and to guide the reader in a critical examination of the OSI approach to specifying rules for computer communication (computer protocols). The text should be particularly valuable for those who are newly moving into positions where they are part of a team developing applications using OSI, either in the International Standards' work or for their own firm. The text would also be useful for those sections of undergraduate and taught masters' courses that deal with OSI, either as the main text or as follow-on reading.

Much of the material of necessity represents personal perceptions and reasoning, as the real reasons for approaches and choices are rarely presented in International Standards or CCITT/ITU-T Recommendations (the primary definitive documents on OSI). The main purpose of ISO Standards and CCITT/ITU-T Recommendations is to present clearly the protocol to be implemented, not to explain the reasons for the choices. Frequently such reasons are buried in old working documents, maybe even only in private or national papers rather than being recorded in official international documents. In some cases reasons are merely in the heads of early workers, and are perhaps not even well articulated. It can also happen that earlier non-OSI protocols provided the basis for the OSI work, and reasons and rationale at the OSI level are simply 'because that is the way it was done in xyz', and the search for real reasons has to go back a level. None the less, I have been active in both progressing the OSI work and in presenting it at conferences and seminars for close on two decades, and the presentation in this text is believed to be a fair one.

The text commences with discussion of the organizations involved in OSI, and with the OSI architecture – the seven-layer model and related concepts, then goes on to consider each of the layers in turn (some in more detail than others), and ends with a single chapter discussing the architecturally interesting features of a necessarily limited sample of application layer protocols.

The text does not attempt to give a complete treatment of OSI application layer standards: the choice of subjects to discuss has been made on the basis of whether the application concerned raises interesting or difficult new concepts, or helps to illustrate features discussed earlier in the text. In other words, the selection of applications treated is based on whether a presentation of a particular application is relevant to a general understanding of OSI and how to produce other OSI applications, rather than on whether the application is considered one of the more important in the market-place.

Most people reading this text will probably have at least heard of X.25, X.400, X.500 and the seven-layer model. This is not assumed in the main exposition, but examples and illustrations occur from time to time that will be less meaning-ful without some background knowledge of these areas. Such examples and illustrations can be skipped without much loss.

J Larmouth

1
Organizational matters

1.1 The subject

OSI (Open Systems Interconnection) represents the totality of protocol definitions and associated additional texts which provide international standardization
of many aspects of computer-to-computer communication. In theory it extends
from the lowest level of signalling techniques to high-level interactions in
support of specific applications.

The work on OSI was initiated in the late 1970s, and came to a level of maturity
in the late 1980s and early 1990s. At the time of writing this text, there are many
OSI standards in place, and implementations of the more popular standards
are available as commercial products. Wide-scale purchase and use of a wide
range of OSI products is still however not yet a reality, with the free Internet
(TCP/IP-based) software still having the greater market share.

It is important to recognize that the main focus of the early OSI work was
largely on autonomous computer systems, performing general-purpose stand-
alone computing functions, and occasionally using communications with
other systems to support some application task. In the 1990s, however, we
increasingly see a client–server approach to computing, with highly specialized
systems performing one or a small number of functions which could not be
performed without the use of communications. Some of the OSI products,
especially the X.400 electronic mail relay systems and the X.500 Directory
systems, will also be specialized server systems. Even in these cases, however,
the host computer systems would normally run as stand-alone systems, with
the communications function used solely to support the X.400 or X.500 activity
that the product implements.

A new area of international standardization of computer communication was
established in the late 1980s and began to show some of its initial shape in the
early 1990s. This is standardization of Open Distributed Processing (ODP).
The ODP work has a slightly different emphasis from the OSI work, and is
sometimes (perhaps incorrectly, perhaps not) seen to be either an advance on
OSI or in competition with OSI. It is beyond the scope of this text to give a
detailed treatment of ODP and of its relationship to OSI. All that can be done
here is to warn the reader to 'Watch this space'. It is at least possible that the
ODP work will merely build on OSI, with new Application Layer protocols for
distributed processing (whatever that comes to mean) using the lower layers of
OSI in the normal way. It is also possible that ODP will produce different
perhaps, better, ways of doing what has already been standardized in OSI.
There is no detailed treatment of ODP in this text, the focus of which is OSI,
but there is a further brief mention in Chapter 11.

This chapter would not be complete without some discussion of the authoritative 'root' document which provides a pointer to all the standards that make up OSI. Such a document does not exist! There is a broad consensus on what standards can sensibly be regarded as in line with the OSI work and effectively part of OSI, but nowhere is there even a definition of the properties of such a standard, still less a definitive index. One could almost argue that OSI is in the eye of the beholder, and has no independent existence!

1.2   The actors

1.2.1   Collaboration

The work on OSI progressed, largely independently, in both CCITT and ISO (see following sections on CCITT and ISO) in the late 1970s and early 1980s. This came to a head in late 1983 when there existed two very large documents, one an ISO working draft and one a CCITT working draft, both called roughly *The Basic Reference Model for Open Systems Interconnection*, and both describing a seven-layer 'architecture' (the 7-layer model). But ... they were completely different texts. The technical similarities (once differences of wording and style were eliminated) were greater than the technical differences, but important differences did exist.

In 1983, CCITT said to ISO: 'The world does not need two different Reference Models for OSI. We will tear up the CCITT draft and adopt the ISO text. But, please, ISO, would you make one or two minor technical changes to your text to accommodate the needs of CCITT.' And that is how the world got the CCITT Reference Model for Open Systems Interconnection!

The watershed year was 1984, and from that point on collaboration between ISO and CCITT on OSI, and latterly on ODP, has become increasingly strong, reaching the point in the early 1990s where almost all international meetings on collaborative work are at least formally, and often in practice, joint meetings of the two organizations, with a single text being progressed by a single editor, and in due course a single document being published under the logos of the two organizations. At the time of writing this text (1995), we have yet to see the first joint publication, the tradition in the 1980s being separately published texts, always with separate editorial style, often separately typeset and hence with different errors introduced, and sometimes with actual technical differences, usually identified in an annex, particularly in relation to conformance statements.

The situation was aggravated by different balloting processes in the two organizations, and by CCITT's tradition of publishing its Recommendations at the end of four-year study periods, and generally at no other time, as opposed to the ISO approach of publishing when and only when the work was considered to be complete. This led in the early 1980s to the publication of CCITT Recommendations that were often immature, and underwent significant corrections and extensions in the next study period, against a very long gestation period for ISO Standards, but with a somewhat better quality in the initial publication. The charge was made: 'Anything ISO can do, CCITT can do quicker: Anything CCITT can do, ISO can do slower but better: CCITT does the work, ISO rubber stamps.' With the increasing collaboration in the late 1980s and the early 1990s, and finally with the publication of joint texts, these charges are likely to be things of the past, with the strengths of both organizations being brought into play.

1.2.2   The club of the PTTs

CCITT is The International Telegraph and Telephone Consultative Committee (CCITT comes from the spelling of the title in French). In crude terms, it was, in the 1980s and early 1990s, the club of the providers of the public telephone and telegraph systems of the world, including both the PTTs, which are arms of government providing postal and telephone services, and the RPOAs (Registered Private Operating Authorities) – private organizations such as Bell Telephone or AT&T, providing telephone services in countries allowing private operators in this area. It is entirely due to the activities of CCITT in agreeing technical standards that world-wide telephone and facsimile communication has become a reality.

The name CCITT ceased to exist at the end of 1992, with a major reorganization of the ITU, but this book talks predominantly about CCITT, for that was the name used in the formative years of OSI.

Formally, CCITT was a sister organization to the CCIR (The International Radio Consultative Committee) which allocated radio frequencies, both being part of the International Telecommunications Union (ITU), which is itself an agency of the United Nations (UN).

A major reorganization of ITU at the end of 1992 replaced CCITT and CCIR with new organizational structures. The corresponding organization to CCITT was called The Telecommunications Standardization Sector of the ITU. This was initially abbreviated for a short time to ITU-TS, but shortly after the current abbreviation of ITU-T was adopted. There is also a Radiocommunication Sector (ITU-R) and a Telecommunication Development Sector (ITU-D), but these are not treated further in this book.

CCITT, and its successor ITU-T, only claimed to provide Recommendations, while ISO produces International Standards. However, because CCITT is within the UN structure, CCITT Recommendations were binding on members of the UN wishing to provide international public services in areas covered by CCITT Recommendations. This in some ways made CCITT Recommendations more powerful than ISO Standards, whose take-up is entirely voluntary.

The major subdivision of CCITT was into study groups identified by roman numerals (Study Group VII is one of the more important for OSI work). (ITU-T has similar divisions, but arabic numerals are now used, so Study Group VII has become Study Group 7.) The study groups tend to have a relatively permanent existence, while lower-level structures (rapporteur groups) are more transient. It is the study group that forms the basis for most international meetings, which are almost all held at the headquarters of CCITT/ITU-T in Geneva, with all the rapporteur groups (and their subdivisions) of the study group meeting together over a period of two to three weeks.

In the past (up to the 1988 Blue Books – the last of the series), CCITT worked to a strict four-year schedule (in particular, 1976 to 1980, 1980 to 1984, and finally 1984 to 1988). At the start of these four-year study periods a set of Questions would be formulated and agreed by a CCITT plenary meeting. These questions were assigned to the study groups, and formed the programme of work for each group in the coming study period. Roughly speaking, each question would give rise to a new or amended Recommendation on completion of the four-year study period. Following the end of the study period, the entire set of CCITT Recommendations, whether changed or not, was republished as a set of volumes in bindings whose colour changed with each study period. Thus people spoke of 'the Yellow Books', which were published after the 1980 plenary which approved the 1980 Recommendations, 'the Yellow Book Era' (1980 to 1984), 'the Red Books' published after the 1984 plenary, and finally 'the Blue Books' published after the 1988 plenary, the last of the set. From 1990 onwards, CCITT/ITU-T will publish Recommendations only when necessary. Complete publication every four years has ceased.

Collectors take note – nostalgia is in order! If you have a complete set of Blue Books in mint condition, keep them!

The above approach had a lot of advantages in controlling and progressing the work, but had significant disadvantages too, not least the costs of republishing every four years. It also gave rise to what was often rudely termed 'the CCITT hibernation period' – there was an approximately 12–15-month period at the study period boundaries when it was almost impossible to progress any technical work within CCITT. This gave rise to a lot of problems in collaborative work with ISO.

There were procedures in CCITT for the appointment of interim rapporteurs to try to progress work across the hibernation period, and towards the end of the 1980s these became increasingly effective. There were also accelerated procedures to permit the publication of new Recommendations at the two-year midpoint in a study period for particularly important work. These procedures were most notably used for the first version of X.25 in 1978, and for the EDI (Electronic Data Interchange) extensions to X.400 in 1990.

The precise working of ITU-T during the 1990s, particularly in the areas of joint work with ISO, remains to be seen at the time of writing this text, but the expectation is of joint work progressing smoothly without regard to study period boundaries, and with a single joint publication at the end of the work.

This discussion of CCITT/ITU-T would not be complete without some mention of the critical differences of emphasis between CCITT and ISO in the 1980s (there is more discussion of ISO in section 1.2.3), as an understanding of these differences of emphasis is important to an understanding of some of the technical differences appearing between CCITT Recommendations and ISO Standards.

CCITT was, as mentioned earlier, largely the 'club' of the PTTs and the RPOAs. One of the unwritten agenda items is to produce Recommendations that will maximize the effectiveness and profitability of these organizations. ISO, by contrast, is much more concerned with the development of international standards for use by a wide variety of public and private organizations, and while the computer manufacturers provide significant input into the work of ISO, there is formally only a very tenuous link between these corporations and the standards-making bodies. Notwithstanding that, one can occasionally (but only occasionally) see the international standards process dominated by and/or unduly influenced by a large multinational computer vendor.

Examples showing the effect of these differences of emphasis between ISO and CCITT can be seen in the early versions of the Network Service specifications, where the CCITT Recommendation text placed more emphasis on X.25 compatibility than the ISO text. Again, for X.400, the CCITT text mandated the use of so-called Transport Class 0, which is effectively a synonym for X.25, while the ISO text allows much more flexibility on the underlying carrier. Yet another example is in the body of X.400, where the CCITT text and diagram envisaged electronic mail crossing international boundaries only through relays provided by PTTs or RPOAs (Figure 1.1), while the corresponding text and diagram in the ISO version recognize direct communication between private systems in different countries (Figure 1.2).

CCITT workers would not necessarily deny that such more general communications will occur – they would merely assert that CCITT Recommendations

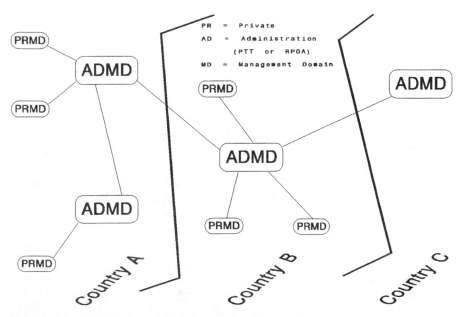

Figure 1.1 *CCITT view of X.400 transfers. PR = Private, AD = Administration (PTT or RPOA), MD = Management domain.*

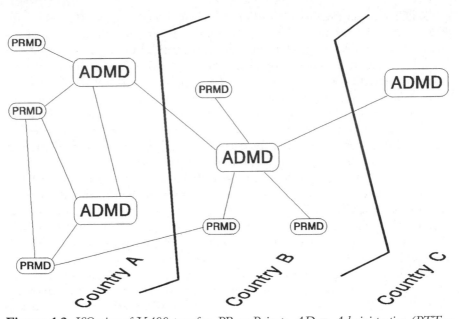

Figure 1.2 *ISO view of X.400 transfers. PR = Private, AD = Administration (PTT or RPOA), MD = Management domain.*

were intended for the use of PTTs and RPOAs, and hence that description of such communications has no place in a CCITT Recommendation!

1.2.3   The club of computer vendors

The International Organization for Standardization, always abbreviated to ISO, is a loose federation of standards institutes (national bodies) from countries around the world, including the USSR, China, and so on. It has a long (but, as far as I can discover, undocumented) history going back into the nineteenth century. Most of the Standards Institutes have some support from or links with their corresponding governments, but are generally largely autonomous bodies. Examples include BSI (British Standards Institute), AFNOR (Association Française de Normalisation), DIN (Deutsches Institut für Normung), ANSI (American National Standards Institute), JISC (Japanese Industrial Standards Committee), and NNI (Nederlands Normalisatie-Instituut).

The major subdivision of ISO (Figure 1.3) is into Technical Committees (TCs), each covering a major division of standardization. The division into TCs is relatively stable; there were 172 Technical Committees in 1991. TCs of interest for OSI include TC68 (banking and related financial services), TC154 (documents and data elements in administration, commerce and industry), TC184 (industrial automation systems and integration), but most particularly TC97 (information technology), responsible for all computer-related standardization, and the parent of OSI. Despite their name, Technical Committees do very little

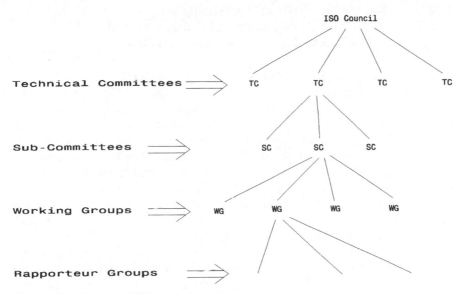

Figure 1.3 *Structure of ISO committees.*

technical work. They are largely administrative, determining the programme of work and the structure of Sub-Committees (SCs) within the TC.

While SCs do break down into working groups and below that into rapporteur Groups, it is the Sub-Committee that is the main unit for ISO meetings – all parts of the Sub-Committee meeting in roughly the same geographical location over a period of two to three weeks. The international meetings of the main OSI-related SCs are now (1990s) annual, and typically rotate round locations in North America, Europe and the Pacific Basin on a three-yearly cycle. The SC structure within TC97 has undergone a number of quite radical changes since TC97 was first established, and can be expected to undergo further changes in the future.

In the mid-1980s, ISO recognized that the work of TC97 overlapped the remit of the International Electrotechnical Commission (IEC). Despite the theoretical overlap, in practice all the work on computer standards had been done in ISO, and there was no overlap of real technical work. None the less, in the mid-1980s, TC97 was renamed Joint Technical Committee 1 (JTC1), and became a Technical Committee reporting to both IEC and ISO. (There is still no JTC2.) This change was not noticed at the grass roots. The Sub-Committee structure of TC97 was copied unchanged to JTC1, the secretariat and officers were unchanged, and the work proceeded without a hiccough. The only difference was that OSI Standards started to be published with both the ISO logo and the IEC logo on the front cover. (Soon – mid-1990s – as discussed earlier, these logos will be joined by the ITU-T logo.)

TC97, in the late 1970s, had three main Sub-Committees which were extremely active in computer standardization, and still existed in the 1990s as SCs within JTC1. These were:

SC2 Responsible for character set standards
SC5 Responsible for programming language standards
SC6 Responsible for low-level data communication standards.

It was in discussions in SC6 and TC97 itself that OSI was born, with the establishment in the late 1970s of a new SC, SC16, responsible for progressing the OSI concept. SC16 developed the Reference Model for OSI, but responsibility for the production of standards in the bottom three layers of that model was given to SC6. Despite some early tensions, there was a lot of cross-membership between SC6 and SC16, and generally a very fruitful and close collaboration.

In the mid-1980s, TC97 reorganized its Sub-Committees. In particular, responsibility for the fourth layer of OSI, the so-called Transport Layer, was passed from SC16 to SC6, and a significant part of the SC5 work (database and graphics languages) was removed and added to the remaining work of SC16, which was disbanded, to produce work for a new SC21. Despite the removal of encryption responsibility to SC20, and the later removal of the graphics work to SC24, SC21 remains one of the largest SCs in the whole of ISO, making the hosting of meetings with many hundreds of attendees a major event requiring a complete small holiday resort, a university campus, or some similar facility. Its future into the late 1990s is again the subject of discussion, and further reorganizations of the work by JTC1 are likely.

1.3 Document names and progression

Understanding OSI, and particularly requesting documents and tracking their status requires some understanding of the terminology used to describe documents, and of the procedure for progressing drafts towards International Standard (IS) status (ISO/IEC) or Recommendation status (CCITT/ITU-T).

Neither ISO nor ITU/T yet make documents available electronically (compare the widespread and easy availability of the RFC – Request For Comment – documents of the USA DARPA Internet – the TCP/IP community, discussed briefly at the end of Chapter 2). This situation is expected to change in the late 1990s, with a move by ISO towards electronic document distribution, but the precise form of this is still uncertain at the time of writing (1995).

Generally, obtaining published CCITT/ITU-T Recommendations or ISO Standards, which are often reprinted as identical text by national bodies and sold at somewhat lesser prices than those of ISO itself, is easily achieved by paying money to buy the published version.

Getting earlier drafts in advance of an agreed Standard or Recommendation is more difficult. ISO national bodies normally make publicly available (at a price, and copyrighted) the text of Draft International Standards (DIS text), and invite comments from the public. Prior to this, documents are formally only available for private circulation to those contributing to the work, but are not copyrighted. There is, however, at least one commercial organization, operating from the USA but with a strong European presence, that will provide copies of almost all CCITT/ITU-T and ISO documents prior to the copyrighting stage (and, with permission from ISO and CCITT/ITU-T, sometimes after) at little more than photocopying and distribution costs. For many, however, the simplest way to track the work is to attend at least national meetings of the relevant ISO feeder committees, membership of which in most countries is open to anyone showing interest in the work.

In the case of CCITT, the document procedures were relatively informal, with any attendee at a meeting being entitled to submit an input paper, and with papers usually containing the name of the author. Drafts of Recommendations had no official status until finally approved for publication as Recommendations, first by the study group, and then by a full CCITT plenary (at the end of the study period in the past). Once approved by the CCITT plenary, the documents input to that plenary were often widely but unofficially circulated as 'white documents' prior to the publication of the 'coloured books', The editorial process often gave rise, however, to minor differences between the whites and the official coloured book version.

In the case of ISO/IEC, the procedures are somewhat more formalized and drawn out. Different Technical Committees in ISO have different rules on the categorization of documents, and on the timing of document submission and circulation, JTC1 being perhaps more formal than most ISO TCs. The following discussions relate specifically to JTC1, but variants on the theme apply to all ISO work.

Input documents to meetings can only be submitted by ISO national Bodies. These documents may, however, have a variety of semi-formally-defined statuses, the most used ones being:

- National body position: usually a short document, commenting on the direction standardization should take, or on a major controversial technical point.
- National body contribution: usually a fairly substantial technical document which has been discussed and worked on over about a six-month period at meetings within the national body.
- Expert contribution: again usually a substantial technical contribution, but often in a more speculative area, or where time has not permitted a lot of discussion within the national body.

Even the latter category usually bears only the identification of the national body concerned, not of the 'expert' who authored it. It should usually have been vetted by other experts in the national body at least sufficiently to be sure that it does not contradict any national body position.

The ISO equivalent of a CCITT/ITU-T question is a New Work Item Proposal (NWI). During the 1980s, the NWI procedures evolved into quite formal mechanisms so that today an NWI involves a substantial amount of work and discussion in its preparation, and is often accompanied by a substantial technical document to form an initial base document for the work. The TC secretariat, which is provided by one of the national bodies – ANSI in the case of JTC1, circulates by post to all national bodies a hard copy of an NWI for a letter ballot. The letter ballot was at the heart of ISO procedures in the 1970s, 1980s and into the 1990s, and while it was sometimes replaced by votes at meetings, this has become increasingly uncommon for major document progression. In the case of an NWI proposal, there is a three-month ballot period in which national bodies are asked to address and answer a number of questions, the most important being:

- Is the NWI well defined?
- Does the national body support the NWI?
- Will the national body contribute to the work if the NWI is added to the programme of work of the TC?

Generally, approval of a New Work Item and its allocation to a Sub-Committee to progress (almost always the SC proposing it) is critically dependent on whether at least five national bodies answer 'Yes' to the last of these questions.

Once approved, the work continues through the cycle of input to international meetings, the production of output documents, which usually include a revised base document, for consideration by national bodies, and then input to the next international meeting, and so on (Figure 1.4). Eventually there is a

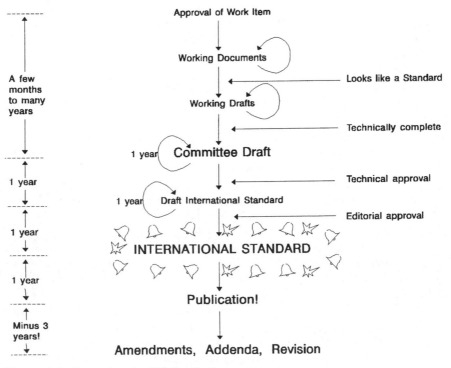

Figure 1.4 *Progression of an ISO Standard.*

consensus that the work is now complete, and a good document is available. In the case of collaborative work with CCITT in the past, this might be quite close to the final text of a Recommendation. At this stage the document is registered by the ISO Central Secretariat as what used to be called a Draft Proposal (DP), but which is now called a Committee Draft (CD). At this time it receives a number which, if it is eventually approved as an IS, is the number of the International Standard. (The number sequence at the end of the 1980s was around the 10 000 mark.) Registration as a CD, which is distinct from the ballot to approve or disapprove of the CD, is normally based on a simple vote of the national bodies represented at an international meeting. In the early 1980s in SC16 this was a very traumatic time, with frequent surprises and upsets. Today, the work is generally time-tabled, and progression to CD registration is generally expected at a particular meeting, and moves smoothly. Once registered as a CD, there is another formal letter ballot in which national bodies are asked if they approve or disapprove (in which case comments are required saying why) of the CD. Usually the volume of comments from each of the national bodies active in the work exceeds the size of the base document, and this is where the fun starts!

The ISO process is a **consensus** process. And ISO has a definition of 'consensus', Consensus has been achieved when 'none of the major participants is extremely unhappy with the outcome.' What this means in practice is that every effort is made to resolve No votes, produced by the letter ballot, by changing the text. There is a phrase engraved on the heart of every person attending an ISO meeting: 'The aim is to produce Standards. If you can't agree, make it optional, or better still, another Standard!' This can easily be justified, for after all: 'If one Standard is good, many Standards must surely be better!' A quotation from the *Encyclopedia Galactica – 2008* version, which is shown in Figure 1.5, redresses the balance.

Humour is only useful if it contains a grain of truth. ISO Standards and CCITT/ITU-T Recommendations often have multiple options and ways of doing things that result from failure to agree on one single standard way. This is both a strength and a weakness of the process. It has, however, given rise to work on Functional Profiles within the USA, Europe and the Pacific Basin, latterly leading to International Standardized Profiles produced by ISO. These Functional Profiles attempt to resolve options which were left in the base standards, often by defining a number of Functional Profiles each of which groups options into what are thought to be useful groupings for the market-place. The success or otherwise of this approach cannot yet (mid-1990s) be determined, as many profiles today do little more than record the minimum subset of the published base Standard, or provide guidance on implementation parameters. The reader should note also that there are documents recording Implementor's Agreements and there are documents recording Functional Profiles, sometimes from the same source. These have a somewhat different emphasis, but are quite similar in what they are doing, and are often confused.

Returning to the progression of documents: the early work in ISO is usually dominated by a **rapporteur** who chairs the meetings and attempts to ensure

In the beginning there was CHAOS,

Then the greater gods descended and begat Standards.

And each begat a new Standard,

And Man worshipped the Standards and said,

"Give us more, give us more".

So the Gods begat more Standards, and more, and more:

And lo, there was CHAOS once more.

Encyclopedia Galactica, AD 20085

Figure 1.5 *Encyclopedia Galactica, AD 20085, p. 10945*

that the work progresses. Identify the rapporteur, and you can often, but not always, identify the source of the key ideas, or of the integration of ideas. The rapporteur is assisted by an **editor** who, in the early work, is little more than an unpaid secretary who takes notes of decisions and produces new base documents. It is following registration as a CD, however, that the role of the editor becomes the dominant one, and the rapporteur has little formal responsibility and often moves on to other work. Following the CD letter ballot, an **editing meeting** is called, sometimes end-on to a main SC meeting, sometimes totally separate in time. This is chaired by the editor, who is responsible for 'resolving No votes,' gaining consensus, producing a revised document, and producing a further document entitled 'Resolution of national body Comments on CD ... ballot' which describes the way in which each national body comment has been dealt with and how 'No' votes have been resolved.

Frequently the Resolution of Comments produces a sufficient volume of technical change to the CD text that there is a second CD ballot (and sometimes a third, and a fourth ...!). Given a good following wind, however, a skilled editor, and a not too controversial area (or one with a strong 'lobby' for rapid progression), it is possible, but generally still fairly unusual, for the text coming out of the first CD editing meeting to be registered as a Draft International Standard (DIS). In theory, technical issues have now all been resolved, and any future comments on the text will be concerned with clarity and editorial matters. The theory is not always the practice, however!

It is following registration as a DIS that national bodies make the document publicly available, and invite public comments. It is also at this stage that the document is translated into French (assuming, as is the case with OSI work, that the original was in English). As an aside: although common CCITT and ISO English language text, with agreed differences, was agreed for the original Reference Model, we narrowly avoided totally independent French versions:

one produced by ISO translation of the jointly agreed English, and one produced by CCITT translation of the jointly agreed English! (Maybe it is a pity this was avoided – comparison of the two translations could have produced years of fun for linguistic students!)

On the main theme, following registration as a DIS text, there is again a formal letter ballot on the text, and a DIS editing meeting, which might result in a second DIS ballot, and then, with luck, registration as an International Standard and finally publication, usually about a year later.

Most of these steps take about 12 months, so that one can often see a period of up to four or five years from the first registered CD text to a published Standard.

Given these procedures in ISO, and the somewhat simpler CCITT procedures linked to a four-year cycle (at least in the 1980s), it is hardly surprising that CCITT Recommendation text and ISO International Standard text often diverged in detail, even where there were no real technical disagreements. The text approved by CCITT and eventually published as a Recommendation has often been the text input into the DIS ballot in ISO, with later changes handled by informal Implementor's Guides, or by simply waiting until the end of the next study period to publish a revised version!

Finally, it is important to know about the procedures for extending or amending ISO Standards and CCITT Recommendations. Again, in CCITT, there were no formal procedures. Once published, a Recommendation was the authoritative text, warts and all, for that study period, and defects were corrected in the next set of Recommendations. Recently, however, Implementor's guides for major Recommendations have been regularly published to record known defects. The procedures for approving the contents of such guides are, however, relatively informal.

In the case of ISO, a published Standard is formally reviewed, and amended or withdrawn or reaffirmed, every five years, but for OSI we have seen during the 1980s a steady stream of addenda to published Standards. The procedure for addenda progression is very similar to that for a base Standard, involving the production and registration of a Proposed Draft Amendment (PDAM) text (equivalent in status to a CD), progressing in due course, following a letter ballot and editing meeting, to a Draft Amendment (DAM) (equivalent in status to a DIS), and after a further letter ballot and editing meeting to a revised or extended Standard. This process is usually used to progress new work in collaboration with CCITT/ITU-T, and it is quite common to find the first amendment nearing the PDAM stage before the base standard is a full IS!

This procedure was recognized as being somewhat cumbersome for correcting actual errors in specifications, and JTC1 has put in place Rapid Amendment Procedures which require simple agreement of the editor and an expert from each interested national body to informally agree on resolution of a defect report which then undergoes a single letter ballot, which is almost invariably approved, to become a technical corrigendum to the Standard. These procedures are intended to mend simple bugs (often in the semi-formal description of protocol exchanges using state tables – see the end of Chapter 3), not major technical defects or new work. The procedures have generated tens of (and sometimes topping one hundred) defect reports and associated technical corrigenda to most OSI Standards. Keeping track of all published defect reports and their status is a major exercise, and only implementors or those very closely involved in the work trouble to track these items.

2
The architecture

2.1 Introduction

Perhaps the best-known aspect of OSI is the **seven-layer model**, formally The
Basic Reference Model for Open Systems Interconnection. Most readers will
have at least heard of it, and can probably recite the names of the seven layers.
What is the purpose of the layer concept? Why do we call it an architecture?
Why seven layers? In this introductory discussion we will take a very broad
look, and develop more detail as we proceed.

First, why seven? Well, why not? Seven has long had magical significance.
The tradition of the seven wonders of the world, the seven labours of Hercules
(actually, it wasn't seven, but it should have been), the seven days of creation
and the seven deadly sins make seven layers for OSI almost mandatory! We
will find a more convincing reason for seven later in this chapter, but who
knows, the power of the human psyche is such that the magic of seven could
well have been the major determinant in the early work.

What is a protocol architecture? Most recent specifications of computer communications protocols (messages, their meanings, and rules for their interchange) provide the total specification for an exchange as a series of related
documents which provide support for a variety of applications when used in
varying combinations. The **architectural description** of the protocol suite
identifies the structure of the specifications that are used to define the communications, the broad functions performed by the protocol in each specification,
and the way the specifications are combined to form complete useful
applications.

2.2 Basic handling of 'holes'

The form of combination of separate specifications in OSI, and in many other
architectures, is as follows.

- The bottom-level set of messages is defined, usually involving some header
  information and some tail information, but with a hole in the middle
  which is left undefined by this level or layer.
- The next layer, which could comprise a set of different independent specifications, any one of which could be used for an actual application, defines
  the contents of the hole, usually in terms of some header information,
  another hole (to be completed by a still higher layer, and so on), and some
  trailing information.

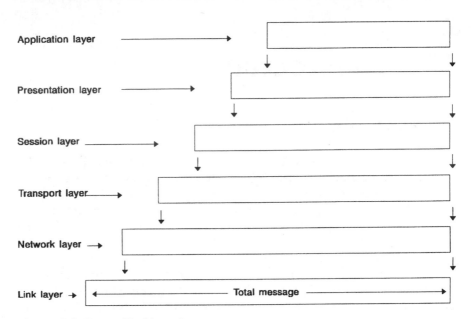

Figure 2.1 *Layered build-up of a message.*

●   Eventually we reach a specification that fills in the last hole (the top layer),
     and have our messages, given an appropriate selection of the specifications,
     completely defined.

   This approach is called **layered protocol definition** or just **layering** (Figure
2.1). Each of the layered specifications adds some value to the functionality of
the layer below or, in OSI terms, uses the services of the layer below to build
an enriched service. Layering, then, is little more than a documentation tool to
assist in the development of a complete specification. It performs two useful
functions: first, if carefully done, it permits independent and simultaneous definition of each layer, allowing a number of committees to work simultaneously
on different parts of the total task; secondly, it enables lower layer specifications
to be reused as parts of wholly different applications without having to repeat
text or reinvent functions and mechanisms.

2.3   Tying things together

An important part of understanding OSI is to understand the differing concepts
of **service standards** and **protocol standards**. OSI talks about protocol **specifications** and service **definitions**. This is a deliberate use of different terms.
'Definition' implies that we are defining terms or a notation, and this is exactly
what a service definition is. 'Specification' implies that we are giving rules that

an implementation must comply with, and this is exactly what a protocol specification is.

The problem with the above discussion on layering is that it is too simplistic. At each layer, there are typically a number of different types of message which can fill a lower layer hole, each type of message providing a 'hole' to the layer above, and each one having a different semantics and different information fields. The Service Definition Standards provide a notational means of identifying which particular hole, in which particular lower layer message, a given message fragment is carried in.

The middle layers of OSI have typically two standards associated with each layer: the first is the service definition for the layer, and the second is the protocol specification. Let us take as an illustration the Transport Layer, which lies beneath the Session Layer and above the Network Layer (Figure 2.2). (For the present, it does not matter what the layers actually do, so if you have little or no current knowledge of OSI layers, just treat these terms as the labels for three adjacent layers that could just as well have been called Jack, Jill and Fred.)

Then we have a **transport service definition** standard that specifies a notation which is used in both the transport protocol specification and the session protocol specification and serves as the glue that enables the two specifications to be combined into a single specification. Once combined, the transport service definition can be discarded. In a similar way, the network service definition notation is used in the Transport Layer to reference procedures and messages defined

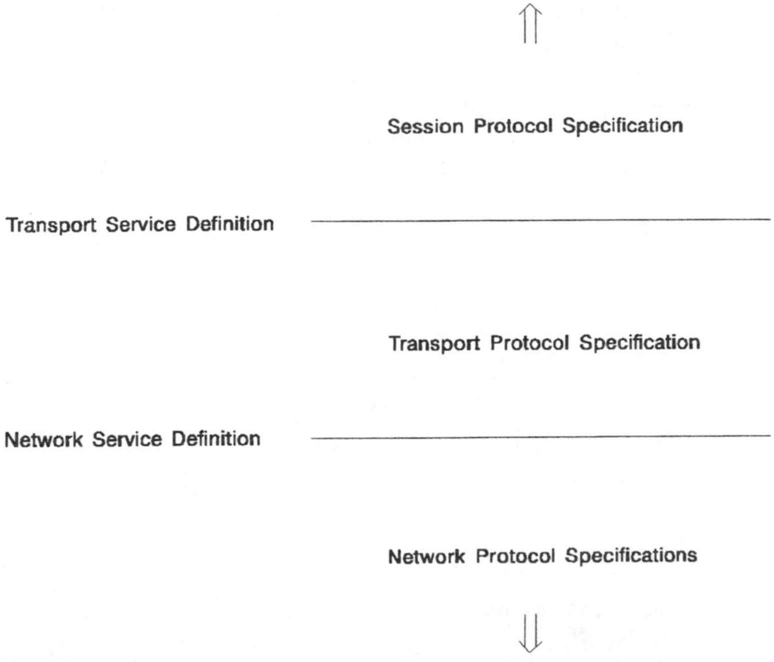

⇑

Session Protocol Specification

Transport Service Definition ————————————————————

Transport Protocol Specification

Network Service Definition ————————————————————

Network Protocol Specifications

⇓

Figure 2.2 *Service and protocol Standards.*

in the Network Layer, and the session service definition notation is used in the session protocol to provide hooks for higher layer specifications.

The form of service definition notations is formalized in OSI, although there are in practice some variations on the general theme. Whenever a message is defined by a layer with a hole in it, the service definition for that layer contains a notation for specifying the issuing of a **service request primitive** identifying the lower layer message to be sent, with parameters of the request primitive corresponding to holes in the message. When a higher layer specification wants to cause a message to be sent, it talks about 'issuing the service request primitive' to the layer below with specific values for the parameters (information to fill in the holes). In the same way, a layer will describe the effect of receiving a message as the issue of an **indication primitive** to the layer above, identifying the type of the received message and with parameters corresponding to the information actually received in the holes. A typical layer protocol has a number of different types of message which need to be visible to the layer above, each with a variety of holes. Each of these has an associated service primitive (request primitive and indication primitive) and parameters defined. It will often also have messages, typically acknowledgements or flow control messages, that aid the operation of its protocol, but have no holes, and are not visible to the layer above. These have no corresponding service primitives.

An example always helps. The Transport Layer has a message used to establish a connection. The corresponding service primitives are the **T-CONNECT request** and the **T-CONNECT indication**. The parameters of these primitives relate to addressing information, properties of the connection, and a limited amount of user data (data provided by the layer above) that can be carried in the connection establishment messages. It has another message used to pass data, and the corresponding service primitives are the **T-DATA request** and the **T-DATA indication**, with a single parameter which is user data. When an implementor reads the session protocol specification, it instructs the implementor to 'Issue a T-DATA request with ... as the parameter' (Figure 2.3). The

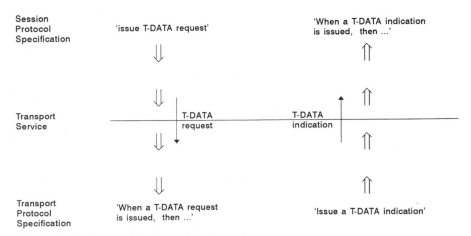

Figure 2.3 *Cross-referencing protocol procedures.*

implementor then turns to the transport protocol specification which says 'When a T-DATA request is issued, then you do ... .' Similarly, the transport protocol specification says that on receipt of certain messages (actually, parameters of network service indication primitives), 'A T-DATA indication is to be issued.' The implementor then goes to the session protocol specification which says 'When a T-DATA indication is issued, then you do ... .' Note that the implementor never needs to refer to the transport service definition. The main purpose of that standard is to ensure that the session and the transport protocol specifications, which are typically produced by different committees, are actually consistent. The main (in principle the only) interaction between the two committees is to jointly agree the service definition which links them. Traditionally in OSI, responsibility for producing the service definition standard has been given to the committee defining the protocol below that service definition, in consultation with the committee responsible for the layer above.

The above treatment has been somewhat simplistic, but should be sufficient for the reader to understand the service primitive concept, more detailed texts on service primitives, or even the actual Standards!

The definition of primitives, with their completely defined parameter types and ranges, looks rather like a computer programming language interface or procedure call definition, and this has led some people to think that the documentation structure and service definition primitives and parameters have to be reflected in implementation structure and visible interfaces and parameters in implementations. This is not so. There is strong text in every service definition saying that this has no implications for implementations. Of course, some of the reasons for modularizing a specification to permit reusability and independent work by different people on the various parts apply equally to the production of computer software. Thus in practice, particularly with prototype or early implementations where speed and ease of production and robustness are perhaps more important than efficiency, one does find software implementations with structures corresponding quite closely with the layered specification structure, and with interfaces and parameters corresponding quite closely with the layer service definitions. Such structures are, however, the implementors' choice, they are not a requirement of the OSI standards, and the match is seldom perfect. Thus it is important for the reader to recognize that the terms Network Layer, Transport Layer, Session Layer are strictly only applicable to the documentation structure of OSI. It is generally inappropriate, and can be very misleading, to talk about 'the presentation layer' as part of an implementation rather than as a grouping of standards.

2.4   The magic seven

2.4.1   From one layer to two

In the earliest days of computer communication, typically when a single link of copper wire or a radio link connected the two communicating computers, a single monolithic specification completely defined all aspects of communication in an unstructured manner. Aspects which were very application-specific, such as signalling the end of a deck of cards or pressing some specific button on one of the communicating machines, were signalled using some specific voltage or current on the wire. In other words, the low-level signalling that was used did not merely indicate zeros and ones that higher layers of specification used to carry information. Rather, the signalling system and the application were inextricably intertwined. Some of these so-called 'link' protocols lasted into the 1990s, mainly in the military communications area, but they are very inflexible because of the intermingling of application matters with details of the signalling system and hence the particular medium of communication. They should be regarded only as interesting historical relics.

   If we are trying to produce International Standards for a large and ever-increasing number of applications (*m* say) to run over a large and ever-increasing number of different types of media and signalling systems (*n* say), then if we were to produce monolithic specifications, we would need *m* times *n* standards, an unmanageable task (Figure 2.4).

   The first and most important step must be to try to separate the application-dependent aspects from the signalling and routing technology-dependent aspects by defining the functionality to be provided by the latter, and assumed by the former. The service primitive definition described above is a suitable vehicle for defining this functionality, so we talk about 'defining the OSI Network Service', that is, specifying the functionality for end-to-end communication to be provided by networks and to be used by application specifications. In principle we have now reduced the problem to an *m* plus *n* plus 1 problem – one end-to-end Network Service Definition, *m* application specifications assuming this functionality, and *n* network technologies providing this functionality to end-systems wishing to communicate. This would produce a two-layer

m applications

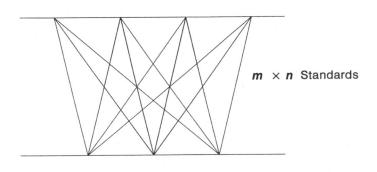

m × *n* Standards

n communication technologies

Figure 2.4 *Monolithic Standards:* m × n *problem.*

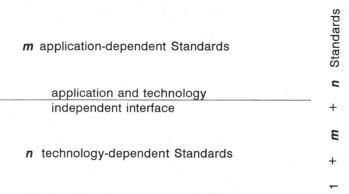

Figure 2.5 *Simple application and media separation.*

model – one network layer and one application layer. There have indeed been (non-OSI) protocol suites that have adopted this architecture. It is the minimum layering that makes any sense today (Figure 2.5).

Notice that this layering fits well with the idea of a network provider as an organizational entity, such as a PTT, providing services for many customers whose computers are end-systems on the network, and all running many different applications over the same network provision. Equally, provided the OSI Network Service is fully implemented by all network providers, and provided the application specifications use only features present in the OSI Network Service Definition, applications can be expected to run over a wide variety of carriers with no additional specifications and minimum changes to software code.

This is a very nice simple approach, but it is unfortunately complicated a little by two quite radically different views of what is the most appropriate end-to-end network functionality to standardize. These two views are discussed later when the network service is examined in more detail.

2.4.2 From two to four layers

It is clear that in providing an end-to-end network service to support the communications of end-systems, the service will be provided by a combination of one or more passive links, each using potentially a different medium and signalling mechanism, and one or more active relay systems or network nodes. In OSI terminology, these nodes are called **intermediate systems**, in contrast to **end-systems** which are the systems containing the applications trying to communicate. (Note, however, reverting back to the discussion of ODP, that this distinction is clear when one focuses on the interconnection of open (end) systems. It is less clear if one's focus is on open distributed processing.)

It is natural, therefore, to consider specifying the provision of the network service by

- specifying media and associated signalling systems capable of signalling just two states – a zero and a one;
- specifying the operation of a single-link protocol which enables messages to be transferred between nodes (end or intermediate systems) over a single link;
- specifying the operation of nodes (end and intermediate systems) to provide the end-to-end network service over various topologies of links.

Following this approach, we introduce three layers at the bottom: the **Physical Layer**, concerned with media and signalling; the **Data Link Layer**, concerned with the operation of a single link; and the **Network Layer**, concerned with the behaviour of nodes to provide the overall network service.

This is again a nice simple concept, but yet again the reality gets more complicated. There is near total agreement that the Network Service Definition, allowing for the two approaches mentioned above, is all that is required, and that it is 'right' for any media, signalling system, and network routing or switching ideas that might arise in the future. (At least, for now!) But when it comes to the separation of functions between the Physical and Data Link and Network Layers, there is less agreement. Physical and Data Link Service Definitions have been produced, but the separation of the total specification of how to provide the network service into three parts glued together by these service definitions is still more an ideal than a reality. The problem is at least partly one of making use of historical systems, but is also at least partly one of logical problems which arise in attempting efficient separation of function between these layers. We will look at two issues of layer separation.

First, let us consider the nature of the Physical Service Definition. It would seem natural to require providers of this service (signalling systems) to provide for the transmission of arbitrary strings of zeros and ones as the fundamental feature of their operation. It turns out, and I don't know if this can be formally proved to always hold, or whether some reviewer will find an exception, that all current signalling systems either:

- can transmit arbitrary strings of ones and zeros, provided there are not too many successive ones (or alternatively zeros), or
- can transmit arbitrary strings of ones and zeros with no constraint, but can also, at no additional cost, signal an additional symbol or state – call it a *t* (but with not too many successive *t*s).

In particular, the signalling mechanisms used in all the Local Area Network (LAN) Standards have an extra state/symbol which is used either to terminate a block of data, or to signal a token being passed. If you are an architectural purist, this is **layer violation**, as such a feature is not part of the Physical Service Definition, and token passing and termination of blocks of data are functions assigned to the Data Link Layer, not to the Physical Layer. This is why, in the LAN Standards, the architectural diagram (Figure 2.6) shows the so-called

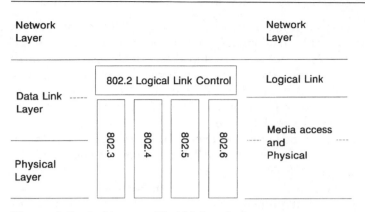

Figure 2.6 *Architecture of LAN Standards.*

'MAC-Service' spanning the Physical Layer, whose upper boundary is shown as a dotted line, and the lower part of the Data Link Layer. There was a time when people worried about this discrepancy between the ideal and the reality, but that time is long past!

The second question we need to look at is the nature of the Data Link Service Definition if the technology we are considering (again, typically, a LAN technology) has a passive link connecting a large number of stations, rather than just two. We typically call such a system a local area network, yet all the standards related to it are, by common agreement, restricted to the Data Link Layer and below. In order to accommodate such systems, the Data Link Service Definition ends up looking remarkably like the Network Service Definition (and in particular needs an address parameter to determine the recipient of data), and the value of separating these layers becomes less clear. But to make the distinction more obvious, and to emphasize an important point, the OSI Network Service is about the provision of a world-wide (and out to the stars in due course) interconnection capability, with sufficient power in the addressing and routing mechanisms to handle such a remit. By contrast, addressing used on passive links such as Ethernet is intended primarily to support the local dissemination of information over the passive link, not for global addressing, despite the fact that allocation mechanisms exist to make Ethernet addresses globally unambiguous.

So ... what is the real OSI architecture of the bottom three layers providing the OSI Network Service? This is contained in a Standard entitled *The Internal Organization of the Network Layer* (IONL). This Standard makes two very important points. First, it accepts that real networks exist, and provide some sort of data transmission service. These are called **subnetworks**. Any particular subnetwork can be enhanced by adding specifications for the behaviour of systems connected to it, which may be OSI intermediate or end systems; these specifications enable the OSI Network Service to be provided across it. Such specifications are called **convergence protocols**. In particular, the X.25 (1980) specification does not provide the OSI Network Service, but can be made to do so with a convergence protocol. By contrast, X.25 (1984) *does* provide the OSI Network Service with no additional convergence protocol. The convergence protocol for X.25 (1980) was developed, but was abandoned before proceeding to International Standard status because everybody thought implementations of X.25 (1980) would have a short life! Yet even well into the 1990s, many PTTs were still offering only X.25 (1980) services, and hence not fully supporting the OSI Network Service.

The real architecture of the bottom layers can be summarized by saying 'It doesn't matter what goes on down below. All that matters is the decking!' The 'decking' is, of course, the OSI Network Service.

The second point made by the IONL is that the OSI Network Service as actually defined has the important property that, given the provision of that service (using some set of protocols) between systems A and B, and given the provision of that service (using potentially different protocols) between systems B and C, then very simple (and specified) behaviour by system B gives us the OSI Network Service between systems A and C (Figure 2.7).

Thus we have the following situation.

- Any real-world network, and in particular those provided by PTTs or standardized as LANs, can have standards developed for them saying how to provide the OSI Network Service over them. This is all broadly in place for X.25, ISO 8802 (IEE 802) LANs, asynchronous PSTN connections and ISDN B and D channels, the main real-world networks (excluding TCP/IP) around today.
- Real-world networks or subnetworks which have specified convergence protocols can be used in tandem, given appropriate behaviour by a gateway between them, to provide the OSI Network Service between end-systems connected to any of them.

This is a very powerful provision, both for linking the world now and for handling future networking developments. In particular, many vendors provide

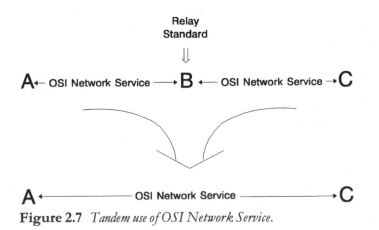

Figure 2.7 *Tandem use of OSI Network Service.*

the OSI Network Service across their vendor-specific networks, with (typically) gateways extending that service across an X.25 network or an Ethernet using the standard protocols on these external networks.

So ... to summarize: despite the above comments, formally at least, we have now justified four layers – three bottom ones providing the OSI Network Service, and a top one which contains a series of application-specific standards, written assuming (and using the notation of) the OSI Network Service Definition.

2.4.3   Going beyond four

We have separated out technology dependence in the bottom three layers from application dependence above them, using a boundary (service definition) which is independent of any application and independent of any networking technology, now or in the future. What else is worth doing?

At least in principle, we can recognize that in writing the m different application specifications we will find ourselves needing to consider similar problems for each application, and write similar (or worse – different) text to solve these problems for each application. In other words, we can conceive of some parts of the total specification that solve problems that are both application-independent and technology-independent. If we can identify such problems, then these are clear candidates for providing solutions by introducing additional layers between the Application Layer and the Network Service.

What can we identify? Do we find three major problems (giving us seven layers), or only two (giving six layers), or four (giving eight layers)? Surprise, surprise, we find three problems. The reader may judge whether maybe two would have been better – or maybe it should have been four? Or maybe one more would have been best? Perhaps the reader will agree that there is no one right layering; arguments over 'the best' separation of layer functions can continue indefinitely: but ... we do have an International Standard architecture, for better or for worse.

The views of *Encyclopedia Galactica – 2008J version* are shown in Figure 2.8.

2.4.4   From four to five

The first application-independent and network-technology-independent problem that we can recognize relates to the quality of the service provided by the particular network connection we are using and the needs of the application we are running. It is again a fact (formally unproven, I think, but I state it as a theorem that no one has disproved) that there can be no combination of signalling system, error detection algorithm and error correction code that can produce a zero probability of error in the transfer of data over computer networks. (We can get arbitrarily close to zero probability of error, but ....) All signalling of zeros and ones is dependent on detection of some threshold being crossed, and all media have some external disturbance that can corrupt the data. Moreover,

"When the Alpha Centaurans and the people of Earth attempted to merge their communications networks, arguments proceeded for several decades. The Alpha Centaurans had established the nature of the application in their lowest layer and error-detection and recovery in their highest. The final compromise was the interleaving of bits in a duo-decahedral envelope.

Encyclopedia Galactica,   AD 20085

Figure 2.8 *Encyclopedia Galactica, AD 20085, p. 29463.*

it is in the nature of economically-viable systems that if you have a low error rate you can increase the speed of transmission (with little extra expenditure on the hardware but with an increased error rate). Thus basic error rates tend to be the product of commercial decisions, not simply the result of properties of the technology.

Suppose we transmit the data, then send it back and check it is still the same as the data we sent. There is still no guarantee that the data has been received correctly, because precisely the corruption that occurred on the forward path can accidentally be exactly reversed by corruption on the reverse path. This is particularly true if we have intelligent human interference: there is nothing humans can do by way of security violations that hardware errors can't do just as effectively, but maybe less predictably!

It would in principle be possible to set the standard for the OSI Network Service at some arbitrary quality level, in terms of residual undetected error rate, rate of detected (signalled) but uncorrected errors, throughput, round-trip time, cost, and so on. This approach would suffer not only from requiring a Rolls-Royce service from all suppliers and cutting Minis and the Model T Ford out of the market, but would more significantly date the Network Service Standard to the expectations of current technology.

Such quality level specifications do not appear. The quality of service (QOS) provided by the Network Service is accepted as being something that will vary depending on the real-world networks being crossed by any particular connection, and perhaps even by trade-offs of cost, bandwidth and error rate selected for a particular hop over a real-world network. Each specification above the Network Service, therefore, needs to address the problem of what additional exchanges to add to ensure that the application can operate over the worst connections that might be encountered as well as over the best.

The problem of designing appropriate mechanisms to provide the QOS required by an application, given the QOS available on a network particular connection, was the task given to the Transport Layer, the layer introduced immediately above the Network Layer. The Transport Layer and QOS issues will be discussed further when we look at each layer in turn, but for now, it gets us from four to five layers.

2.4.5   From five to six

OK. So we now have an end-to-end connection capability on a world-wide basis, and have allocated responsibility for producing any necessary specifications to address the QOS issue. What other problem will most application specifications have to solve that can sensibly be addressed by a specification that is independent of both the application and the networking technology? This one is not so obvious or clear as the Transport Layer or (to come) the Presentation Layer. It is also difficult to find a similar separation of the problem we are about to address in other communications architectures. The layer we are going to introduce, above the Transport Layer, is the **Session Layer**.

The jargon phrase, repeated in so many textbooks on communications, is that 'The session layer is concerned with dialogue control and dialogue separation'. What does that mean? What real problem are we trying to solve? Even worse, some older textbooks equate the word 'session' with 'login-session' and think the problems addressed are all about usernames and passwords, that is, security. In fact, the Session Layer is the one layer in the OSI model which, in the Standard for OSI Security Architecture, has been given no security responsibilities.

There are rather a large number of functions performed by the Session Layer specification, and to understand the need for some of them (particularly the so-called 'orderly termination'), the reader needs rather more detail about the nature of the Network Service and the Transport Service than we have been able to provide so far. So a detailed description of all the problems the Session Layer group was asked to solve must come later. For now, however, let us concentrate on two problems. The first relates to the 'style' of message exchange that an application protocol designer wants to adopt. There are those who would argue that it is easier to produce a correct protocol specification (and to produce a software implementation) if the lower layers guarantee that normal messages do not cross in transit. Of course, we have to allow for signalling of exceptions, but some would claim that the basic protocol design is easier if one end is always the sender and the other the receiver of messages, with a mechanism provided by a lower layer for signalling the passing of the turn to send (or in Session Layer terminology, passing the data token). The Session Layer therefore provides the means of operating in two-way alternate (TWA) mode in addition to (no added value) two-way simultaneous mode (TWS) for those application designers that prefer that mode of operation. This is what is meant by **dialogue control**.

The second problem relates to the establishment of checkpoints. Here it is important to recognize that in the late 1970s, when the OSI architecture was developed, checkpointing and associated restart mechanisms to cope with system failure during long-running tasks was an absolute necessity. The reader must judge whether the same imperative exists today, but let us none the less assume that many applications will need to make provision for checkpointing their activity from time to time to guard against system failures. What protocol support is needed, can be provided in an application-independent fashion, to make it easy for application-protocol designers to incorporate checkpointing into their designs? Why is the specification of checkpointing such a hard problem that it warrants major discussion as part of a separate layer of specification?

Let us consider checkpointing of an application on a stand-alone machine. It is a simple problem. The designer merely says that after some specified time, the complete state of the application is to be recorded on disk. (My word processor has as I write this said '* Please Wait *' while it did precisely that.) What is the problem?

Now let us consider an OSI application involving the interconnection of two computers (two will do for now – more is a different problem). What we need to do is to arrange for them both to checkpoint their state at some agreed point in time. Oh dear – help us please, Einstein: simultaneity (synchronization) of events at different points in space is a hard problem!

In reality, the problem is even harder – the total state of the application includes the state of network relays that contain messages that are currently in transit. So we need not merely to checkpoint, simultaneously, our two end-systems, but also to ask our friendly network provider to please checkpoint (and later restart!) the network switches when we need to do our checkpointing. Now the problem is rather clearer, and we can see why it may warrant assignment to a special group as part of the functions to be provided in a separate layer of specification.

Of course, if the application involves a very simple use of the connection to transfer sequential data in one direction only, checkpointing is not so much of a problem. What we do is put a marker in the flow of data that separates an earlier part of the transfer (the dialogue) from a later part, and we checkpoint at the sending end when we insert the marker and at the receiving end when we receive it. The marker provides a **dialogue separation** between the two parts of the dialogue, and enables checkpointing to take place, if the application designer specifies it. In terms of Session Layer jargon, separation of this rather simple one-way dialogue (not really a dialogue at all, rather a monologue) is called 'establishing a minor synchronization point'. It is minor because it only works for this rather simple, but very common, dialogue (Figure 2.9.)

In the general case of messages flowing in both directions, perhaps with some exception signals that might overtake normal data flow, providing a separation of the total interchange into dialogues A and B such that checkpointing can be applied, should the application designer so wish, between the two dialogues is a more interesting problem. This is solved by what the Session Layer terms **major synchronization** – a steam-hammer that can crack any nut! (The handshakes for major synchronization are discussed in Chapter 6.)

The whole issue, then, of the different forms of synchronization (to permit different forms of checkpointing) and how to provide them is an interesting and

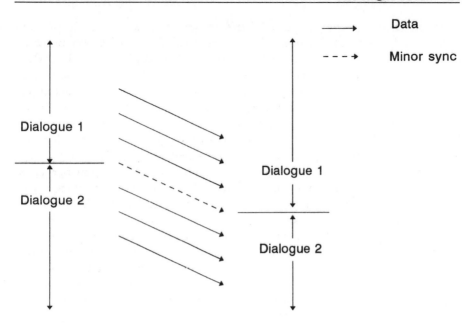

Figure 2.9 *Minor synchronization dialogue separation.*

complex study, and provides the second major problem that justifies (? – the reader must judge) the existence of the Session Layer.

2.4.6   From six to the magic seven

So ... we have an end-to-end connection capability, we have all we need by way of QOS improvement mechanisms, and we have all we need by way of dialogue control and establishment of synchronization points for a variety of types of dialogue. What else can usefully be separated out as a sufficiently important problem to warrant writing another layer into the architecture?

When that question is asked in seminars and lectures, the answers are often either 'Management' or 'Security'. The idea of a management layer that monitors traffic, introduces charging information, or whatever, is an interesting possibility, but in fact management functions are not seen as an integral part of all applications, but rather as applications in their own right. This is probably an appropriate view. Thus not providing a management layer can be fairly easily justified. Justifying the non-provision of a security layer is certainly harder. There is no doubt that security features must permeate the operation of all applications. However, the OSI architecture sees security features being provided by many (most) layers, with some additional support in the Application Layer that is discussed briefly in Chapter 11, but does not include a layer specifically concerned with security.

So what is the application-independent problem that gets us to the magic figure of seven layers? Let us consider the tasks an OSI application protocol designer has to undertake, and see if there is anything we can do to provide assistance. Is there any identifiable problem that most application protocol designers will face, and which may be amenable to application-independent treatment? First, the designer must examine the application and determine the broad nature of the information that has to be exchanged. We talk about 'determining the semantics of messages'. Next, the designer somehow needs to specify the data structures (message formats) that are going to be used. We talk about 'defining the abstract syntax of messages'. Finally, the designer needs to determine an appropriate bit representation for values of the data structures in use. The bit representation has to be independent of any particular compiler or computer system. In particular, if messages contain integer elements, real numbers or character strings, the designer has to determine the representation of these elements, and of any structuring information that groups them into composite elements. We talk about 'defining the transfer syntax of messages'. In the early days, the names **abstract transfer syntax** (for the form of messages without concern about bit-pattern representation) and **concrete transfer syntax** (for their bit-pattern encoding) were used, but these were later abbreviated to **abstract syntax** and **transfer syntax**, which are the terms exclusively used today.

It is clear that the application designer needs to define the semantics of protocol exchanges, and once we require this specification to be done formally rather than in English, the designer has effectively also defined an abstract syntax for the messages. There is, however, no reason to force the designer to worry about the transfer syntax (bit-pattern encoding). We ought to be able to at least provide some support in this area in an application-independent manner, and hence a layer concerned with the representation of information during transfer is an appropriate one to introduce. This is the **Presentation Layer**. The term 'Presentation' Layer is a little misleading. (In retrospect 'Representation Layer' or 'Encoding Layer' would have been better.) A number of early books on OSI contained text saying that the Presentation Layer was all about the presentation of information on a terminal display to a human being – in other words, entirely concerned with a terminal handling application. This is, and always was, a wrong statement.

The Presentation Layer, then, is concerned with bit-pattern representation during transfer. In particular, in the OSI architecture, we recognize that any particular set of application messages (abstract syntax) can have associated with it multiple possible representations (transfer syntaxes) to be used in different circumstances (Figure 2.10). The presentation protocol is given the responsibility for negotiating the encodings to be used in any particular connection, and the Presentation Layer group was later also given the responsibility for standardizing a language (notation) for specifying abstract syntaxes (Abstract Syntax Notation One – ASN.1) and a set of encoding rules associated with use of that language.

In the early days of OSI, the importance of clearly separating the definition of abstract syntax and semantics from transfer syntax was recognized, but without a formal notation for abstract syntax definition, it was considered necessary

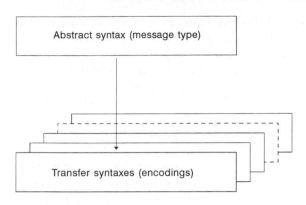

Abstract syntax (message type)

Transfer syntaxes (encodings)

Figure 2.10 *Multiple transfer syntaxes.*

to have, for each application, at least two Standards – one specifying the semantics and abstract syntax, and others, which would be application-specific, specifying possible bit-pattern encodings for that application. With the emergence of languages for abstract syntax definition, all Presentation Layer matters (representation issues) can now be treated in an application-independent manner, and there are today no application-dependent Presentation Layer Standards.

The questioning reader might still be asking why it is appropriate to recognize the idea of different encodings that are negotiated, and what the advantages are of a clear separation of the transfer syntax definition from the abstract syntax definition. After all:

- Other protocol architectures generally do not have this flexibility as a general feature, handling things like compressed representations as an ad hoc matter in application designs that are concerned with bulk data transfer.
- Lower layer protocol designers are well used to drawing pictures showing the form of their messages as a set of named bit-positions within a set of octets, that is, defining a fixed transfer syntax as an integral part of their protocol definition.

So why isn't that approach good enough in the OSI Application Layer? There are a number of points to be made which show why the Application Layer is different from other layers, and why the introduction of the Presentation Layer as a separate layer is at least arguably a 'good idea'.

First, if we look at the complexity of the data structures needed for the messages in the different layers, we find that in the Data Link and Network Layers we have very simple structures, with a fixed set of parameters of fixed length in fixed positions in the messages. Drawing a picture of the message is easy. In the Transport Layer, we find the need for optional parameters, and variable-length parameters. In the Session Layer we see the introduction of the further concept of **parameter groups** – sets of parameters appearing together in the message, or omitted in their entirety. When we get to Application Layer protocol design, the complexity of the data structures we need becomes even greater, with optional groups of information, arbitrary repetition, groups within groups to any depth, and so on. A more powerful and user-friendly descriptive technique than simply drawing a bit-map of the message is needed.

A second point relates to the skills needed in protocol design in the different layers. In the lower layers the skills needed are largely those of the communications expert, to whom 'bit-twiddling' to produce efficient bit-pattern representations is a natural pastime. In the Application Layer, however, the most important skill is a good knowledge and understanding of the application domain, not of communications or computer software. Detailed design of bit-pattern representations is likely to be at best a boring chore to those with application domain skills.

A third point relates to the nature of the protocol definition in the different layers. In the lower layers, we are concerned with some header (and perhaps trailer) information, with the bulk of the message left as a hole to be completed by the next higher layer. If the OSI protocols work efficiently, the total of all the headers and trailers in all the lower layers will not account for more than perhaps 10% of the total communications traffic. By contrast, the Application Layer data is the 90% bulk of the transfer. Thus getting the 'best' encoding for the lower layer protocols is not likely to be significant. For an Application Layer protocol, it could be very important.

So what is the 'best' encoding? This is where we see the desirability of introducing the idea of multiple encodings selected on a per-connection basis by negotiation between the two end-systems. Consider two systems communicating over a high-bandwidth line with a low-level encryption device in place at both ends. The 'best' encoding of the application protocol will be a clear encoding with no compression which minimizes the number of CPU cycles needed by the two end-systems to convert between their local representation and the transfer syntax. But suppose that a bulldozer goes through the high-bandwidth line, and the back-up provision is a dial-up telephone connection with modems – low bandwidth and insecure. The 'best' representation is now likely to be one that introduces selective encryption of some fields at the presentation layer and does as much compression as possible, regardless of the cost in CPU cycles.

Let us look at another scenario (Figure 2.11) for determining the 'best' encoding. Suppose the application (not unrealistically) involves the transfer of a few gigabytes of information comprising a highly structured and standardized document format for a large technical document. The way that is represented on disk will be chosen by computer vendor A to suit his system, and could, for example, be an EBCDIC encoding of characters, with some highly indexed set of files for holding the structure of the document. Computer vendor B, on the other hand, might use a more embedded structure with less indexing and an ASCII representation of the text. If, in an instance of communication, a machine from vendor A (A1) is communicating this document with a machine from vendor B (B1), we will need a vendor-independent transfer syntax, and both machines will need to convert the few gigabytes of data between the local repre-

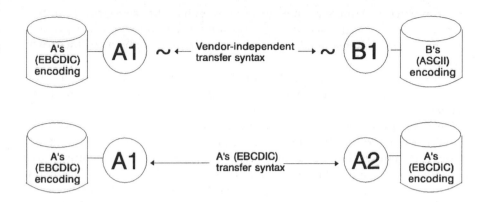

Figure 2.11 *Conversion versus vendor-specific encoding.*

sentation and the vendor-independent transfer syntax, despite the CPU-cycle and possible disk-churning costs. On the other hand, if, in this instance of communication, the machine from vendor A (A1) happens to be communicating with another machine from vendor A (A2), it is highly desirable to allow a transfer syntax that is as close as possible to the local representation on the vendor A disks. If OSI did not permit this, there would be tremendous pressure from vendor A customers for a vendor-A-specific protocol to be made available and used, and OSI protocols would only ever be used between dissimilar machines.

This discussion of the Presentation Layer would not be complete without some mention of a few problems.

First, the Presentation Layer of OSI was the last of the non-application layers to mature and stabilize. One major application (X.400 electronic mail) was first published in 1984 before the Presentation Layer Standard was ready, and was written to sit directly on top of the Session Layer, assuming effectively a six-layer model. (This was corrected in the 1988 version, but not without a lot of difficulty – see the discussion in Chapter 7.) Moreover, X.400 is very much concerned with relaying information from a mail originator through mail relays to a mail receiver. In this relay situation, negotiation of appropriate encodings becomes at first sight problematic, and even, on further thought, difficult. Thus the Presentation Layer concepts were not strongly supported by CCITT workers (a situation that to some extent persisted into the 1990s), despite their formal acceptance of the Presentation Layer in their Reference Model (CCITT/ITU-T Recommendation X.200).

Second, the Presentation Layer concepts will only be exercised in reality if a number of transfer syntaxes (some of which will be vendor-specific, some standardized with varying verbosity and CPU-cycle properties) have been defined. Up to the start of the 1990s, such definitions of transfer syntaxes did not exist. In practice, there was precisely one transfer syntax defined at the international level for each application layer standard, based on the Basic Encoding Rules of ASN.1. Thus negotiation of transfer syntax was a nice theory, but did not occur in practice. Moreover, implementors were far more concerned to implement a standard transfer syntax to get open interworking with other vendors than to bother defining an efficient transfer syntax for use between their own machines.

Third, the level of understanding of the Presentation Layer and sympathy with its aims (even among implementors and some OSI application protocol definers) has not always been as great as might be wished.

This situation changed quite rapidly in the early 1990s, with a number of additional encoding rules for ASN.1, with much improved properties over the Basic Encoding Rules, being progressed to International Standards. Thus encoding choices and real negotiation of encodings will become possible in the late 1990s. The reader should note, however, that there is a very real danger of a proliferation of encodings, with any one vendor implementing only a small subset (and with some pairs of machines having no implemented encoding in common), resulting in new interworking problems. In the ideal world, we would have a small number of internationally standardized encodings, each with important useful properties in relation to trade-offs on compression, CPU cycles and security, with all of them implemented by all vendors and the most appropriate selected for each instance of communication according to circumstances. At the present time there is no real thought being given to the set of encodings and their characteristics that are needed, standardization of new encodings being somewhat haphazard. (The reader should, however, note that the last time I made a similar sort of remark in a text for publication, the situation was rectified before the text was published!)

2.4.7 And going beyond seven ...

We said that the OSI architecture had a magic seven layers. But the above discussion will surely have alerted the reader to the fact that there are potentially a pretty large number of other problems that occur in application layer standardization and which will be common to a number of applications and hence worth specifying as separate application-independent Standards. Can the architecture embrace this situation without requiring the addition of more and more layers?

To be fair to CCITT (see section 1.2.1), the main difference between the CCITT Reference Model in 1984 and the ISO Reference Model was a recognition by CCITT that one had to accept the situation that there would be some application-independent specifications, Common Application Service Elements (CASEs), in the Application Layer that would be referenced by real application-dependent standards, Specific Application Service Elements (SASEs), to provide the total layer seven specification.

In the late 1980s, however, it became clear that it was hard to distinguish between SASEs and CASEs. The process was really one of producing more and more building blocks, with a gradually increasing amount of application dependence. What to some people was a very specific application (file transfer or electronic mail) was to others (for example the banking or international trade communities) merely a carrier standard to be used to support their 'real' application. The S and the C were therefore dropped, and today we merely talk about **Application Service Elements** (ASEs) as the jargon term for Standards in the Application Layer that combine with each other to form either bigger building blocks, complete rooms or livable-in houses.

A discussion of the more important ASEs which form low-level building blocks appears in Chapter 9, but it is worth noting for the present that when the first of these building blocks, the Association Control Service Element (once known as the unique CASE), was being discussed, there was a significant lobby from the experts of one national body for that to be effectively inserted as an eighth layer between the Presentation Layer and the real Application Layer, with a complete set of service primitive definitions. In the event, this approach was not adopted.

The model now is that an ASE will 'steal' some of the service primitives from the Presentation Layer or from some other ASE (that is, if a referencing Standard wants to reference the service primitives of that ASE, it is not allowed to reference the 'stolen' services) and provide a richer service with its own service primitives on top of these (much as layers do), but leaving all other service primitives for direct access by a referencing Standard (as layers do not). The position (Figure 2.12) can be summarized as follows.

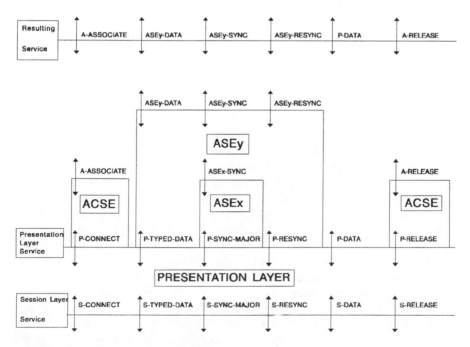

Figure 2.12 *Stealing service primitives.*

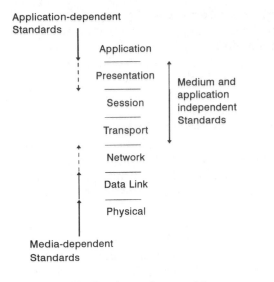

Figure 2.13 is the final Figure depicting the OSI 7-layer architecture.

Figure 2.13 *Final seven-layer model.*

- A layer 'hides' all the service primitives of the layer below, and provides a complete set of service primitives that are the only primitives a higher layer can access.
- An Application Service Element 'hides' some service primitives from the Presentation Layer and/or from some other ASE(s), but leaves the remainder available for direct access.

The elaboration of the concept of ASEs and the way they work together occurred after the completion of the Basic Reference Model, and is included in a Standard called Application Layer Structure. This underwent some further development in the early 1990s to provide an Extended Application Layer Structure, discussed more fully in Chapter 9.

Figure 2.13 is the final Figure depicting the OSI 7-layer architecture. The architecture envisages a never-ending set of Standards in the Physical Layer, perhaps involving additional Standards right up to (but not beyond) the Network Layer as signalling and switching technology advances. OSI standardization will never be complete in these layers. Equally, in the Application Layer, we expect to see an ever-increasing set of ASE Standards as new applications are proposed for standardization. Again, OSI standardization will never be complete in this layer. In the middle layers of application-independent and technology-independent standardization (Network Service, Transport Layer, Session Layer and Presentation Layer – the heart of OSI), the standardization work is largely complete now, with only minor changes and extensions likely in the future. (But ... see the end of Chapter 4!)

2.5   Comparison with other architectures

There is no doubt that the OSI architecture is richer and more complicated than any other protocol architecture. It may be illuminating to compare the *de facto* architecture of another major suite of protocol specifications with the architecture of OSI. The suite we compare with is that of the USA Department of Defense (DoD) Advanced Research Projects Agency (DARPA) **Internet** Community better known as **TCP/IP**.

There is no formal document specifying the architecture of the TCP/IP-related (Internet) specifications, so there can be different views by different authors on the *de facto* architecture, and particularly on its relationship to the OSI architecture. The following treatment would probably be accepted by most workers, however.

The Internet became widely known and talked about in the early to mid-1990s. It is a world-wide collection of interlinked (hence the 'Inter') wide-area networks, with associated local area networks. In the 1970s it was better known as the Arpanet, when it was the first network to establish the viability of wide-area computer communication. It later became known as the Darpanet, but the term the Internet is preferred today. Up to the mid-1990s it was largely a research, military and educational network, with a very limited and restricted amount of commercial traffic over it. This situation changed dramatically in the mid-1990s with the growth of interest in the provision of World-Wide Web pages. (While all the early TCP/IP protocols have equivalent or better OSI equivalents, there is no OSI equivalent for the protocol underlying the World-Wide Web, although the markup language used to author pages (HTML – Hyper-Text Markup Language) is based on an ISO Standard (SGML – Standard Generalized Markup Language).)

Communication over the Internet is characterized by the use of Transmission Control Protocol (TCP) and Internet Protocol (IP), but particularly the latter, with a variety of other protocols on top. All the protocols in the suite are generally collectively known as 'the TCP/IP protocols' (even if they do not actually use TCP), or more accurately as 'the Internet protocols'.

The Internet protocols are vendor-independent, and their specification is controlled by open public discussion that is not dominated by any one vendor. They are also widely implemented by a variety of vendors and hence fulfil the definition of 'open' as used in OSI. Today, when people talk about 'open networking', they can mean implementation of either OSI or TCP/IP, and advertisements need to be examined carefully to see which is meant.

Originally, TCP/IP was very much aimed at wide-area networking, but its adoption in the early 1980s by the UNIX developers led to its widespread use in the late 1980s on local area networks. It is probably fair to say that much of the success of UNIX in the 1980s was due to its incorporation of TCP/IP. At the end of the 1980s and in the early 1990s, stand-alone LANs running UNIX workstations were frequently being linked by high-bandwidth leased lines and cheap commercial routers, so that wide-area TCP/IP company networks, which were initially not necessarily part of the Internet, grew up rapidly in the

UK and other parts of Europe. It is probably true to say that while in the 1980s TCP/IP local area communications sold UNIX systems, in the 1990s the widespread use of UNIX systems sold wide-area TCP/IP.

So ... what is the TCP/IP architecture? It has strong similarities with parts of OSI, but is broadly much simpler. As with OSI, there is critically an end-to-end network service provided by the use of IP, with network switches understanding only the IP protocol and associated routing and management protocols. Beneath the IP layer there is whatever real networks are around, and there are a series of specifications (Internet specifications are called, somewhat misleadingly, **Requests for Comment** (RFCs)) that specify how to transmit IP messages over a whole range of real-world networks, including some vendor-specific ones. This part of the architecture then is very similar to the OSI 'Internal Organization of the Network Layer' described earlier. Above the IP layer, there is a layer corresponding quite closely to the Transport Layer of OSI, and containing TCP and another very simple protocol called User Datagram Protocol (UDP). On top of these sit monolithic specifications for applications.

To avoid learning wrong lessons at this stage, it is important to note that the IP and TCP are roughly equivalent to half – the so-called connectionless half – of the corresponding OSI layers. This issue will be discussed later, and should be ignored for now. Also ignore UDP for now – UDP is not a difference between TCP/IP and OSI – OSI has an equivalent protocol which will again be discussed later.

The main difference between the OSI and the TCP/IP architectures is that in TCP/IP the Session and Presentation Layer functionality is not factored out into separate specifications, nor are application specifications normally broken down into a set of ASEs. For those readers that know TCP/IP well, one can discern some elements of the ASE concept in the TCP/IP TELNET protocol, which is used both as an actual application (terminal login) and also to support other application protocols (file transfer and electronic mail). With this exception, however, Internet specifications above TCP or UDP tend to be self-contained.

In summary, and to simplify slightly, the main difference between the OSI and the TCP/IP architectures is 'monolithic over TCP' versus 'session plus presentation plus ASEs over OSI Transport'. Which is best? Does it matter?

Certainly one must not confuse discussions of the architecture (how specifications are structured) with the quality of the final protocol. A bad protocol can be specified in a highly structured manner, a good one in a monolithic way, and vice versa. In principle one would expect more commonality in the way functions are performed with the OSI approach than with the TCP/IP approach. In practice ....

The lack of a separated-out Session Layer seems to cause few problems in TCP/IP, although one major feature of the Session Layer (orderly termination) comes out as part of TCP because of detailed technical differences between the OSI Transport Protocol and TCP, so the comparison is not quite fair. As far as the Presentation Layer is concerned, one can discern in the more recent TCP/

IP protocol specifications elements of the Presentation Layer approach, and of tools very similar to ASN.1. (For those wanting to probe further, and knowing TCP/IP, look at the XDR specification that supports the SUN network file servers (NFS).) TCP/IP also introduced in the 1980s its own Remote Procedure Call (RPC) Protocol which is being used as an ASE comparable to the Remote Operations Service Element ASE of OSI. Thus some of the concepts present in the OSI architecture can be seen in the latest TCP/IP work.

3
Direct connection, formally!

3.1 General

There are no ISO/IEC International Standards or CCITT/ITU-T Recommendations covering specifications of signalling systems and protocols that have been developed especially with the OSI Physical and Data Link Layers in mind (the layers concerned with direct connection of two systems).

As was discussed in Chapter 2, the specifications in these layers either predate OSI, or were developed to support networks such as ISDN or Ethernet or Token Ring, that can, with suitable Network Layer protocols, be used to provide the OSI Network Service, and hence form part of OSI, but which can also be used to support other protocol suites.

There do exist two Standards – the Physical Service Definition and the Data Link Service Definition – that were produced as an integral part of the OSI work, but their importance, as described earlier, in gluing together layer specifications is minimal.

Another remark can be made justifying the shortness of this chapter on the bottom two layers: the principles of signalling systems and of link layer protocol design have been well understood for a long time, and any of the many books on data communications will give a good treatment of the principles of design in these layers. We therefore include only three short further discussions in this chapter, covering these two layers in turn, followed by a discussion of **Formal Description Techniques** (FDTs).

3.2 Getting the bits across

How to convey a string of bits from one system to another over some sort of connection (copper, radio waves, optic fibre) is the province of Physical Layer specifications.

There are a number of signalling systems in common use today, including those using parallel channels to convey eight bits at a time plus a clock signal, those conveying bits serially using wave-forms close to square-waves, those that transmit bits over the telephone network using a series of 'whistles' in the voice range, and so on.

As an aside, a lower-layer purist from a telecommunications background would object to the use of the term signalling to describe the means of transmitting general information, and in particular data consisting of zeros and ones, because in telecommunications the term is traditionally restricted to the transmission of information related to the setting up and tearing down of a connection (dial-tones and the like), not to the means of transferring information for the user of the connection. In this text, the term is used as it would be by a lay person to describe more generally the mechanism (voltage, current, flashes of light) used for the transmission of any sort of information by some disturbance of some physical medium. The purist would probably use the term **data transmission system** for this more general activity.

There are interesting problems to be solved in the design of Physical Layer features, particularly problems of skew due to the charging and discharging of the capacitance of a line, and related clocking (bit synchronization) problems. There are also many interesting concerns in the design of optical fibre systems for very high-speed transmission. While the development of new and better and faster signalling systems is vital to computer communications as a whole, it is not particularly related to OSI, and is outside the scope of this text.

There is only one thing I usually say about signalling systems in the Physical Layer of OSI: 'If you can waggle it, and someone else can feel it, then you have a signalling system.' When I put that slide up in my lectures, the brighter students come back with 'No, no, no! Communication needs understanding. You have to know what the wiggles mean.' Of course they are right – the slide should really have added 'And you have an agreement on the type of wiggles to use, and on the meaning of each wiggle, as a zero or a one for example.' But that would not be so snappy, and the students would not remember it so well!

There are two further points to be made about the Physical Layer: first, that bandwidth (how fast you can signal zeros and ones) is really the main concern in this layer, and bandwidth improvements are the main reason for research and development; second, that for the past 20 years or so it has been easier (cheaper) to get higher bandwidth over local area distances (a few kilometres) than over wide-area distances. The reader should question whether this situation will continue, or whether the electronic equivalent of motorways will emerge providing higher bandwidths than congested town driving. A further quotation from the ***Encyclopedia Galactica – 20085 version***, shown in Figure 3.1, summarizes the position.

Obtaining high bandwidth over stellar distances remained a problem. Attempts to modulate a Cepheid Variable failed dismally, but experiments with Black Holes were more spectacular.

Encyclopedia Galactica, AD 20085

Figure 3.1 *Encyclopedia Galactica, AD 20085, p. 30608.*

This also brings out the point that we will always go on producing new and better signalling systems (and means of routing and switching too). OSI will never be complete in these lower layers.

3.3   Handling the link

3.3.1   *Historical*

Many of the remarks made about the Physical Layer also apply to the Data Link Layer – the work and the Standards were not produced just to support OSI, and there are many data communications textbooks that give a good treatment of link layer protocols.

None the less, there are a few points to make about the Link Layer which will help in a general understanding of the provision of the Network Service, the main starting point for understanding OSI, and which we should deal with here.

The earliest link layer standards predated OSI, and were concerned with communication when a single link, typically copper wire or a radio link, directly connected two end-systems. In the very earliest days of data transmission (1960s), such connections were engineered specifically for the two end-systems that were to communicate, but this was soon replaced by the introduction of the ISO Basic Mode protocol standard. This was a short standard, and no one except implementors has ever heard of it. The variant of it used by one well-known vendor – commonly called BiSync – became somewhat better known, although in the 1990s even that is not often mentioned (or used). Basic Mode was character-based, and was the origin of the so-called **control characters** in the ASCII character set. The first 32 bit-patterns in this character set are designated as having a 'control' meaning such as

SOH	Start of header
STX	Start of text
ETX	End of text
DLE	Data link escape
ACK	Acknowledge

In the ISO Basic Mode Standard we see an attempt to transmit messages, not just a stream of bits or of characters. Each message starts with an SOH, then some addressing information (to cope with multiple stations attached to the link), then an STX, then the actual text, then an ETX, then a two octet checksum. The single ACK character is used to send a reply saying the message has been successfully received (Figure 3.2).

In the original Basic Mode standard, the message could contain only text – control character bit-patterns were not allowed within it to avoid confusion with their use as message terminators, etc. A later version introduced **transparency** – messages were allowed to contain any bit-pattern including those assigned to control characters, and were pre-processed to ensure that their end

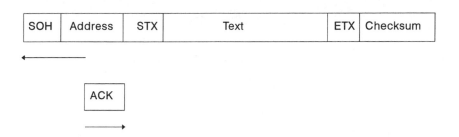

Figure 3.2 *ISO Basic Mode messages.*

could still be detected by the receiver no matter what they contained. The tech-nique was to use DLE followed by ETX as the terminator, and to double any DLE in the original message, sending it as DLE DLE. On receipt, the double DLE was turned back to a single DLE before being passed up to the user (Figure 3.3).

We also see in these early Standards recognition that errors do occur in trans-mission, and that these errors require detection using some form of sum-check, with some form of acknowledgement and retransmission mechanism if reliable communication is to be achieved.

If we move into the mid-1970s, we see the development of the so-called bit-oriented link layer protocols, of which **High Level Data Link Control** (HDLC) is now extremely well known and the *de facto* Standard, with support from chip-sets.

It is called bit-oriented because transparency – the ability to transmit arbitrary bit-patterns in its messages – is not obtained by examining the message as a sequence of characters (octets), but rather by treating it as a pure string of bits. The technique, called bit-stuffing, is to insert a zero bit after any sequence of five successive one bits in the message, using transmission of a zero followed by six one bits to terminate the message (Figure 3.4). This is all very easy to do in transmission chip-sets, but would not be a very nice task if it had to be done by computer software!

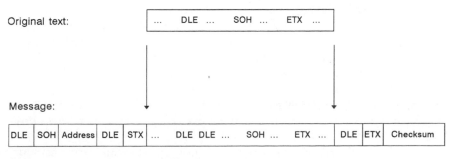

Figure 3.3 *Transparency with DLE.*

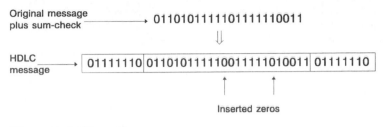

Figure 3.4 *Bit-stuffing.*

HDLC is the Grand Old Man of Data Link Layer standards, with very many options and extensions, and is still very much alive today. The LAP and LAP-B protocols used as level 2 of X.25 are a subset of HDLC. So are LLC1 and LLC2, used in the IEEE 802 (ISO 8802) set of protocols for Local Area Networks. So is the LAP-D protocol used on the D-Channel of ISDN.

3.3.2 Essential features

For the purposes of this text, we need to recognize the following essential features of the link layer protocols that have been developed.

- Message orientation: the protocols provide for the transmission of a sequence of messages, perhaps of limited size, which form the unit for error detection (and perhaps correction); enabling messages containing arbitrary bit-patterns to be delimited (**framed**) is a main concern of the link layer.
- Error detection: the inclusion of some form of sum-check which allows received material to be recognized as a good message or as something else; the 'something else' might be two or more messages with the framing corrupted, or one message turned into what looks like two or more by a frame pattern inserted by corruption of data, or a single message with the data corrupted; we don't know which of these has occurred, and all such material is usually simply discarded and ignored.

In HDLC, the 'sum-check' is a **Cyclic Redundancy Code** (CRC) whose design is based on some quite sophisticated mathematics (Galois Field Theory – the study of polynomials with coefficients modulo 2) which predates computers. The mathematical analysis ensures that, for the number of bits added, the probability that corrupt messages will pass the check is minimized. Again, discussion of this area is outside the scope of this text.

These framing and error detection features can usually be provided relatively simply and cheaply, with virtually all the work being done in special-purpose chips.

If the rules for the receiver are to simply ignore frames with erroneous sum-checks, then the service being provided is one of transmission of a sequence of messages with arbitrary bit-patterns, with those messages that are delivered to the user having a high probability of being uncorrupted (depending on the 'strength' of the 'sum-check' algorithm in use), but with the occasional message being lost.

Note that the probability of a message being lost in this service is dependent on both the underlying error rate across the link and the length of the message. For any given error rate there is some message length such that virtually all messages are lost! Thus we see the need to impose maximum message lengths if sensible transmission is to occur. (It is also necessary to impose maximum message lengths when several logically separate transmissions are sharing a channel, in order to ensure that maximum waiting times are kept small.)

3.3.3   Additional features

Beyond framing and error detection, we find HDLC providing (optionally) two further features which add considerable complication, but provide a much improved service to the user.

The first additional feature is error correction by retransmission. In simplest terms, this involves sending a message, waiting for an acknowledgement of correct receipt, and resending it after some time-out period if an acknowledgement is not received. The design of this protocol is quite complicated: you have to allow for the possibility that the acknowledgement and not the original message got corrupted (lost); you have to avoid round-trip times too often; you have to worry about an acknowledgement being delayed rather than lost; and so on. It is an interesting tutorial exercise to develop a simple protocol (that none the less correctly does the job required) for error correction by retransmission. A number of data communication texts describe this protocol – the thing to look for is a discussion of the **alternating bit protocol** (including a treatment of **parasitic transmissions**, which arise if ACKs with the wrong sequence number produce retransmission of the data rather than being ignored, resulting in the double transmission, to no useful effect, of all subsequent messages). The protocol is a simplified version of HDLC. Such a detailed tutorial is beyond the scope of this text, but the important point to recognize is that the provision of error recovery by retransmission adds considerable complexity over the basic functions.

The second additional feature uses many of the same mechanisms as are developed for error correction by retransmission. This is flow control – the ability for a receiver to say 'Hey, slow down, you are sending me stuff faster than I can handle it, my buffers are filling up, and we are in danger of hitting an overrun situation.' Again, problems arise if a 'stop-sending' message gets corrupted (lost), but even worse problems arise if an 'it's OK to go on now' message gets corrupted, because this produces a deadlock situation. (One end thinks flow control is released and that the other end has nothing to send, while the other end has material to send, but thinks that flow is still blocked.) The detailed design of flow control provision is usually integrated with retransmission mechanisms, and is similarly an addition of considerable complexity to the basic protocol.

HDLC has within it not only defined subsets containing only the essential framing and error detection features, but also defined subsets with full error correction by retransmission and flow control.

The main purpose, however, of this amount of detailed discussion is to identify the sorts of features that we need to provide between end-systems, and to encourage the reader to think about how we should use concatenated (multiplexed) links (see section 4.2).

3.4 Formal Description Techniques (FDTs)

This discussion is something of an 'aside', but the reader who wishes to progress to reading OSI Standards needs to be aware of the FDT work, and a brief treatment of this comes appropriately after the discussion of the complexity of protocols which is what gives rise to the need for some notation (an FDT) which will enable clear, unambiguous and error free specifications to be produced.

If you pick up any of the main OSI Standards specifying a protocol, you will find some more-or-less readable English language text, usually followed by several pages of **State Tables**.

The State Table concept is a fairly simple one, particularly for those readers familiar with spreadsheets. It has been used from the earliest days of OSI specification work. An example is given in Figure 3.5 for what is there called the EG-service and protocol (EG for 'example'). This is an asymmetric service and protocol so the State Tables for the EG-sender and the EG-receiver are different. The protocol being defined is actually the Alternating Bit Protocol, with the parasitic transmissions bug.

In developing a State Table, the designer identifies a number of states that an implementation can be in (the first is the initial state, the others are the result of earlier exchanges). For each state, there is a single column in the State Table. (In the example, the sender initial state is S-WAIT0 (S for State), with the other states S-WAIT1, S-WACK0 (meaning that an ACK0 is awaited) and S-WACK1, and the receiver initial state is S-WAIT0 with other state S-WAIT1.) Note that it is often the case in practice that a State Table is too large to print in its entirety on a single page, so the logically single State Table is often printed over several pages as a set of related tables. We are describing the single logical State Table here.

The State Table has one row for each **event** that can occur in an implementation. The most important events are the receipt of the different types of message that constitute the protocol, and the issue of service primitives (requests for transmission of messages) by the layer above, together with the expiration of any timers that might be running.

(In the example, events at the sender are the issue of an EG-DATA request service primitive from the layer above, arrival of an ACK0 or ACK1 message from the link, or expiry of a timer.)

The cells (row-column intersections) contain the action to be taken when that event occurs in that state, which is usually either the issue of a service primitive

EG-Receiver

State / Event	S-WAIT0	S-WAIT1
DATA0	ACK0 EG-DATA indication →S-WAIT1	ACK0 →S-WAIT1
DATA1	ACK1 →S-WAIT0	ACK1 EG-DATA indication →S-WAIT0

Primitives: EG-DATA request and indication

Messages: DATA0, DATA1, ACK0, ACK1

States: As column headings

Actions: SET-TMR, RESET-TMR

EG-Sender

State / Event	S-WAIT0	S-WAIT1	S-WACK0	S-WACK1
EG-DATA request	DATA0(NEW) SET-TMR →S-WACK0	DATA1(NEW) SET-TMR →S-WACK1	X	X
ACK0	→S-WAIT0	→S_WAIT1	RESET-TMR →S-WAIT1	DATA1(OLD) SET-TMR →S-WACK1
ACK1	→S-WAIT0	→S-WAIT1	DATA0(OLD) SET-TMR →S-WACK0	RESET-TMR →S-WAIT0
TIMER	X	X	DATA0(OLD) SET-TMR →S-WACK0	DATA1(OLD) SET-TMR →S-WACK1

Figure 3.5 *A simple pair of State Tables.*

to the layer above, or the transmission of a protocol message, followed by the new state to be entered as a result of that event and action. (Thus the EG-DATA request in state S-WAIT0 at the sender results in transmission of the new data as a DATA0, setting the timer, and entering state S-WACK0. Arrival of an ACK1 message in state S-WACK0 results in retransmission of DATA0 with the old (previous) data, resetting the timer, and staying in the same state. The reader should note that this cell (and its equivalent in S-WACK1) is what produces parasitic transmissions, and may care to modify the State Table to correct this bug!)

For local events (issue of service primitives), an event may be forbidden in some states (for example, a T-DATA request cannot be issued until a connection has been established), and the State Table can indicate simply that that event cannot occur in that state – enforcing that is a local matter. On the other hand, for external events (arrival of messages), the events can occur in any state if the other communicating system is non-conforming. The State Table has to reflect this by specifying actions and new states in such cases. Thus in the example, the EG-DATA request for the sender can be decreed never to occur in certain states because it is a local matter to prevent it. Similarly, the TIMER event cannot occur where marked X because it is logically impossible for it to occur in these states (the timer is not running). All other events can, in theory, occur in all states (perhaps only if the peer is non-conformant) and must be covered.

The State Table approach is usually called a 'semi-formal description technique', to distinguish it from 'true' Formal Description Techniques. In the example, the precise actions indicated by 'DATA1(OLD)', for example, need English language specification (it means 'resend a DATA1 message, with the same data as was sent last time'). This is common in the state table approach, and is what makes the technique only semi-formal.

Formal Description Techniques are part of what the reader may have encountered more generally as **Formal Methods** – the use of a language or notation for specifying systems that is formally rooted in mathematics, and which can be parsed and understood by computers. (Perhaps the best-known such languages for general system design are Z and VDM – not yet standardized. If you have never heard of them, it doesn't matter.)

In the case of Formal Methods for OSI protocol specification, two languages (FDTs) have been developed and standardized. One is called Estelle, and the other LOTOS (Language of Temporal Ordering Specification).

There is a third language, favoured by some CCITT/ITU-T workers, called System Description language (SDL) which is closer to Estelle than to LOTOS, but it does not have an ISO Standard, and is not generally regarded by ISO workers as part of OSI in the way that Estelle and LOTOS are accepted, nor is it normally used for specifying the mainstream OSI protocols. (It is, however, standardized as a set of CCITT/ITU-T Recommendations in the Z.100 series.) SDL will not be discussed further in this text.

Estelle is an extension of Pascal, and critics of Estelle make the following points.

- It specifies too much that should be left unspecified (implementation matters), because it is effectively writing a complete computer program for the implementation of the protocol.
- It is very verbose, Estelle specifications frequently being several times the size of the corresponding English text.
- Specifications written using it are hard to transform and analyse for correctness because it contains all the features of a general programming language (so you can't, for example, even prove in general that it will terminate).

On the other hand, much of an Estelle specification is fairly easily readable by anyone with a programming background. Figure 3.6 is a piece of Estelle. We shall not attempt to explain it, but the careful reader will recognize a certain similarity to Figure 3.5!

LOTOS, by contrast, produces much shorter specifications that are amenable to computer analysis. It does, however, use symbols such as ? and ! with a very specialized meaning, making a LOTOS specification extremely hard to read by anyone who has not been steeped in the language. Figure 3.7 is a piece of LOTOS, but it is too small a fragment for useful discussion of its meaning.

```
specification Example;
  default individual queue;
    type T = 0..1;
    channel U(R1,R2);
      by R1:put;
    channel S(R1,R2);
      by R1:dt(p:T);
      by R2:ak(p:T);
    module E systemprocess;
      if U:U(R2); S:S(R1);
    end;
    body E1 for E;
      state S0,S1;
      var x:T;
      initialize to S0 begin x:= 0 end;
      trans when U.put
              from S0 to S1
                begin output S.dt(x) end;
            when S.ak(p)
                provided p=x
                  from S1 to S0
                    begin x:= 1-x end;
    end;
end.
```

Figure 3.6 *A piece of Estelle.*

```
process Transmitter
[ul,mt,t])
(tws:Nat,hs:Nat,lu:Nat,rq:PduQueue)
  : noexit :=
  (
    Sender [ut,mt,t] (tws,hs,lu,rq)
  >>
    accept hs:Nat,rq:PduQueue in
      Transmitter
      [ut,mt,t](tws,hs,lu,rq)
  )
[]
  (
    AckRec [mt,t] (hs,lu,rq)
  >>
    accept lu:Nat,rq:PduQueue in
      Transmitter
      [ut,mt,t] (tws,hs,lu,rq)
  )
[]
  (
   TimeOut [mt,t] (hs,lu,rq)
  >>
   Transmitter
   [ut,mt,t] (tws,hs,lu,rq)
  )
[]
  (IgnoredPdu[mt] (hs,lu)
  >>
  etc.
```

Figure 3.7 *A piece of LOTOS.*

In very crude terms, workers on the European side of the Atlantic Ocean tend to favour LOTOS, while workers on the other side tended to favour Estelle during the 1980s.

Most OSI protocol Standards have the authoritative specification done using English text and State Tables. In addition, there is sometimes an informative annexe containing an Estelle or LOTOS description, but more commonly such a description, if it exists in a published form at all is published as an ISO Technical Report, not as a Standard or part of a Standard. There is one exception, where the latest work in the FTAM (File Transfer, Access and Management)

In the beginning there were Mathematicians, who built   345 triangles and pyramids and ruled the world ... and lo, it was good. But then there grew up physicists and chemists and engineers and *technologists* who built bridges and computer systems and *business applications* ... and the study of mathematics waned,   and it was bad.

But then there was invented Formal Methods to control and govern the work of the engineers and technologists ... and lo the mathematicians again ruled the world,   and lo it was good.

Encyclopedia Galactica,   AD 3045

Figure 3.8 *Encyclopedia Galactica, A D 20085, p. 49576.*

Application Layer Standard (FTAM is discussed in section 10.4) makes very heavy use of LOTOS as the main authoritative text for specifying the overlapped access extension to FTAM.

I will end this discussion with another quotation from the ***Encyclopedia Galactica – 20085 version***, and two slides I sometimes use. The quotation is shown in Figure 3.8, and the first slide asks:

Why FDT's?
Prevent omissions
Prevent ambiguity
Allow machine analysis of specifications
And because they are fun!

FDTs can help to ensure a specification is complete and unambiguous, and potentially allows a computer to analyse it in various ways to detect some errors, or to generate test suites, and with the right sort of (warped?) mind, you can get a lot of fun out of developing a detailed and correct FDT specification!

The second slide redresses the balance:

Why not FDTs?
Specs take a long time to produce
Too much detail, too easy to get wrong
Shortage of people with FDT skills
And they are boring! (and hard!)

It takes a lot of care and time to develop a specification in an FDT, and there are few people with the necessary skill, or even with the skill to check that the result is correct. If you add the need for protocol design skills and knowledge of an application area to the FDT skill, the number of people able to do the work gets even smaller. And finally, it would be hard for anybody to enjoy a piece of FDT as bedtime reading (too many trees obscuring sight of the wood), whereas I have on many occasions fallen asleep reading English language text specifying protocols!

4
World-wide connection

4.1 Introduction

In this chapter we will discuss in somewhat more detail the most important piece of standardization in the whole of OSI – the Network Service Definition. First, let us review the concepts introduced in the architectural discussion. We are here concerned about

- agreeing on an end-to-end functionality (the nature of carrier services) for data transmission over networks on a world-wide basis;
- identifying the types of message exchange to be provided and the parameters of those messages;
- defining a notation to support the linkage between Network Layer protocols claiming to provide support for this functionality (to arbitrary Transport Layer protocols) and Transport Layer protocols wishing to make use of this functionality (over arbitrary carrier protocols).

In the architectural discussion, we described the Network Service Definition as 'the decking', summarizing the Internal Organization of the Network Layer Standard by saying, 'It doesn't matter what goes on down below. All that matters is the decking.' At this point in the text, however, we have to explain to the reader that there are two styles of 'decking' that are standardized for the ship: 'Her Majesty's Ship the Network Carrier One has a flat deck with scrubbed bare boards. It needs little beneath it, and travels very fast. By contrast, Her Majesty's Ship the Network Carrier Two has very ornate decking, beautifully crafted, with mahogany filigree inlays, and sails beautifully across the roughest seas.'

The reader will ask why it was necessary to standardize two types of decking. We address this in the next section, and consider the details of the interchanges (the Network Service Definition) and addressing and routing issues in the remaining discussions of this chapter.

4.2 End-to-end functionality

Following the description of the functions of traditional single-link protocols, we recognize the need to provide (at least on an end-to-end basis):

- framing of bits into messages
- error detection for corrupted messages

- error correction by retransmission of messages
- flow control to prevent over-run.

We have protocol standards in place (HDLC) which can provide all these functions over a single link, and as our first attempt at defining the Network Service, we will assume we simply put end-to-end a set of links to provide an end-to-end service with these properties. An alternative approach is introduced later, where we do not exercise all these functions on a per-link basis, but rather defer some for end-to-end (only) provision.

Of course, there are some further features that we need to introduce, as part of the Network Layer standardization providing a world-wide service, that go beyond what is needed in the link layer.

- Multiplexing: We need to recognize that at least our internal links between nodes will have to carry, simultaneously, communications relating to the transmissions of many pairs of end-systems, not just one, and that it is probably desirable to provide flow control on an individual channel of communication, so that a 'stop-sending' message from one end-system does not cause a complete internal link to be blocked for transmissions which are not related to the one for which the 'stop-sending' was issued.
- Addressing and routing: We need to solve the problem of how an internal node can determine which outgoing link to send a message on, and to recognize that multiple paths may be possible between different end-systems, with different overall properties.

If we are to handle the multiplexing and flow-control questions, then we are forced into recognizing the concept of sequential messages forming part of some **connection** which threads its way through the network between a pair of end-systems (each end-system pair potentially having more than one connection between them, each one being treated independently). We also have to recognize that 'stop-sending' messages may need to be generated by internal nodes, not just by end-systems, if overrun is to be prevented when, for example, one particular output link from the node is getting overloaded. Such messages need to be applied to only those connections on other links that are 'feeding' the overloaded outgoing link: it is not satisfactory to simply choke off all communication on all other links.

Thus we are led to the concept of logical channel identifiers that are known to (remembered by) internal nodes, with this information stored when a logical connection is first established, and forgotten when the connection is released. Flow-control messages can now be designed which contain a logical channel number, and hence affect only data on that single logical channel.

We get a small bonus from this arrangement. If a node detects that the link accessed by one of its ports has failed because the Link Layer protocol is not being honoured, it can use its knowledge of what connections are running through that link to send messages back saying the connection has broken.

Equally, if the buffer allocation mechanism for a node occasionally fails, causing it to have to discard some data messages for some particular connection (but the connection is still in place), it again becomes possible to signal this in both directions. We talk about a **network-generated disconnect** and a **network-generated reset** in these two cases.

One final point, and we are almost there! Once we provide a flow-control mechanism, we really need to provide for an end-system some means of signalling (in violation of the flow control) 'Look, we are blocked, do something about it.' This is commonly called an **interrupt message**, or in OSI terms, the transmission of **expedited data** – 'expedited' because it can overtake normal data if flow control, perhaps transiently, is blocking the normal data.

So ... we have a variety of messages which are understood by internal nodes and end-systems (set up a connection, disconnect, reset, expedited data, normal data), and a pretty complicated protocol to be implemented by those systems, on top of the already pretty complicated full-function link-layer protocols they are implementing. What has been described and developed above is in broad terms the **X.25 protocol** which is both the *de jure* and the *de facto* protocol for provision of public data communication services by PTTs, and is also widely used in private networks.

But ... can we do any better than this? Is this really the best way of putting together a set of links to provide an end-to-end service (Figure 4.1)?

The above treatment seemed to follow logically from chaining together full-function links (Figure 4.1(a)). But maybe some of the things done in the link level protocol for a single link between a pair of end-systems would be better done on an end-to-end basis, not on each link, when we chain links together through network nodes to provide a world-wide network service interconnection? Suppose, in particular, that we take only the essential link layer functions of framing and error detection (with resulting discard), and leave all question of flow control and error correction by retransmission as matters to be solved by exchanges between the end-systems involved, with internal nodes having no knowledge of such exchanges (Figure 4.1(b)). What happens then?

We no longer need to introduce the concept of logical channels as far as the network nodes are concerned (in the Network Layer). These, together with any associated retransmissions and flow control, can be part of a higher layer specification (the Transport Layer). As far as the Network Layer is concerned, we have only one message, the data message. We ensure that each data message contains the address of its destination, solve the routing problem (section 4.4), and treat each message independently. We have no concept of a 'connection': we have designed a **connectionless** communication protocol. (The term 'datagram service' has in the past been used to describe this form of operation, but the term is not used in OSI.)

What then does this **connectionless mode**, to use the OSI terms, give us compared with the X.25 **connection-oriented mode**? First and foremost, it gives us a very simple set of protocols to be operated in relation to the main data transfer by network nodes. Such nodes can therefore be fast and cheap (in comparison to X.25 switches). Secondly, the end-to-end service results in the

Single link (pre-OSI):

Single channel over tandem links:

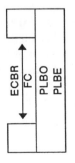

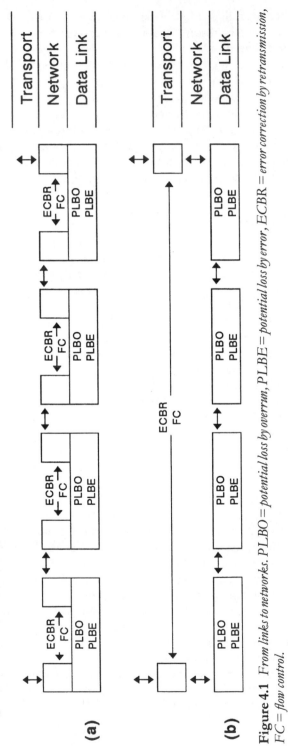

Figure 4.1 *From links to networks. PLBO = potential loss by overrun, PLBE = potential loss by error, ECBR = error correction by retransmission, FC = flow control.*

following features occurring on a fairly frequent basis that probably have to be addressed by a protocol between the end-systems if applications are to run successfully:

- occasional loss of messages due to corruption on one of the links in the path;
- occasional loss of messages due to congestion in a network node (if you can't say 'stop-sending' when your buffers are getting full, your only other option is to discard any other incoming material), dependent on the amount of traffic being generated by other end-systems;
- occasional delivery of messages out of sequence because the 'best' route changed between the transmission of the two messages;
- retransmission (if done by end-system to end-system exchanges) following loss or corruption involves a delay corresponding to a full network-wide round-trip time, rather than to a single-link round-trip time
- no notification to a sender that the communication has failed.

In fact, on the latter point, we can relatively cheaply provide some sort of facility in this area. We probably want to carry the address of the sender in every message anyway, so that the end-system knows where the message has come from, and if we make this visible to the network nodes, then we can arrange to send a message back to the sender if a network node discards messages for some reason or other. Note, however, that in contrast to the network-generated reset and disconnect messages in the 'connection-oriented' approach, there is no guarantee that these messages will actually get back – they also may get discarded through corruption or congestion.

So ... where are we now? We recognize two different ways of approaching a world-wide network service. We can take either the connection-oriented approach of a 'reliable' service over each link, but with quite complex protocols for network nodes, or the connectionless approach of a very simple network protocol, but with more work to be done by end-system to end-system exchanges that are transparent to network nodes. Which is best? If you are a PTT, trying to make money from a public service to customers, I wonder which you would choose? How do you charge a customer if you throw away five per cent of everything the customer gives you? Still worse, the percentage you throw away will be dependent on what other customers are doing! Maximizing the size of your own market sector clearly leads to provision of the 'reliable', but perhaps more expensive, service. In practice, the connection mode of operation was adopted by CCITT in the X.25 protocol. It was the only mode of operation in the first Reference Model Standard, but the connectionless mode of operation was added to both the ISO and the CCITT text as an addendum. Why? (See the following text.)

While focus on the provision of a public network service might lead to a favouring of the connection-oriented approach, if computer vendors are to market networking products using their own switches, connected by leased lines, they are likely to favour fast cheap switches (sorting out any resulting mess in their end-systems) and hence the connectionless approach. In practice a number of computer vendors adopted the connectionless approach, and this is the approach also used in the Internet (the TCP/IP community), discussed earlier, where IP is the connectionless network protocol known by nodes and carrying data and global addresses, and TCP is the connection-oriented error correction, reordering, flow-control-providing protocol run by end-systems.

Quite clearly then, both approaches are viable ways of providing a network service, and there was a substantial lobby for the standardization of both approaches. As an aside, there are clearly some possible halfway houses, such as end-to-end transmissions in which loss of order does not occur, or in which reliable link protocols (error correction by retransmission) are used but loss due to congestion remains possible. Current interest in frame relaying and in the most appropriate network service to provide using very high bandwith (a few hundred gigabits per second) optic fibre networks is focusing on intermediate types of service that may in the future become sufficiently important to be added as recognized types of OSI Network Service. For the present, however, there are just the two extreme services standardized, with no suggestion of producing standards for any service that is part way between the two.

I have so far described the favouring of the two approaches as a PTT versus computer vendor divide. This is not wholly true. Some computer vendor networks are connection-oriented in nature. It is also the case that there was in the 1980s something of an Atlantic divide, particularly between the academic communities, with the USA firmly favouring the connectionless approach because of their large Internet investment, and the UK (and to some extent other countries in Europe) building large private X.25 networks. (This divide broke down in the 1990s, with a growth in the use of TCP/IP – connectionless – private networks in Europe.)

Which approach is best? There are experts who will argue very cogently on behalf of both approaches. There are uncontested advantages for each approach, as well as contested points, such as which approach degrades more gracefully if a lot of nodes and links fail? Some further discussion of the pros and cons of Figure 4.1 (a) and (b) is presented in Chapter 5.

Which approach will stand the test of time? Again it is hard to express an opinion. PTTs will be slow to abandon X.25 and hence the connection-oriented approach, but there are some features of internal ISDN operation that are connectionless in nature, and the overall impact of ISDN, particularly broadband ISDN (B-ISDN), is yet to be determined. Equally, it is clear that the Internet community and a number of computer vendors see any migration to OSI as being to the 'connectionless' Standards, and once such migration is complete the connectionless approach is likely to have a very long life. It looks fairly likely that we will be left with both approaches for some time, with any move to a single approach being dependent on the transition to very high bandwidth real-time networks.

Is it a good or a bad thing to have the two approaches standardized? At one level, it was essential. If OSI had contained in the 1980s only the connectionless approach, it would never have been accepted by the PTTs. Equally, if it had only the connection-oriented approach, it would never have been accepted by some computer vendors, or by the Internet community, and any move from TCP/IP to standardized protocols would be even more difficult than it is now.

What of interworking? There are a few points to make. First and foremost, it is always possible to treat an X.25 connection (or any other connection, such as an ISDN connection) simply as a link between internal network nodes, and to use that link to form part of a connectionless network service. (This is sometimes called 'tunnelling through' X.25 – an approach frequently used for LAN to LAN interconnection.) If the X.25 link actually provides a direct connection between the two end-systems, then the frequency of loss over it will be very small, but that does not prevent it being used as if the frequency was high! Secondly, two end-systems, one implementing only the connectionless network service over an X.25 interface and the other implementing only the connection-oriented network service over an X.25 interface, will not interwork over a direct X.25 connection between them.

If one accepts that both connection-oriented and connectionless approaches will be around for a long time, it would seem desirable for the majority of computer vendors to implement both the connection-oriented set of protocols and the connectionless set of protocols over both their X.25 interface and their Ethernet interface, for example. Moreover, it would be desirable for network nodes with Ethernet or leased line or X.25 interfaces to be capable of routing both connectionless and connection-oriented traffic over all their interfaces. There are signs that this (particularly the latter) is beginning to happen, but once such a situation is achieved, making both connection-oriented and connectionless communication possible between most pairs of end-systems, the way a decision will be taken in an instance of communication to use one or the other mode of communication is unclear. Certainly there is nothing in the standards today to permit any form of negotiation of which to use, nor is there any real consensus on which is best in various cases, except for the following.

- Where the interconnection between a pair of end-systems is formed by a single PTT-provided X.25 connection, it is probably more efficient and less expensive for the end-systems to run in the connection-oriented mode.
- Where an X.25 path is used between internal nodes to connect two Ethernets, and there are multiple communications running between different end-systems on the two Ethernets, it is probably more efficient and less expensive for the end-systems to run in the connectionless mode (because that enables use of a single X.25 connection for all the communications, while the connection-oriented approach in this scenario needs a separate X.25 connection for each end-system communication).

In the absence of most vendors implementing both approaches, there is a real potential for the world of conforming OSI systems to divide into two non-communicating parts – those containing implementations of the connection-oriented

protocols and those containing implementations of the connectionless protocols. To address this problem, an ISO Technical report (TR10172, 'Network/
Transport Interworking Specification') has been produced describing the operation of an **Interworking Unit** that relays at the top of the Transport Layer to
provide interworking between these two worlds. This is strictly in violation of
the OSI architecture, as the Transport Layer protocols are supposed to be for
'QOS (Quality of Service) improvement' directly between the end-systems and
have no role in the provision of end-to-end connectivity. It also suffers from
the practical disadvantage that the QOS (undetected error rate, or frequency of
signalled errors – resets or disconnects) actually seen by the application is not
dependent solely on the two end-systems, but also depends on the quality of
the Interworking Unit. For these reasons, the Technical report has a health warn-
ing saying, roughly (but in more guarded language): 'This Technical report
was produced by the group defining OSI Standards. It is not, however, an OSI
Standard, and never will be an OSI Standard, but it is an agreed specification
that may be useful under some circumstances.'

The extent to which such an Interworking Unit is actually deployed in the
field, if at all, remains to be determined.

4.3   The OSI Network Service Definition

This text is largely a summary of what has gone before. Formally, the OSI
Network Service is a single service that contains both connectionless and
connection-oriented exchanges.

The connectionless exchanges at the service level are particularly simple – a
single message carrying up to (just under) 64K bytes of data. This is reflected
in the service as the N-UNITDATA request and indication primitives. The service definition also includes a **queue model** that gives, in an abstract way, precision to the fact that there is no flow control, may be loss of messages, and may
be reordering. As an aside, the Connectionless-mode Network Protocol
(CLNP) is actually not as simple as the above discussion implied, as it needs to
address the problem of limited message sizes on various carrier links (not necessarily known to the end-systems involved), and hence the need for network
nodes to fragment the messages and for reconstruction at the receiving end.
This is, however, buried in the protocol, and is not visible in the service definition. The 64K limit is, however, present in the service, and reflects limitations
in the protocol on the number of bytes used for various length fields. It should
also be noted that it is not expected that connectionless messages will normally
be anywhere near the 64K limit, due to the point made earlier that the probability
of loss of the whole message depends on its total size (there is no mechanism
for retransmitting fragments, so if one fragment is lost by corruption or congestion, the whole message is lost).

The connection-oriented exchange involves many more service primitives.
Again there is a **queue model** that is used to abstractly describe the existence

of flow control, the in-order delivery, the possible bypassing of normal data by expedited data, and the potentially destructive nature of resets and disconnects in relation to data sent but not yet delivered. The service primitives, with corresponding message types, are as follows.

- The N-CONNECT request, indication, response and confirm to set up a connection (and which can also carry up to 128 octets of user data in each direction).
- The N-DISCONNECT request and indication (the indication resulting from either an N-DISCONNECT request or from a network-generated disconnect), again carrying up to 128 octets of user data.
- The N-DATA request and indication carrying an unlimited length of user data (in this connection-oriented case, the unlimited length is fully usable, because retransmission of fragments occurs across each link in the communication). For those familiar with X.25, the fragmentation corresponds to the use of the X.25 more bit, with the service primitive corresponding to the transmission or receipt of a complete X.25 M-bit sequence.
- The N-RESET request and indication (carrying 128 octets of user data). This is used to signal loss of N-DATA primitives, but without loss of the connection. Although the request primitive is formally defined, it is expected that resets in OSI use will normally arise only from network nodes.
- The N-EXPEDITED request and indication (carrying 32 octets of user data). This primitive bypasses flow control.
- An N-DATA-ACK request and indication (no parameters).

Of the above, only the N-DATA-ACK may seem curious to the reader. Acknowledgements are normally internal matters to the protocol, operating on a link-by-link basis, so why do we need such a service primitive? When X.25 was first implemented, some PTTs produced networks where an acknowledgement for receipt of the last fragment of a complete M-bit sequence was only given to a sending system when the message had been acknowledged by the receiving end-system (end-to-end significance of acknowledgements), while others gave an acknowledgement when the last fragment had been received by the first network node. (The first X.25 Recommendation did not make it clear which was intended.) The main difference for the user is that in the former case a later disconnect request could not overtake and destroy the acknowledged data, while in the latter case it could. In the 1980 revision of X.25, the situation was clarified by the introduction of the so-called D-bit (D for delivery) by which a sender could request, on each message, whether end-to-end acknowledgement was needed or not. The N-DATA-ACK, and a corresponding parameter on N-DATA to request end-to-end acknowledgement, is a formalization and abstraction of this end-to-end acknowledgement provision in the X.25 service. The way this feature is used in the Transport Layer is discussed in the next chapter.

It is beyond the scope of this text to give a more detailed treatment of the parameters of these primitives, but there are no new concepts involved, and the interested reader should now be well able to read the actual Standard.

You will no doubt have noted from the above discussion a very close relationship between the *de facto* service provided by X.25 and the formally defined, connection-oriented OSI Network Service. The match is actually extremely close, but not total. (Skip to the end of this discussion if you are not familiar with X.25.) In particular, the X.25 Q-bit does not appear in the OSI Network Service. The main (only, in international specifications) use of this bit is in the X.29 protocol supporting terminal login over X.25 to remote systems. This protocol is an application protocol, and hence in the OSI architecture should not be running directly over X.25 anyway, so in principle the loss is not too great. Moreover, the OSI Network Service is in practice provided over Ethernet (and other LANs), leased lines and ISDN by the use of the X.25 protocol, so the Q-bit is in practice if not in theory available end-to-end provided only that it is correctly mapped by actual relay systems.

As far as the provision of the OSI Network Service is concerned, it has already been stated that X.25 (1984) does indeed fully support the (connection-oriented part of the) service. In the 1980 version, there were problems with support of N-EXPEDITED, which carries 32 octets of user data, by the X.25 INTERRUPT packet, which could carry only eight octets of data. There was also a problem that in some cases the X.25 DISCONNECT packet did not make provision for carrying the 128 octets of user data specified in all circumstances for N-DISCONNECT. The major impact of these problems was that the OSI Network Service Definition introduced an option into the definition. The availability of N-EXPEDITED was made optional and subject to negotiation. This had a somewhat unfortunate knock-on effect when we get to the Transport Layer, and indeed on up to the Application Layer, as we shall see later.

4.4   Addressing and routing issues

There has probably been more written on addressing and routing in traditional data communications texts than on any other single subject. It is not the purpose of this text to add to that coverage, and the reader who is interested in a more theoretical treatment of the issues and options should consult those other texts.

There are many aspects of naming and addressing, some of which go beyond the Network Layer, but are treated in this discussion because an understanding of them is needed to set the scene.

There are two levels of naming in OSI, much as there is in TCP/IP. At the top level, there is a relatively user-friendly, organization-structure-related naming scheme for end-systems and the applications running on them. These names are called **system-titles** and **application-entity-titles**. (For those that know TCP/IP, they correspond closely to the domain names of the Internet). This top level of naming is converted by local look-up tables or by a directory query into a 20-octet **Network Service Access Point** (NSAP) **Address**

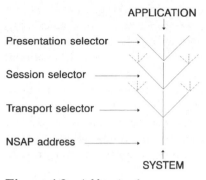

Figure 4.2 *Addressing fan-out.*

(which globally identifies the associated end-system, be it attached to an X.25 network, an ISDN connection, an Ethernet, or whatever) together with a set of **selectors** (one for the Transport Layer, one for the Session Layer, and one for the Presentation Layer) which provide fan-out to applications within an end-system (Figure 4.2). In TCP/IP, by contrast, there is a 32-bit **Internet Address**, carried by IP, corresponding to the 20-octet NSAP Address, and a single fan-out parameter, the **port number**, carried by TCP (Figure 4.3). Provision for three selectors in OSI, of which typically all but one will be null, allows for various implementation structures of the upper layer code in actual systems and is discussed further in Chapter 9.

The OSI Network Service Definition requires that supporting protocols carry the NSAP addresses of the called and calling systems end-to-end. This is essential to support the use of these addresses by relay systems in progressing the total network connection. It is again a failing of X.25 (1980) that it has no provision for carrying such addresses, and hence cannot be used for anything other than a single-X.25-hop direct connection between a pair of end-systems. This is corrected in X.25 (1984).

The allocation of IP addresses in TCP/IP is a very centralized matter. By contrast, OSI NSAP addresses allow an address for a system to be constructed out of a whole variety of other globally unambiguous information. This is partly why the NSAP address space is so large. In particular, the address can be formed

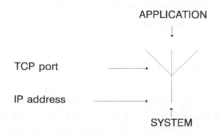

Figure 4.3 *TCP/IP address fan-out.*

using a combination of an X.25 and an Ethernet address, or using a telephone number, or using an ISDN number, or using a number obtained by an existing Registration Authority that allocates International Code Designators (ICDs) to international organizations, or using an allocation from an ISO/IEC national Body. Note, however, that the sole purpose of the NSAP address (like the TCP/IP IP address, but unlike X.25 addresses) is to provide an unambiguous identification – the internal structure is irrelevant. The fact that it might be constructed using some specific telephone number, or some specific X.25 address, carries no implication that the corresponding end-system can be accessed, either directly or indirectly, by a call to the corresponding telephone socket or X.25 port.

So much for addressing – the provision of world-wide unambiguous names for end-systems. Now what about routing? How do network nodes learn where to send connectionless packets or connection requests that they receive? In the case of X.25 addressing, address space is allocated initially to a PTT or RPOA, and is then typically allocated in accordance with the topology of the X.25 network run by that PTT or RPOA. In particular, it is necessary to change people's addresses if the network configuration is changed by the splitting of one switch into two (for example). Routing tables in these circumstances can be based on the hierarchical structure of the address, and are typically manually configured and fairly static.

This feature of X.25 addresses has led some people concerned with connection-oriented communication to tend, incorrectly, to ignore routing problems. Even where an end-to-end public X.25 connection is possible, this is not necessarily the optimum route between a pair of end-systems if bandwidth and cost are taken into account and if private network overlays are present. Most of the running in producing Standards for protocols to support the distribution of routing information has come from those mainly interested in connectionless communication, despite the fact that both communities have precisely the same requirement for the distribution of routing information related to NSAP addresses. Fortunately, the emergence in the early 1990s of new products that were primarily developed to support connectionless traffic (and hence the routing protocols supporting that traffic), but which were also capable of routing connection-oriented traffic (using the same routing tables), largely eliminated the problem.

So how does routing work in OSI? It is very similar to the latest routing approaches in TCP/IP, recognizing three levels of division of the world for the purposes of routing activity. The highest level comprises a complete routing domain, and would normally correspond to a complete organization. (Geographically, of course, routing domains are really overlapping planes. They are rarely disjoint, and permitted cross-connections between organizations are links between these overlapping planes – see Figure 4.4.) The next level allows the organization to have what is essentially a backbone of **level 2 intermediate systems** serving a number of areas consisting of **level 1 intermediate systems**. Within the lowest level (a level 1 area), every intermediate system (network node) maintains a complete picture of all end-systems and intermediate

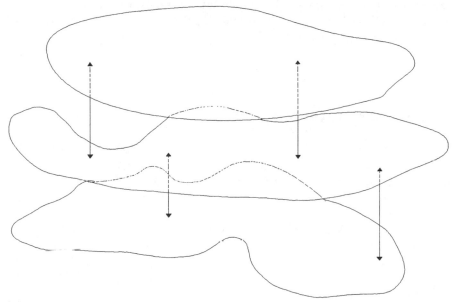

Figure 4.4 *Overlapping planes.*

systems and the available links between them (each link having a set of 'costs' associated with it), and calculates 'least-cost' routes to each system in the domain. 'Cost' can be based on money charges (**the expense metric**), on bandwidth (**the default metric**), on expected delay (**the delay metric**) or on the probability of undetected errors (**the error metric**), resulting in four potentially different routes to each destination in the level 1 area, one for each metric. The actual route chosen depends on flags in the data messages being routed (and reflected as QOS parameters in the Network Service) that indicate trade-offs requested for this connectionless message or connection.

The most common algorithm for calculating least-cost routes is based on work done by Dijkstra, and is well described in many textbooks. The actual protocol (ISO 10589) involves each intermediate system noting the state of each of its links, including the metrics for that link, and flooding that information throughout the entire level 1 area. Routing between these lowest level domains does not involve complete flooding, and routing at the highest level, between independent organizations who may not wish to make their internal structure or connections to other organizations known generally, was still under development in the early 1990s, and is likely to involve manual configuration to at least some extent.

Within the lowest level of domain, where the traffic will be greatest, there will be optimal routing. Between independent organizations, however, routing will, in general, and of necessity, be sub-optimal. Thus two routers connected to the same local PTT X.25 exchange in Europe, but owned by two different international organizations, may not know about or be allowed to use the direct route between them, but will instead know about and use a route halfway round the world and back, via their head offices in the USA, and pass through the local PTT exchange going out and coming back.

4.5   Network Layer protocols

There are broadly four categories of protocol that have been developed for the Network Layer (Figure 4.5). We have met them all implicitly in the earlier text, and this short discussion merely draws the earlier work together.

First, there is the protocol which forms the main back-bone for connection-oriented services, either over a LAN, over ISDN, or over a PTT network. This is called the **X.25 Packet Layer Protocol**, reflecting its origins in the X.25 Recommendation. In fact, it is a slight generalization of the CCITT X.25 Recommendation, reflecting the fact that for OSI use, particularly over LANs, leased lines and ISDN, we have two identical implementations (DTEs in X.25 terminology) directly communicating, whereas in a PTT's network, the standardized communication is always between a DTE and a DCE (a network node) which are configured to know their role, and implement slightly different rules of procedure. (Internal DCE to DCE protocols are not the subject of CCITT Recommendation, and are a matter for individual PTTs and/or implementors of X.25 switches. This is why X.25 is sometimes described as being only an interface protocol, not a network protocol.)

Similarly, there is the protocol that forms the main back-bone for connectionless services. This protocol (Connectionless Network Protocol – CLNP) is very strongly related to the IP protocol of TCP/IP, with almost identical functions and fields in messages, although it is not quite bit-for-bit compatible. There are two main differences. The first is that the addresses being carried are 20-octet NSAP addresses, not 32-bit TCP/IP addresses. The second is that the protocol for sending 'we can't deliver it' messages back to a sender is a separate protocol in TCP/IP (ICMP – Internet Control Message Protocol), but is a part of CLNP in OSI. Other differences are minor, but do exist.

Main connection-oriented protocol   (X.25 PLP)

Main connectionless protocol   (CLNP)

Convergence protocols, relay
operation, subnetwork access

Routing and address formats

Figure 4.5 *Categories of network layer specification.*

The third group of specifications provide the convergence from existing real networks to the OSI Network Service. They generally reference one or other of the above specifications, saying how the Network Layer protocol is to be carried over the actual real network.

And finally, we have a collection of specifications related to the routing problem, starting with a Technical report introducing the concept of **Inter-domain Routing** (within a single organization) and **Intra-domain Routing** (between independent organizations), and extending to protocols for communication between intermediate systems (generally of the 'flooding' variety) and communication between end-systems and intermediate systems to make themselves known. Further details on these protocols is beyond the scope of this text.

4.6 New approaches

In the late 1980s, stability of the network service was largely assumed (and hence of the middle layer protocols and services – Transport, Session and Presentation – which were defined to be independent of network technology and applications). In the early 1990s, however, new approaches began to be developed which introduced some instability into these areas.

The history of networking has been one of questioning the obvious and developing new approaches. Thus in the early 1980s it was apparent that one could signal down links at speeds far in excess of the ability of cheaply available computers at that time to switch the traffic between different links. How then to build high-speed (megabit per second) networks switching traffic between different links? The answer is blindingly obvious once presented: 'Don't switch!' – send to everybody and let the destination select traffic destined for it. This was one of the key ideas which allowed the development of local area networks: cabling systems in which traffic floods to all stations with no switching. Of course, there remained the problem of determining who had control of the medium (was allowed to transmit) at any point in time, and a variety of contention and token-controlled mechanisms were developed to provide 'fair' access to the medium by each station in a controlled and shared manner. In most, but not all cases these mechanisms were distributed, with the only intelligence in the network being in the attached stations. None of this, however, really impacted the Network Service. Ethernet and Token Ring Local Area Networks were just another hop in the provision of either a connection-oriented or a connectionless Network Service.

The developments in the early 1990s, however, were more significant. The issue being addressed in this case was how to cope with congestion and potential overrun within the network. Traditionally we have seen two approaches to the problem of 'What happens if a network node is receiving traffic on one or more of its links faster than it can dispose of it on some other link?' (A similar problem exists if an end-system cannot accept traffic as fast as the network is trying to deliver it.) The first approach to the congestion problem introduces the relatively complex X.25-like protocols to say 'stop' and 'go on', and produces the connection-oriented Network Service. The alternative approach simply discards traffic when congestion occurs, producing the connectionless Network Service. At first sight, these are the only two possibilities if a node gets overloaded.

There is, however, another option. Why not agree the bandwidth that is to be provided, using some negotiation at the start of a connection, and then have all parties support, and keep within, that bandwidth? There are still quite complex protocols needed, but they can now operate once at set-up time and do not affect the speed of handling the main traffic. We thus get a 'lightweight' but connection-oriented-like (no discard) service. Moreover, the error rate on signalling systems using optic fibre has dropped to about 1 in ten to the power 14, even for extremely high transmission speeds, compared with about 1 in ten to the power 7 for old-fashioned signalling on copper wires, so loss due to detected errors becomes less of a feature.

There is one other important advantage of this so-called 'managed bandwidth' approach: because queues are no longer needed to smooth out statistical variations in traffic, much better network delay characteristics and delay jitter (variation in delay) can be achieved, making it possible to handle real-time voice and video over such networks in an effective manner. The disadvantage, however, is that it assumes a steady flow of data and is clearly inappropriate for traffic that is inherently bursty. Queues, however, are not the only source of delay. If a packet is to be stored (for error detection or routing analysis) before being forwarded, there is inherently a delay introduced by the node equal to the time taken to transmit the packet, and hence proportional to the packet size. Equally, whatever multiplexing or medium access control mechanism is provided, the unit of multiplexing will be the packet, and hence the delay before it will be possible to send material related to some channel of communication is proportional to the packet size in use. Both these issues give rise to a need to work with small packets if low-delay characteristics are needed; these small packets are called **cells** and are 48 bits in length.

Another important development was the approaches to compression of video data that emerged in the 1990s. One important technique requires a base transmission of information (relatively low bandwidth) whose correct transmission needs to be guaranteed, and which is sufficient to produce a 'reasonable' picture, while additional transmissions are needed to produce a good picture, but their loss is not disastrous. With this approach, the network needs to guarantee the base transmissions (vital, high priority), but can afford to provide only a probabilistic service for the rest (enhanced picture, low priority). Discard, due to occasional millisecond congestion, of the low priority data will show itself only as a temporary degradation of picture quality and can be accepted – it may not even be noticed by the human visual system. Traffic with these sorts of characteristics clearly opens up a number of additional options for network design and bandwidth management.

There are a number of approaches emerging in support of these broad concepts, expected to culminate in the late 1990s in a wide availability of a 'broadband' wide-area network service giving speeds up to a few gigabits per second, and potentially rising to a few tera (ten to the power 12) bits per second, and with very good delay characteristics. Interested readers should investigate books and papers on 'Broadband Integrated Services Digital Networks' (B-ISDN), on 'Synchronous Digital Hierarchy' (SDH), on 'Cell and frame relay', and on 'Asynchronous Transfer Mode' (ATM). Such topics go beyond the scope of this book, but their impact on OSI in the late 1990s is likely to be important.

There was formal recognition in ISO during 1991 that these new technologies would require at least a refinement, and perhaps a more substantial reworking, of the OSI Network Service, and a consequent extension of the services and protocols of the Transport Layer designed to improve the 'quality' of the end-to-end Network Service. This formal recognition took the form of the establishment of New Work Items covering these layers to develop appropriate standards to meet the needs of high-bandwidth low-delay networks and the applications that they made possible.

At the time of writing this book (1995) the precise direction of these new or extended Standards is unclear, and will be ignored in the rest of this text. It is, however, clear that the old arguments between proponents of the connectionless approach and the connection-oriented approach to provision of an end-to-end connection are likely to be overtaken by approaches based on ATM-based communication systems. The views of the **_Encyclopedia Galactica – 2008J version_** are given in Figure 4.6.

In the beginning the two giants CONS and CLNS fought for supremacy on the copper wires, but in the days of flashing light the fibres thrilled to the tingle of ATM—mode transmissions with its small cells and good delay characteristics, and the giants quietly died.

Encyclopedia Galactica, AD 20085

Figure 4.6 _Encyclopedia Galactica, AD 20085, p. 21076._

5
Sorting out the mess

5.1   Introduction to the middle layers

In the next three chapters, we introduce and discuss some of the concepts under-lying the three layers that are at the heart of OSI, the Transport Layer, the Session Layer and the Presentation Layer. Whereas one could argue that a net-work is 'OSI' if and only if it runs protocols providing the OSI Network Service (connectionless or connection-oriented) across it, one could equally argue that an application protocol is 'OSI' if and only if it runs over these three middle-layer protocols. It is also appropriate to remind the reader at this time that it is in these three layers that we are expecting to address issues that are inde-pendent of both the technology used for communication *and* the application that is the subject of the communication.

Thus in these three layers, and these three layers alone, one can reasonably expect OSI to become 'complete' and 'stable'. Such stability is inherently depen-dent on stability in the specification of the OSI Network Service, which provides the technology independence to these layers, and on stability in the broad identi-fied application-independent requirements that determine the functions to be performed in these layers. As discussed above, it became evident in the early 1990s that assumptions of stability in these two areas were becoming invalid, and new work was initiated to extend the functionality of the transport layer and surrounding services. None the less, it remains the principle that once com-pleted, OSI standards in these middle layers should remain relatively impervious to future changes in technology, or to the need to develop standards for new applications.

As a final introductory point, it should be noted that the issue of connection-less versus connection-oriented services was originally discussed in relation to end-to-end transport mechanisms, with the expectation underlying earlier text that applications would want a connection-oriented type of service. There are two concepts that are important to this discussion:

- individual messages that might or might not get through (connectionless); versus
- a stream of messages delivered in sequence with any loss or failure signalled to both end-systems (connection-oriented).

These twin concepts can be applied to the actual service used by an applica-tion. One can conceive of some applications (but maybe not many!) where use of connectionless communication without attempting any form of error recovery is acceptable.

To support this, and paralleling the UDP (User Datagram Protocol) that is a lesser known but equal partner to TCP in the TCP/IP suite, the OSI stack includes connectionless services mapped right up to the Application Layer. The connectionless services and protocols in the middle layers are much simpler than the connection-oriented services and protocols, and are ignored in the following discussion until a final section of this chapter covers this material. Thus the following discussion is concerned solely with the provision of connection-oriented services to the application, albeit obtained, in the case of the Transport Layer, using either a connection-oriented or a connectionless Network Service.

5.2   Overview of the Transport Layer

The Transport Layer Standards address the issue of providing mechanisms that will improve the overall quality of the end-to-end service which is in use. The quality of an end-to-end communications path will normally be highly dependent on where it is going. For some paths there may be heavily overloaded and unreliable switches in use, while for other paths from the same end-system there may be no congestion problems and highly robust switches. In the former case an application will frequently need mechanisms operating between the two end-systems (a Transport Layer protocol) to correct from network failures and to provide a reliable communications path. Such protocols can clearly be made independent of the actual application in use, and can sensibly be standardized as an application-independent standard. We say protocols (plural), because the functions to be performed will depend on the quality of the end-to-end communications path and could vary from a do-nothing protocol for use over a highly reliable path to a very complex protocol if the path is very poor. There is, of course, an infinite range of possible variation in a network communications path, and hence a potentially infinite set of 'useful' Transport Layer protocols. Standardization requires the selection of a small number of such protocols to meet the range of needs.

In OSI, we talk about the **class** of Transport Protocol, Transport Protocol Class 0 to Transport Protocol Class 4 – effectively five protocols (Figure 5.1). The usual abbreviation in the literature for, for example, Transport Protocol Class 4 is either TC4 or, more commonly, TP4. The principle of the OSI Transport Layer is that all five protocols will be supported by a general-purpose implementation, with an appropriate selection made for each instance of communication. Of course, if an implementation is designed for a rather specialized environment (for example, for use only over network paths consisting of a single high-quality PTT-provided X.25 hop), then corners can be cut and protocols designed for a less reliable path need not be implemented. In the early days of deployment of OSI implementations, one frequently found systems implementing only one protocol class, resulting in serious interworking problems (this is discussed in section 5.11), but increasingly today one finds implementations

Name	Summary of functions
TP0	Do nothing
TP1	Signalled-error recovery
TP2	Multiplexing
TP3	TP1 and TP2 functions
TP4	All singing and dancing: Error detection Works over connectionless

Figure 5.1 *Classes of transport protocol.*

with the full range of capability, and with the ability to select and negotiate with the other end-system about which one to employ.

5.3 Quality of service

In order to give some precision to a discussion of 'quality', it is necessary to define what constitutes the 'quality' of a network path. The Network Service Definition includes the concept of the quality of service (QOS) provided by a connection-oriented or a connectionless transmission in terms of a number of parameters such as cost, delay, probability of loss, probability of undetected errors, throughput, and so on. Values associated with some, but not all, of these parameters are carried in network protocols, and can in principle be used to affect the route taken by a connectionless transmission or by a connection.

These same parameters are passed down in service primitives from an application when a connection is being established, to reflect its needs, and are passed to the Network Layer which can use them to help determine the best route to be taken by this communication. They are, however, also used in the Transport Layer, in conjunction with knowledge of the quality of service being provided by the network for this particular communication path, to determine which of several possible protocols to employ in the Transport Layer to meet more nearly the QOS needs of the application. Of course, not all aspects of quality of service can be improved by an end-to-end protocol. An obvious example is the round-trip delay time. If this is poor, there is nothing the two end-systems can do to improve it. None the less, there are a number of aspects of QOS that an appropriate choice of Transport Protocol can improve.

The idea of improving on a poor underlying service is fundamental to the use of the connectionless Network Service, where the lossy nature of the network path makes it necessary to improve the service by end-to-end error recovery and reordering in order to support most applications. In the TCP/IP suite, it is

TCP (Transmission Control Protocol) that performs this role. This protocol is often compared with TP4. While there are many similarities, there are none the less differences in the details of the service provided.

There are five main aspects of quality that the Transport Layer addresses. These are:

- cost of the communication (see section 5.4);
- available bandwidth (see section 5.5);
- recovery from errors which are signalled by the Network Layer (the network generated N-RESET and N-DISCONNECT primitives) in the connection-oriented service (see section 5.6);
- recovery from unsignalled loss or reordering of messages (predominantly in the connectionless service, but potentially in the connection-oriented service too) (see section 5.7);
- detection of corrupted messages where the corruption was not detected and dealt with by a lower layer (see section 5.8).

5.4   Cost reduction

How does one reduce the cost of transmission? One obvious suggestion would be to provide data compression to reduce the amount of data transmitted. Provided charging over this network path was based on the number of bits transmitted, and not simply on a message count, this could be quite effective. (It could also improve the effective bandwidth seen by the application.) For better or for worse, this is not a feature of the Transport Layer of OSI. Compression is seen as an issue related to the way in which information is represented, and hence as something which is the concern of the Presentation Layer, and compression features are not present in any of the transport classes.

So how else can cost reduction be achieved? The trick is to consider the possibility of several connections running between the same pair of end-systems. In the tariffing of many PTTs, the cost of an X.25 connection is a combination of a volume charge for the amount of data sent and a holding charge for the length of time the connection is kept open. For certain types of traffic, for example that generated by a user on a terminal logged in to a remote host computer, the two charges are often about equal.

Suppose, then, that we have 20 terminals physically attached to one computer system, and all logged in to the same remote computer system. In the simplest approach, each would have its own X.25 connection, and we would be paying, say, 60 pence per minute. But now suppose we were able to introduce a protocol that provided multiplexing of all those 20 logical channels of communication onto a single X.25 connection. This would not affect the volume charges, but would effectively eliminate the holding charges, resulting in a halving of the total cost to about 30 pence per minute. This is one of the functions performed

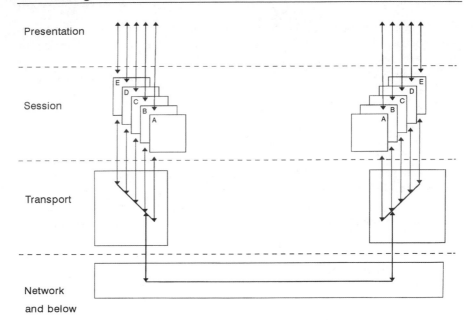

Presentation

Session

Transport

Network
and below

Figure 5.2 *Transport Layer multiplexing.*

by the OSI Transport Layer (in classes 2, 3, and 4): multiplexing. Multiplexing in the Transport Layer is in principle no different from multiplexing in the Network Layer: it involves tagging each message with an identification of the logical channel (transport connection) it relates to, transmission over the shared carrier (the single network connection), and separation at the receiving end. Figure 5.2 shows multiplexing of five channels onto a single network connection carrier.

5.5   Bandwidth improvement

Again, we recognize that, for better or for worse, standards for compression are not a part of the OSI Transport Layer. So how do we improve bandwidth?

The recognition here is that it might be possible to establish multiple network paths which are wholly independent (different links at the two ends, different networks involved) but which can be used together to provide what appears to the application as a single communication path whose bandwidth is the sum of the individual paths.

Figure 5.3 shows a single logical path being split between five carrier paths. If the Transport Layer part of Figure 5.3 is turned upside down, it looks remarkably like Figure 5.2, so this technique is often called **downwards multiplexing**. The necessary features in the protocol are, however, very different. The problem with downward multiplexing is that packets sent in sequence (alternately say) on the two paths will not necessarily arrive in sequence at the receiving end,

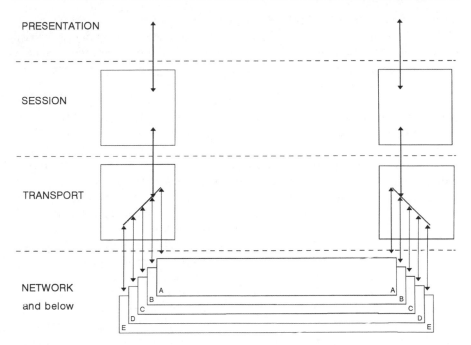

Figure 5.3 *Transport Layer splitting.*

due to delay variations. Thus there is a requirement to number each message and to resequence at the receiving end. This requirement is, however, no different from the requirement to resequence messages that have got out of order because a connectionless Network Service is being used. Thus support for bandwidth improvement is indistinguishable from support for error recovery when operating over the connectionless network service.

5.6   Recovery from signalled errors

This is a feature which relates only to the connection-oriented service. The connectionless service has only the N-UNITDATA primitives, and does not provide any signalling of loss.

In many countries, the introduction of X.25 in the late 1970s produced an initial service in which unreliability and overload in the network switches produced a relatively high frequency of network-generated N-RESET primitives (signalling loss of data, but with the connection intact) and of N-DISCONNECT primitives (signalling loss of a connection). If you were using the connection for a terminal login session, the loss of data was usually fairly easily recovered, but the loss of the connection meant you were usually forcibly logged out, with all that that implies in terms of loss of work in progress. Providing protection against such transient network failures seemed like a high priority. Today, the reliability of PTT-provided X.25 services is generally much higher, and in many countries network-generated resets and disconnects hardly ever appear. None the less, private networks can still be configured in such a way that overloads are frequent, or can be based on older equipment where hardware reliability is poor.

Protection against such signalled errors requires the numbering and storage of every message that is sent, with discard of the stored message when its receipt at the remote end-system has been acknowledged. Following a network-generated reset, or after re-establishing the connection on a network-generated disconnect, when messages may have been lost, a simple exchange can determine which messages to resend, and the communication continues with the break largely invisible (except for a possible time delay) to the application. There are no retransmissions on timers: action is taken to see what has been lost and retransmit only when a signalled N-RESET or N-DISCONNECT occurs.

One of the more sophisticated features of the Network Service is the provision, within that service, for so-called end-to-end acknowledgement of data (the D – for *d*elivery – bit of X.25, mapping into the N-DATA-ACK service primitive). If the D-bit is used, the Network Layer signals acceptance of a message if and only if it has been accepted by the Transport Layer of the remote end-system, not just by the nearest network node. This provides a ready means for discarding stored messages without introducing additional message exchanges in the Transport Layer. Unfortunately, from the point of view of the Transport Layer, the D-bit facility (the N-DATA-ACK service primitive) is optional in the Network Service. Thus the Transport Layer protocol needs to be able to provide explicit acknowledgements if the N-DATA-ACK is not supported on this communications path.

Transport Classes 1 and 3 provide recovery from signalled errors using this approach.

5.7   Recovery from unsignalled errors

This requirement produces the most complicated protocol features. The errors being addressed here are loss of messages and reordering of messages – precisely the sorts of error that are a characteristic feature of the connectionless network service. Thus only those classes (and in fact it is only one class – TP4) that support this feature are capable of being used over the connectionless network service. In addition to numbering and storing messages, the lack of any concept of a D-bit in the connectionless service makes it necessary to transmit explicit acknowledgement messages, which of course may get lost due to error or overrun, and to set timers running with retransmission when material is not received. This protocol is also characterized by a 'heart-beat' transmission based on the expiry of an idle timer. If the protocol is operating over the connection-oriented service, it takes no account of N-RESET and N-DISCONNECT primitives, nor is any use made of N-DATA-ACK: 'recovery' takes place only when a message has been unacknowledged for too long, and an attempt is made to re-establish a lost network connection only when the connection is needed to transmit or retransmit data.

The resulting protocol (TP4) is considered by many to be both complex and also expensive on network bandwidth, particularly if used when it is not in fact needed (for example, over a reliable PTT-provided X.25 connection). None the less, it is the only protocol that can cope with the connectionless network service and is capable of being used over a connection-oriented service as well, and hence it provides the realistic option for those wishing to implement only a single class of transport protocol.

5.8   Extra error detection

There is a potential problem with the error detection features provided in the lower layers. These are based on the Data Link Layer's so-called cyclic redundancy codes (CRCs). No matter how good the CRC is at detecting errors, the fundamental problem with this approach is that errors are detected only if they occur on an actual link. Thus a CRC is calculated and appended to a message on transmission, checked on reception, and recalculated for what is usually a slightly changed message (header fields often change from link to link) before transmission on the next link. Errors which are introduced due to bus or memory failures within the network node thus go undetected. Again, in the late 1970s, when OSI was developing, computers used for network nodes often had less inherent internal error detection circuitry than the mainframes that formed the end-systems. Thus there was considerable attention on trying to provide an error detection capability that was as reliable as the communicating end-systems.

The connectionless internet protocol (the main protocol supporting the connectionless network service) made some attempt to address this problem. It required that, if the header of a message was modified by a node, the redundancy check information was not recalculated from scratch, but rather was amended in accordance with the amendment made to the header. This makes undetected errors less likely, but still possible. The necessary cure is to generate redundancy check information using only that part of the message that should be transmitted unchanged end-to-end, to carry that redundancy check information with the message transparently through the network, and to check it at the receiving end-system. This feature is provided only in TP4, which again strengthens the case for TP4 implementation.

5.9   Packaging into TP0 to TP4

What then are the main characteristics of the TP0 to TP4 Standards? (Refer again to Figure 5.1) TP0 is a very simple protocol. Apart from identifying itself in connection establishment, it is a do-nothing protocol. Each request for a transport connection involves the establishment of a single new network connection, and messages received as T-DATA requests from the Session Layer are passed as N-DATA requests to the Network Layer, unchanged. TP0 is even more basic than that. Because fielding network-generated N-RESET messages is the job of the Transport Layer, there is no corresponding T-RESET primitive defined in the Transport Service, so if an N-RESET indication is received, TP0 has no choice but to generate an N-DISCONNECT request to drop the network connection, and to signal upwards a T-DISCONNECT.

There is one other problem with TP0. In the early discussions on the definition of the connection-oriented Network Service, that part of X.25 which supported N-EXPEDITED (messages that bypass flow control in a nondestructive manner) – the so-called X.25 INTERRUPT packet – carried only one octet of user data. It was determined that, because of the need to carry headers for upper layers, a minimum requirement for the N-EXPEDITED primitive was 32 octets of user data. At the time, it looked as if X.25 (1980) would not be changed, but there was a strong 'political' lobby for the Network Service to be completely supported by X.25, so the N-EXPEDITED service was made an optional feature of the Network Service, and TP0, the do-nothing service, was designed to make no use of N-EXPEDITED. This means that, with TP0 in use, even though X.25 did eventually modify the INTERRUPT packet to support N-EXPEDITED with 32 octets of user data, the T-EXPEDITED service primitive cannot be used. This has some important knock-on effects on the upper layers, which will be discussed later.

Turning now to TP1: the TP1 protocol provides for recovery from signalled errors (N-RESET and N-DISCONNECT indications) as described above. It provides a simple and low-overhead option for operation over the connection-oriented network service when the rate of signalled errors is too high for TP0 to be a reasonable option. If an N-DISCONNECT indication appears, and the connection cannot be re-established in a reasonable (agreed by the two ends) time (a bulldozer has gone through the line), then a T-DISCONNECT indication is issued. TP1, by contrast with TP0, is a 'respectable protocol', in that it fully supports and maps T-EXPEDITED. If N-EXPEDITED is not available, or if the D-bit is not available, then TP1 will introduce its own acknowledgement messages in order to provide acknowledgements and its own flow control. By never exercising Network Layer flow control, it can provide support for T-EXPEDITED even if N-EXPEDITED is unavailable.

Transport Protocol classes are not hierarchical. The next in sequence is TP2, but this does not provide the functions of TP1. TP2's sole function is the provision of multiplexing (see the cost reduction discussion in section 5.4). If TP2 is in use, a new logical channel can be added using a network connection without any disruption to any existing channel. However, if an N-RESET or an N-DISCONNECT indication appears, a T-DISCONNECT indication is issued on all the multiplexed channels. Thus in circumstances where such indications are a frequent occurrence, any cost-savings in TP2 may be more than balanced by the increased disruption that such indications cause.

TP3 is simply a combination of the features of TP1 and TP2 – multiplexing and recovery from signalled errors.

TP4 is the all-singing all-dancing protocol described above which will operate over a connectionless or connection-oriented service, provides multiplexing of multiple transport connections onto a single network path, can map onto multiple network paths (downward multiplexing), ignores signalled errors, and detects and recovers from lost, out of order, and corrupted messages. TP4 does, however, have some problems, the most significant being its treatment of expedited data. The 'rules' written into the Reference Model require that while expedited data may overtake normal data, normal data should never overtake expedited data. When expedited is provided within a connection-oriented service in which all messages are sequenced, simply as a relaxation of flow-control rules, then this is clearly and easily achieved. When, however, an attempt is made to support expedited data in the Transport Layer over a connectionless service, it is somewhat harder to guarantee that a later normal message will not arrive ahead of an expedited message, due to them taking different routes. TP4 solves this problem by delaying the transmission of subsequent normal data until receipt of any expedited data has been acknowledged by the receiving end-system. This introduces an effective round-trip-time blockage on the normal flow whenever expedited data is sent. The problem does not arise in any other transport class. This property leads some experts to oppose protocol options above the Transport Layer that make use of expedited data, and particularly to oppose use of the Session Layer major synchronization primitives that are described later.

5.10   Interaction with Teletex

One of the major developments within CCITT in the late 1970s was the development of the Teletex service, with the definition of the relevant protocols to operate over X.25.

Teletex was intended to provide a similar service to the rather ancient Telex, but with a much broader character set, and operating over normal (X.25-based) public data networks, rather than requiring a dedicated network.

While today there are few people who would argue that Teletex compatibility is an important requirement for anything, in the late 1970s and early 1980s there was an important and powerful lobby for such compatibility. In particular, there was, in relation to the Transport Layer, a desire to be able to rewrite the specification of S.70 (now T.70) in terms of the issue of T-service primitives, in such a way that the actual bits transmitted down the line in the use of X.25 would be identical to the existing specification.

The Teletex Transport Protocol was essentially a do-nothing protocol, with the only added value being extra parameters in the connection establishment messages for further addressing fan-out within end-systems. It made no use of expedited data. The TP0 protocol was specifically designed to provide the requested Teletex compatibility, and it was this as well as the decision to make N-EXPEDITED optional (see the previous section) that led to TP0 not supporting the T-EXPEDITED primitives.

There was a further problem. If the Transport Layer is going to work by having all classes of protocol implemented by most systems, with the appropriate protocol 'plugged in' for each connection, then there has to be an agreement between the two end-systems on what is 'the appropriate protocol' to plug in. This requires parameters in the initial connect messages to offer and agree one of the classes (class negotiation). Such a feature was not, of course, present in the Teletex protocol, which had just the one class, so negotiation of classes cannot be bit-compatible with Teletex. The Standards permit an implementor of class 0 to handle zero only, and not to negotiate, to cope with Teletex, but implementation of full negotiation is none the less recommended to allow full open working with non-Teletex systems.

5.11   Implementation of transport classes

In the ideal world, all classes will be implemented by all end-systems. Deployed systems in the 1990s do not, however, represent the ideal world. Pressure to get OSI products onto the market quickly have led to selection of a single transport class for initial implementation, and selection of specific classes in procurement profiles. Purchasers of OSI products should look carefully at the transport classes that have been implemented or are promised for implementation. The different classes do not interwork. Even in the case of TP3 versus TP1 and TP2 (where each of TP1 and TP2 is a subset, functionally, of TP3), an implementation of TP3 alone will not interwork with an implementation of TP1 alone. This is even more true for TP0 and TP4. The views of the *Encyclopedia Galactica – 20085 version* are given in Figure 5.4.

The ISO Standard and the CCITT/ITU-T Recommendation both contain conformance clauses requiring specific classes to be implemented in order to try to ensure interworking, but in this area the desires of the two groups (ISO is broadly the club of computer vendors, and CCITT/ITU-T is broadly the

𝔗𝔥𝔢 𝔭𝔬𝔯𝔱𝔯𝔞𝔶𝔞𝔩 𝔬𝔣 𝔱𝔥𝔢 𝔗𝔯𝔞𝔫𝔰𝔭𝔬𝔯𝔱 𝔆𝔩𝔞𝔰𝔰𝔢𝔰 𝔦𝔫 𝔍𝔩𝔟𝔬𝔱𝔰𝔬𝔫'𝔰 𝔯𝔢𝔫𝔬𝔴𝔫𝔢𝔡 𝔭𝔩𝔞𝔶 (𝔢𝔫𝔱𝔦𝔱𝔩𝔢𝔡 '𝔄𝔫𝔦𝔪𝔞𝔱𝔦𝔬𝔫 𝔬𝔣 𝔒𝔖𝔍') 𝔴𝔞𝔰 𝔰𝔦𝔤𝔫𝔦𝔣𝔦𝔠𝔞𝔫𝔱. 𝔇𝔢𝔠𝔩𝔞𝔯𝔢𝔡 𝔗𝔓4 𝔱𝔬 𝔗𝔓0: '𝔍 𝔴𝔬𝔯𝔨 𝔥𝔞𝔯𝔡 𝔴𝔦𝔱𝔥 𝔟𝔞𝔯𝔢 𝔡𝔢𝔠𝔨𝔰 𝔞𝔫𝔡 𝔭𝔯𝔬𝔳𝔦𝔡𝔢 𝔞 𝔳𝔞𝔩𝔲𝔢𝔡 𝔰𝔢𝔯𝔳𝔦𝔠𝔢. 𝔜𝔬𝔲 𝔞𝔯𝔢 𝔞 𝔡𝔬−𝔫𝔬𝔱𝔥𝔦𝔫𝔤 𝔱𝔥𝔞𝔱 𝔯𝔢𝔮𝔲𝔦𝔯𝔢𝔰 𝔩𝔲𝔵𝔲𝔯𝔶 𝔟𝔢𝔫𝔢𝔞𝔱𝔥 𝔶𝔬𝔲. 𝔍 𝔴𝔦𝔩𝔩 𝔫𝔬𝔱 𝔱𝔞𝔩𝔨 𝔱𝔬 𝔶𝔬𝔲.'

𝔈𝔫𝔠𝔶𝔠𝔩𝔬𝔭𝔢𝔡𝔦𝔞 𝔊𝔞𝔩𝔞𝔠𝔱𝔦𝔠𝔞, 𝔄𝔇 20085

Figure 5.4   *Encyclopedia Galactica, AD 20085, p. 31945.*

club of the PTTs) diverged, and different text appears. In Recommendation X.224, implementation of TP0 is mandatory. All else is optional. In ISO 8073 implementation of either TP0 or TP2 is mandatory, with a fairly complex set of rules which say, in particular, that if TP4 is implemented, then TP2 shall be implemented.

If we turn to the GOSIP specifications (Government OSI Profile), which specify requirements for government purchases, we find, slightly confusingly, a USA GOSIP and a UK GOSIP. These differ significantly in coverage, have totally different text even in common areas, but more importantly express differing requirements in some important areas. Transport Classes is one of these. USA GOSIP requires TP4, but recognizes TP0 for connection to a PTT X.25 public network, and recommends TP2 because that is a requirement of the ISO Standard if TP4 is implemented. By contrast, UK GOSIP requires TP0, but recommends TP2 again for ISO conformance.

What is happening in practice? Interest in TP1, 2 and 3 is minimal. Many implementations support either TP0 (particularly over X.25) or TP4 (particularly over the connectionless Network Service), and frequently little or nothing else. Note also that TP4 over the connectionless Network Service over an X.25 tunnel is a very different protocol from TP4 over the connection-oriented Network Service over individual X.25 virtual circuits. Implementation of the latter is very much less common than implementation of the former. At this point the reader is cautioned that situations like these change quite rapidly, and that in this area the above discussion may soon be little more than a description of past history. None the less, the issues are very real ones for procurement in the 1990s.

5.12   Selection of classes for an instance of communication

Let us assume the best possible scenario.

- All network switches (nodes, intermediate systems) support protocols on each of their links to other intermediate systems which permit that link to form part of an end-to-end connectionless path or to form part of an end-to-end connection-oriented path.
- All end-systems similarly support connectionless or connection-oriented communication with each of the intermediate systems that they are connected to.
- All end-systems support all transport classes, including TP4 over both the connection-oriented and the connectionless Network Service.

It is important here to remember the 'Internal Organization of the Network Layer': the connection-oriented Network Service can be supported by an X.25 link with no additional protocol over X.25, and with one X.25 virtual circuit for each Network Service connection; the connectionless Network

Service can also be supported by an X.25 link using what is termed 'tunnelling through', where a single X.25 connection is opened up when needed to transmit traffic to that intermediate system, and closed down when there is no traffic. Both uses of X.25 are fully standardized and implementable. In the same way, a simple link to a router can be used to pass connectionless traffic in a straightforward manner, but can also be used to carry the X.25 protocol to support the connection-oriented service. Thus the above assumption that any route which works for connection-oriented will work for connectionless is not an impossible one.

Having said that, deployed intermediate systems today usually either:

- handle connectionless traffic (received from a dedicated line, from Ethernet, or from an X.25 public network interface) using the Connectionless Internet Protocol on all links, and 'tunnelling through' X.25; or
- handle connection-oriented traffic (received from a dedicated line, from Ethernet, or from an X.25 public network interface) using the X.25 protocol over the dedicated line and the Ethernet;

They do not normally do both. Similarly, end-systems packages will often support only the connection-oriented use of network interfaces and links or only the connectionless use of those interfaces and links. In both cases, however, the situation is changing rapidly in the mid-1990s, with a number of intermediate systems and end-system packages becoming available that have the dual Network Service capability. This situation can be expected to increase, and our scenario essentially says: 'Let us assume that the choice of which Network Service and which Transport Class to use is not dictated by which have been implemented, but rather by which will get us to a particular end-system, or which is possible through a particular set of routers: all are available.'

What then are the pros and cons? The advantages and disadvantages of running an end-to-end connection using the connection-oriented approach as opposed to using the connectionless approach is something on which there is no general agreement. It frequently becomes a religious war, and can also get confused with the TCP/IP versus OSI debate, where OSI is frequently equated to X.25 (connection-oriented) and TCP/IP uses the connectionless approach. (The reader of this text should by now recognize that OSI should not be equated to X.25, and has both approaches firmly established within it.)

Here are some points, some almost contradictory, which some people will argue strongly for, while others will argue that they are either not true or not important! It is hard to make a reasoned technical judgement:

- Connectionless networks are more robust in establishing new routes if links or nodes go down.
- Connection-oriented networks degrade more gracefully if loss of nodes or links produces a major traffic overload on the remainder of the network.

- Loss of messages is recovered with at worst about a single-link round-trip delay in the connection-oriented case, but can require an end-to-end round-trip delay in the TP4 over connectionless case.
- TP4 over connectionless works well with traffic losses of up to 5%, but degrades badly, in terms of throughput and delay, at higher traffic losses. The connection-oriented approach (because recovery is done on a link by link basis and flow control prevents loss due to overrun) performs better in lossy and congested situations.
- In pure connection-oriented (relaying using the OSI Network Service mapping from link to link) as opposed to real X.25 networks (where additional protocols operate) the route taken by a connection is established once and for all at connection-establishment time, and loss of a link or node produces an N-DISCONNECT indication to both ends and requires major end-to-end action to re-establish a new connection on a different route. In the connectionless case, routes are dynamically established on a per-packet basis, and loss of a node or link at worst produces loss or duplication of a small number of packets.
- Highly dynamic routing protocols to support the automatic dissemination of routing information to intermediate systems have been developed to support the connectionless network service, and routing for connection-oriented has in the past tended to be based on human configuration of relatively static routing tables.
- There is no reason why routing techniques developed for connectionless traffic should not be used to route connections, and increasingly implementations supporting both approaches will use dynamic routing techniques and a single routing table for both sorts of traffic.
- The basic protocol for connectionless communication is much simpler and cheaper to implement than that for X.25 (because of the additional flow control and error recovery), and runs faster on cheap routers.
- The full Connectionless Internet Protocol is at least as complicated and slow to run as X.25 because of its fragmentation and reassembly capabilities, per-packet routing based on quality of service optimization, and notification of discard.
- The cost, in terms of network traffic/charges and in terms of end-system CPU utilization, of running TP4 over the connectionless network service and tunnelling through a PTT's X.25 network for a single transport connection to a remote end-system on that PTT's network is very much higher than supporting that transport connection with TP0 directly over X.25.
- If a PTT's X.25 network is being used to link two Ethernet sites, with a large number of independent connections running from different end-systems at one site to different end-systems at another site (Figure 5.5), the connection-oriented approach requires a separate X.25 virtual circuit for each connection (TP2 and TP3 can't help in this case, because the end-systems are all different), whereas the connectionless approach with TP4 automatically multiplexes the traffic over the PTT's X.25 network onto a single X.25 virtual circuit, reducing costs.

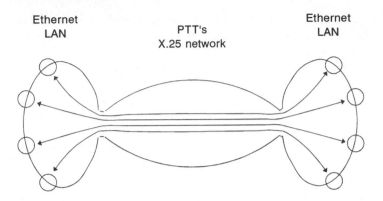

Figure 5.5 *Multiple communications over X.25.*

- TP4 over connection-oriented has slight CPU-usage advantages over TP4 over connectionless over an X.25 interface, but these are small and unimportant.

So where does that leave us on selection of transport classes? If both end-systems are directly connected to a PTT's reliable X.25 network, the simplest option is TP0, and it should be selected if there is unlikely to be another simultaneous but independent connection required between the same end-systems. If more than one connection is likely, then using TP2 does not add a great deal of complexity, but does allow the same X.25 virtual circuit to be used for all connections, and hence gives cost savings with many PTT tariffing systems.

By contrast, if a PTT's network is used by a pair of intermediate systems to handle traffic between them, and that traffic is the result of a number of transport connections running between different end-systems, then TP4 and connectionless is likely to produce cost savings.

If a PTT's network is not involved, then the choice is less clear-cut, and the general points made above about connectionless versus connection-oriented become more prominent. If the connectionless approach is taken and the path is predominantly one of linked X.25 (private network) connections, then this probably involves unnecessary CPU cycles and network traffic compared with the connection-oriented approach, perhaps using TP1 or TP3 if one of the linked X.25 networks is a bit unreliable.

Use of TP4 over the connection-oriented Network Service will provide advantages over TP1 or TP3 only if there is a significant unsignalled corruption or loss of packets, as opposed to network generated resets and disconnects.

Little more can be said. It is one thing to act as God (full knowledge) to determine the 'best' choice in particular circumstances; it is a somewhat different matter for an end-system to obtain enough knowledge about the possible network paths to an intended destination in order to make sensible decisions.

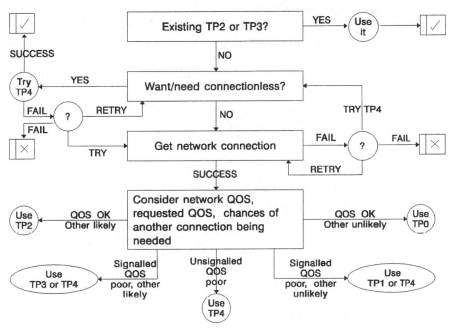

Figure 5.6 *Choice of transport protocol class.*

For a sending implementation requested to make a new transport connection to an end-system, the decision-taking process might go as follows (Figure 5.6).

- Do I have an existing TP2 or TP3 connection to this end-system? If so, it is probably sensible to add this new connection into the existing multiplex, provided the quality of service matches reasonably that requested for this transport connection, otherwise ...

- Should I attempt to use connectionless traffic, or should I establish a new network connection to this end-system? This will bring in most of the considerations above. If the decision is connectionless, then we use TP4 and that ends the matter, but if the decision is connection-oriented then ...

- We establish a network connection, requesting a quality of service based on what is required by the application, and note the actual quality of service parameters returned. Based on the actual quality of service parameters and/or some in-built knowledge, we can decide whether we need TP1 or 3 for reliability, or maybe even TP4. We can also decide, again based on in-built knowledge, whether we are likely to want another connection to the same end-system, and if so whether network charges would be reduced by use of TP2 or TP3 instead of TP0 or TP2 with the further possibility of using TP4.

- We further decide which other classes to offer as alternatives. If we have implemented them all (which we are assuming), we list as alternatives all other classes, or maybe we exclude only those that we know will be unworkable (for example, if we know the path is unreliable, the other end-system might not, and we should avoid offering TP0 or TP2).

- The Transport Layer connect packet is then despatched, using an N-DATA request, and the remote end-system then goes through a similar process to determine whether to accept the class we said we preferred, or to accept one of the alternatives we offered, or to reject the connection.
- If the transport connection attempt fails (using connectionless network service or using connection-oriented), we can then decide to retry the transport connection establishment using the other form of network service, or using a different selection of classes over the connection-oriented service. (This really applies if our scenario is not wholly true: network routes may only be possible using connectionless or only possible using connection-oriented, or the remote end-system may only have implemented some transport classes.)
- Eventually we have a transport connection, or have decided to give up!

The above sounds pretty horrendous. Computer software would be hard to configure to take these sorts of decisions in a sensible manner. It is, therefore, not surprising that people tend to say: 'To hell with it, if we are going out over an X.25 link we will use TP0 over connection-oriented, and otherwise we will use TP4 over connectionless. It may not be optimal, but it is simple!'

Where it is known that certain heavily used end-systems have paths for which one of the other options is the best, these can be built in specifically and relatively statically as a selection table. The situation is, of course, further complicated by the knowledge that, at the present time, some end-system connectivity can only be obtained using connectionless, some only using connection-oriented, and by differing recommendations from profiling and procurement groups. Deployment of the Interworking Unit of TR10172 (described in section 4.2) may be the only option.

5.13   The OSI Transport Service

The formal definition of the Transport Service as a set of primitives parallels very closely the Network Service Definition, which is not surprising as the main purpose of the Transport Layer is Quality of Service improvements, not the introduction of new types of service. In fact, the Transport Service Definition is actually significantly simpler than the Network Service Definition for two reasons.

- The end-to-end versus link-by-link acknowledgement of the Network Service (the N-DATA-ACK primitives) is there largely to support TP1 and TP3, and has no equivalent in the Transport Service.
- The N-RESET primitive is there to support partial failure of the network. Recovery is either undertaken by the Transport Layer, or, if this is not

possible (TP0 or TP2 in use), a more serious 'disconnect' failure is generated. Thus N-RESET is also absent from the Transport Service.

All this makes the Transport Service the slimmest, simplest, and cleanest of all
the layer services. In the description below of the mapping of T-service
primitives to N-service primitives, the use of the connection-oriented Network
Service is assumed. Where the connectionless Network Service is in use, all
primitives map to N-UNITDATA. The Transport Service consists of the
following.

- The T-CONNECT request, indication, response and confirm primitives,
  with corresponding protocol messages carried in N-DATA primitives,
  used to negotiate the Transport Class and to set up a connection
  (including adding a new connection to a multiplexed set of connections).
  It carries 128 octets of user data, but the user data is not used by the OSI
  Session Layer protocol.
- The T-DATA request and indication primitives (also carried in N-DATA,
  with a header octet to distinguish this usage of N-DATA from that supporting T-CONNECT, and with some extra parameters in those classes
  that need to number messages, perform acknowledgements, add flow control, and so on) which has a single parameter that is unlimited user data.
  (Note that the Transport Protocol provides segmentation, and segment
  sizes are negotiable. If one end-system requests 128-octet segments in the
  protocol, then the other end-system has to accede. This means that implementation of segmentation in the Transport Layer is mandatory: if 128-
  octet segments are negotiated, then under normal X.25 operation there
  will be no use of the M-bit for segmentation in X.25 level 3.)
- The T-EXPEDITED-DATA request and indication primitives used to
  carry data which non-destructively bypasses flow control. Where N-
  EXPEDITED-DATA is available, the T-EXPEDITED-DATA maps to
  N-EXPEDITED-DATA, otherwise it is not available (TP0) or is mapped
  to N-DATA, with flow control within the transport protocol. It carries
  up to 16 octets of user data.
- The T-DISCONNECT request and indication primitives that are used to
  tear down a connection when it is finished with. This is a destructive service, and will bypass flow control and cause the discard of any data not
  already delivered. These primitives, like the T-CONNECT primitives,
  also carry 128 octets of user data.

In order to understand fully the Session Layer, two points should be noted
about the Transport Service. These are discussed below.

First, it is a two-way simultaneous service, with normal data and expedited
data flowing in both directions, with normal data not overtaking normal data,
expedited data not overtaking expedited data, normal data not overtaking

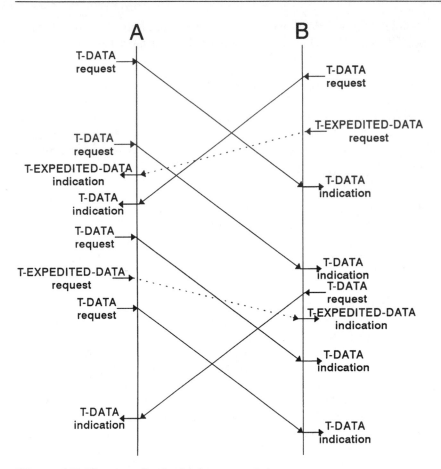

Figure 5.7 *Transport Service for data transmission.*

expedited data, but expedited data possibly, but not necessarily, overtaking normal data (Figure 5.7).

While the OSI Transport Service is frequently equated with the service provided by TCP in the TCP/IP suite (with TCP being functionally very similar to TP4 – but certainly not bit-compatible), there are some significant differences in detail, one of which relates to expedited data. The roughly equivalent concept in TCP is **urgent data**. Urgent data can be submitted when flow is blocked, but it does not overtake normal data. To obtain it, the receiver must read (and store or discard) all earlier normal data. What TCP does provide is a notification, effectively a single bit, that there is urgent data stacked up waiting to be read. If the OSI Session Layer had been built on the TCP style of service, it would have been very different: not necessarily better, not necessarily worse, but different. There are specifications of how to map protocols designed for OSI onto

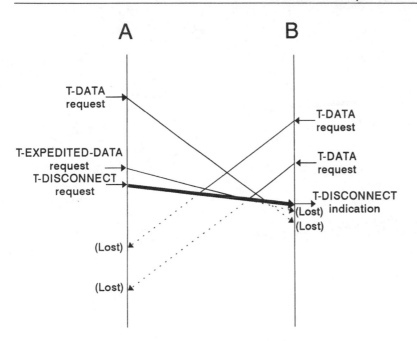

Figure 5.8 *Destruction of data by T-DISCONNECT.*

TCP, and vice versa, and there are even implementations of OSI stacks on top of TCP. The differences between expedited and urgent are usually not properly covered, but as most applications in both TCP and OSI make little or no use of these services (and if they do they are in unusual circumstances) the differences tend not to be critical.

The second point to make is the disruptive nature of the disconnect primitives. If a disconnect is issued, earlier normal or expedited data can potentially be overtaken and is discarded. Equally, messages in the reverse direction may have been issued, but will never be received due to the issuance of the disconnect (Figure 5.8). It is also possible for two disconnects issued by the two ends of the connection to collide inside the network (or within lower layer handlers), and to mutually cancel each other with non-delivery of the user data carried by them, or for a disconnect to collide with a network-generated disconnect and mutually cancel, with one side seeing only a disconnect issued with user data and the other side seeing only a network-generated disconnect (Figure 5.9). Thus the issuing of a disconnect is somewhat fraught with problems, and usually needs to be preceded with some form of 'Have we finished?', 'Yes, we have', 'OK, I'll disconnect' dialogue to provide what is usually called an **orderly termination** for the application's dialogue. In TCP, there is added functionality (to provide orderly termination as well as disorderly abort) that is missing in the ISO service. (It is added by the OSI Session Layer.)

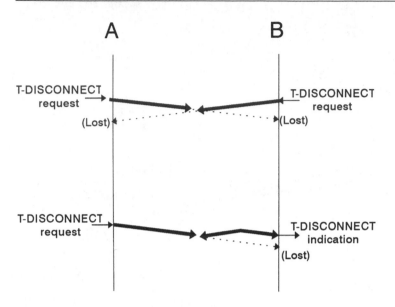

Figure 5.9 *Collision of disconnects.*

5.14 The Connectionless Transport Service

The Connectionless Transport Service is normally seen as a simple passing through (much as TP0 passes through the connection-oriented Network Service) of the connectionless network service, with little added value. There is just one service: a T-UNITDATA request and indication primitive.

There are, in fact, two main pieces of added value. The first is some additional addressing information that can provide fan-out within the end-system; this is called the **transport selector**. Addressing selectors exist in both the connection-oriented service (when they appear as parameters on connect primitives) and in the connectionless service (when they appear as added parameters with every data message – the UNITDATA request and indication primitives) in all the three middle layers. The need for this wealth of addressing information and their general function is described later.

The second piece of added value is the addition of an end-to-end checksum in TP4 to provide protection against undetected corruption of messages in the network. The Connectionless Internet Protocol (CLIP) provides a checksum on every message, but that protects only the header information, not the up-to-64K (about) of user data. Detection of any corruption of the user data relies either on error detection (and perhaps correction) by the subnetworks carrying the CLIP message, or on the end-to-end checking of the Transport Layer. If errors are detected, the message is simply discarded, and it is invisible to both users of the Transport Service whether discard occurred in the Transport Layer for this reason, or at a lower layer, or by complete loss within the network.

6
Dialogues and all that

6.1 Overview of the Session Layer

Having spent a lot of time thinking about service improvements on the QOS of the Network Service (by some error correcting protocol), it requires a mind-shift to appreciate the Session Layer. Here we are not concerned with errors, reliability, or multiplexing. If such concerns cannot be adequately addressed by the standards of the Transport Layer, they go unaddressed. In this layer and all the above layers, we assume that the reliability of the communications path provided by the Transport Layer is as good as we need, or at least, as good as can be obtained by end-system protocol exchanges. The only failure we will see is a T-DISCONNECT indication, but it is important to realize that that can occur at any time, with loss of data in transit in both directions – this cannot be prevented, and application designers have to be prepared for it.

What we can hope to do, however, is to control the issuing of disconnects (provision of orderly termination), except when they are the result of a network generated N-DISCONNECT or N-RESET that the Transport Layer cannot resolve: these latter occurrences should be infrequent if we are using an appropriate transport class, but cannot be totally eliminated. In the Session Layer they are called **aborts**. Thus in the Session Service, there is no mention of 'disconnecting'. Instead we speak of **releasing the connection** (or **orderly termination**) and of **aborting the connection** (or **disorderly termination**).

This is one example of the sort of problem that might have faced application designers who had to design a protocol to support some application if there were no Session Layer, and they had to design a direct interaction with the Transport Layer. Thus an important focus of the rest of this discussion on the middle layers (and a part of the discussion on the Application Layer) is an attempt to answer the question: 'If I am asked to design a protocol to support a distributed application in my own specialized domain of knowledge, what facilities/tools are available to me beyond opening a connection, transmitting octet-string messages in both directions, and disconnecting?'

So we ask ourselves: 'Given the nature of the Transport Service, what might application designers have to worry about that is not really anything to do with their application? What sort of tools might be wanted?' The broad answer, given earlier, is 'dialogue control and dialogue separation'; we now need to cover this in some detail.

We have already touched on some possible problem areas when discussing the Transport Layer, and in the earlier discussion of the Session Layer when we were concerned with the overall OSI architecture. The main points to be discussed further in this section are:

- the use of tokens to provide two-way alternate operation and to prevent collisions (requests in two directions crossing in the network or in the buffers of lower layers);
- orderly termination and negotiated release of a connection;
- dialogue separation by minor and major synchronization points (the reader is invited to revisit section 2.4.5);
- resynchronization (going back to a previously established synchronization point);
- bypassing of token control (as with flow control, produce a control and somebody wants to bypass it!);
- the activity concept (not yet introduced) and Teletex;
- negotiation in the Session Layer;
- exception reports (failures) in the Session Layer;
- lengths of user-data fields.

Before ending this overview, it is important to recognize that the Session Layer is not really a single monolithic protocol. Rather it is an almost random collection of largely independent service primitives, each of which invokes a quite limited exchange of messages over the Transport Service and represents one particular tool that is available for use by an application designer. These service primitives and the corresponding messages are grouped into what are called **functional units**, and at the start of a session connection there is agreement on the functional units to be used on that connection.

In the case of the simplest possible use of the Session Layer by an application designer, the only primitives used are S-CONNECT, S-DATA, S-P-ABORT (P for provider – an upcoming T-DISCONNECT), and S-U-ABORT (U for user – a disorderly termination by one or other user), mapping simply and directly to the corresponding Transport Layer primitives with little added value and little complexity for implementors.

In addition to this set of primitives, which is called the **kernel functional unit** – actually the kernel includes one other, discussed later, an application designer makes a conscious choice that some (or none) of the other functional units of the Session Layer (negotiated release of the connection, token control of data transfer, the expedited service, minor synchronization, etc.) are useful in support of his or her application, and obtains the required functionality by specifying that the corresponding service primitive be issued.

The alert reader will be beginning to ask the question: 'How can application designers specify that a Session Service primitive is to be issued when the Presentation Layer is between them and the Session Service?' In fact, it is a correct question. Application designers indeed cannot invoke Session Service primitives, but what they can do is invoke Presentation Service primitives that correspond in a direct and almost one for one manner to the Session Service primitives, so we can loosely talk about the issuing of Session Service primitives.

6.2 Historical development

In order to understand fully the 'Why?' of the Session Layer, it is necessary to appreciate some of the historical background. In 1984, there was a well-developed Session Standard produced by ECMA (European Computer Manufacturers' Association), which is the 'club' of European computer manufacturers. However, all major computer manufacturers have some European manufacturing plant, and are eligible to become members of ECMA. Despite its name, ECMA is effectively the club of all computer manufacturers world-wide, with a primary role of contributing to OSI standards development. As such, ECMA has from the beginning had a very strong input into ISO standardization activity in the OSI area. Its influence in the development of the OSI Reference Model and of most of the main OSI standards has been strong and has far outweighed what would be expected from the name 'European'. If the reader is interested in looking at the archives of early OSI papers, the technical content of the very first input into the OSI Reference Model makes an interesting study. There were papers from the USA, from France, from Japan, from the UK, and from ECMA. Only the ECMA paper had a seven-layer model, broadly similar to what eventually emerged as the standard. So in 1984, ECMA had a Session Layer Standard with most of the features we have suggested as candidates for support in the Session Layer, and there was a strong lobby for this to become the ISO Standard. Unfortunately, there was also in existence CCITT Recommendation S.62 (later renamed T.62), part of the Teletex suite, with an even stronger lobby for that to be adopted as the Session Layer Standard.

Teletex has already been referred to in connection with the Transport Layer, and the pressures on Session were just as great. CCITT wished to be able to rewrite the Teletex specification to use the Session Service Definition, with no change to the bits on the line. This meant that the S.62 protocol had to be imported lock, stock, and barrel into the OSI Session Layer.

There were some areas where the ECMA work and the CCITT work were very similar, some areas where they noticeably diverged but with identical functionality, and some areas of completely different functionality. During 1984 a major effort was expended to a tight time-scale to merge together the CCITT work and the ECMA work. The result was the current ISO Session Standard. In broad terms, the protocol and much of the terminology in it followed the S.62 specification (as it had to), with added protocol messages where appropriate to support ECMA features. The service notation more nearly followed the ECMA work, and hence there are some mismatches between the names given to protocol messages and their corresponding service primitives, but these are unimportant.

What was the end result? Importantly, the work was completed in a timely manner. But instead of finding just one screwdriver and one hammer in the tool-kit, the application designer finds two of each! One is ECMA-derived, and one is CCITT-derived. These tools differ slightly, but not significantly, in their functionality, and there are no very good technical reasons for using one rather than the other.

The bad side-effect, however, was that from that day almost to this (mid-1990s), arguments continue among application designers on whether to use 'activities and two-way alternate' (the CCITT legacy) or 'major synchronization and two-way simultaneous' (the ECMA legacy). This argument has been particularly important in preventing the adoption of common building blocks for bulk data transfer, discussed later in section 10.4 on FTAM (File Transfer, Access and Management), and for RTSE (Reliable Transfer Service Element).

Did the result enable the Teletex specification to be rewritten using the Session Service primitives? Yes and no. When CCITT went on to develop the X.400 Recommendation, it was originally written to use Session Service primitives (the Presentation Layer was not sufficiently far developed to be usable at that stage – late 1984), but there was a strong lobby for the bulk data transfer part of X.400 (RTSE) to be compatible with Teletex. The Session Layer was sufficiently faithful to S.62 that people were able to claim that that had been achieved. In practice it is doubtful if anyone has attempted to interwork an existing Teletex implementation to an X.400 implementation, and even more doubtful that it would actually work! But what mattered was that the 'political' issue was resolved – nobody today even mentions Teletex compatibility. All parties were happy to accept that, in writing X.400 to use Session Service primitives, the bits on the line would be compatible with Teletex – provided, of course, that TP0 was used, with no offering of other classes. And so we find the CCITT X.400 Recommendation requiring the use of TP0. But we must now return to the technical content of the Session Layer.

6.3   Tokens and collisions

One of the problems with designing protocols is that when an application A receives a message over the network from application B, the receiver A generally does not know whether, at the time that the message was sent by B, the state of the sender B was based on the most recent message sent by A, or whether, at that time, the most recent message had not yet been received. In many cases of protocol design this can produce uncertainty and complications, and failure to analyse fully such **collision cases** can be one of the greatest sources of errors in protocol design.

A similar problem can arise in the implementation of protocols that use two-way simultaneous transmission: the implementation does not know whether to wait for a queue to become free to transmit a message or to wait for a message to arrive. Put another way, the operating system interfaces have to permit the implementation to be able to handle the two partially independent processes of sending and receiving at the same time, in a way which does not soak up CPU cycles. In languages and systems with a well-developed process concept and with an interrupt capability, this generally poses no problems, but with simpler systems and languages a protocol based on two-way simultaneous traffic can be difficult to handle.

A solution to both problems is to use the communications medium in a strictly two-way alternate manner: application A transmits a series of messages, identifies the end of the series of messages, then waits for messages to come in; application B waits for received messages and processes them until it receives the message identifying the end of the sequence and then proceeds to transmit a series of messages in reply, again identifying the end of that sequence. Thus the right to send alternates between the two applications, and we say that they 'pass the turn' between them. If an application designer wishes to work in this way, then managing that two-way alternate dialogue needs to be planned out, and standardization of messages and functions (and hence service primitives) to support such a mode of operation is one of the functions of the Session Layer.

Of course, where round-trip times between A and B are long, this can be a very inefficient way to work, and it would be better to design a protocol using two-way simultaneous transmission, and to put the effort in to get it right and to implement it using an appropriate infrastructure. The decision of which approach to take has to be the application designer's, and the Session Layer therefore provides both the option of two-way simultaneous (TWS) operation (effectively a do-nothing Session Layer in this regard) and also the option of two-way alternate (TWA) operation, in which protocol messages (supported by Session Service primitives) are defined to allow management of the two-way alternate dialogue.

The Session Layer Standards use the concept of a **data token**. This is a conceptual token that gives the right to transmit data (to issue the S-DATA request primitive). At the start of a session connection, there is agreement on whether to operate in two-way alternate mode or not (this cannot later be changed – perhaps a mistake in the design), and if so, where the token is to be positioned initially. Thereafter, if you have the token, you can issue S-DATA requests, and will not get any S-DATA indications. You can pass the token by issuing an S-TOKEN-GIVE request, which results in an S-TOKEN-GIVE indication at the other end of the communications path. If you do not have the token, you can request it with an S-TOKEN-PLEASE request, which produces a corresponding indication. The receiver of an S-TOKEN-PLEASE indication may completely ignore it (this is an unconfirmed service), or may respond with an S-TOKEN-GIVE request, perhaps after completing some set of transmissions related to current operations.

The above text implies some degree of 'free will' on the part of the application. What it really means is that what happens is not determined by the Session Layer. The application designer may (and often will) completely determine when an S-TOKEN-GIVE request or an S-TOKEN-PLEASE request is to be issued, and the action to be taken on an S-TOKEN-PLEASE indication. Equally, application designers may determine that, for their application, there is no useful purpose served by S-TOKEN-PLEASE, and that primitive will never be issued or received. This discussion has again illustrated the 'tool-kit' nature of the Session Layer.

Once a token concept has been introduced, it can be used for other purposes to help avoid collision problems in the operation or use of the Session Layer itself. Thus in addition to the data token described above, there are also tokens called the minor synchronization token, the major/activity token and the release token. These are described in more detail in the relevant section below.

Using the S-TOKEN-GIVE primitive, one or more of the tokens held by an application (including all of them) can be passed to its peer. The Session Service also, however, contains an additional primitive (and a corresponding protocol message) which passes all tokens that are held. This is the S-CONTROL-GIVE request and indication. This is, of course, an example of having two almost identical screwdrivers in the tool-kit – a consequence of the ECMA and Teletex merger (S-CONTROL-GIVE is largely there to support Teletex). However, it is important for the reader – a potential application designer – to recognize that while passing all tokens using S-CONTROL-GIVE or using S-TOKEN-GIVE may be identical as far as the Session Layer is concerned, it is perfectly permissible for the application designer to carry different application semantics (different meaning at the application level) to these two ways of passing tokens. In principle, S-TOKEN-GIVE could be restricted to pure session semantics – passing tokens for the right to transmit certain session primitives – while S-CONTROL-GIVE could transfer rights to initiate some very application-specific actions. This is one of many examples in the Session Layer where there are primitives whose effects in terms of the Session Layer itself are identical, but where, because they are different primitives, they provide the opportunity for signalling different application semantics associated with the same session effect.

6.4 Orderly termination and negotiated release

We have already discussed at some length the problems of disorderly termination – the uncontrolled issuing of a T-DISCONNECT. The Session Layer provides two orderly release mechanisms, both supported by the S-RELEASE request, indication, response and confirm primitives. In the simplest case (the facility in the kernel functional unit), the Session Layer provides a very simple exchange. Application A issues an S-RELEASE request to its Session Layer with the semantics 'I want to end this connection as soon as possible in an orderly manner', and ceases all transmissions, but still receives any incoming material. The Session Layer then uses a T-DATA transmission to provide delivery of an S-RELEASE indication to application B, which then completes any further data transmissions (normal or expedited) that it considers appropriate before issuing the S-RELEASE response to its Session Layer with the semantics 'OK I am done, you can disconnect when you get this'. Again T-DATA is used to transmit the corresponding session message, causing an S-RELEASE confirm, and the Session Layer supporting application A would then normally issue a

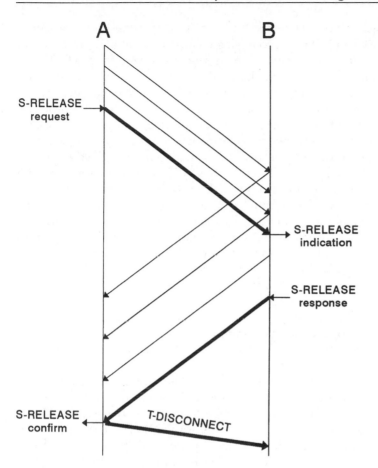

Figure 6.1 *S-RELEASE handshake.*

T-DISCONNECT. This exchange is shown in Figure 6.1, and it can be seen that there is no data in transit in either direction when the T-DISCONNECT is issued, so orderly release has been achieved.

There are a few problems with this basic mechanism, and a few additional observations to make. First of all, it may be useful to retain the transport connection for future use for another session connection (perhaps for another application). This is, of course, invisible to the application, and is not shown in the Session Service Definition. It is, however, part of the session protocol supporting S-RELEASE that there is negotiation in the S-RELEASE exchange of whether to retain the transport connection for possible reuse or not. (The session implementation where the S-RELEASE request was issued says – on the message supporting the S-RELEASE request/indication – whether it is happy to have the connection retained, and the peer session implementation confirms or refuses retention on the message supporting the S-RELEASE response/confirm.) This retention of the transport connection is not permitted (an easy way of solving problems) if transport expedited is in use on this transport connection, as use of S-EXPEDITED in the following connection could, in principle and in some circumstances, arrive before the message supporting the S-RELEASE response/confirm, and hence arrive during the lifetime of the previous session connection and be delivered to the wrong application. There have been recurring discussions within the Session Layer group about 'mending' this problem, and allowing retention even when transport expedited is in use, but this has not yet (1995) resulted in a change to the Standard.

The second point to make is that one cannot remove all access to T-DISCONNECT. An upcoming T-DISCONNECT indication (as a result of a network failure from which the Transport Protocol in use cannot recover) can occur at any time, and cannot be avoided. This loss of the connection has to be passed up to the application, and this is handled by the S-P-ABORT indication in the Session Service. Application designers must clearly specify the action to be taken when such an indication occurs. (As an aside, an action involving immediately re-establishing the connection is not appropriate. If such action is wanted, then the appropriate class of Transport Protocol should be used.) It is also important to allow an application designer the freedom to specify a disorderly termination, either because there is no response in a reasonable time to an S-RELEASE request, or because of the immediacy of the situation requiring termination. To support this, the S-U-ABORT request and indication primitives are provided.

Thirdly, the S-RELEASE primitives (request/indication and response/confirm) all carry user data, so the application can, for example, pass charging information as part of the release process. Of course, if the release collides with (is disrupted by) an upcoming T-DISCONNECT (resulting in an S-P-ABORT), or an S-U-ABORT is issued by the peer, the user data on the S-RELEASE will not be delivered. But that is expected. A more interesting situation arises if both sides issue an S-RELEASE request at the same time (a **collision** situation). The effect in the first Session Standard was as shown in Figure 6.2. One of the S-RELEASE response/confirms (and its associated user data) was not delivered, because the transport connection was prematurely terminated. This illustrates the sort of problems that can arise from collisions. This was reported as a defect in the Session Standard, and a number of solutions were discussed to resolve the problem and ensure the delivery of both S-RELEASE confirms in the collision case. The result was an amendment to the Standards, using something called the **rapid amendment procedures** (which involve much less balloting and time than a normal amendment or revision to a standard). The amendment required the acceptor of the connection to delay the issue of an S-RELEASE response if he had already issued (the collision case) an S-RELEASE request until the S-RELEASE confirm was received, and to leave disconnection to the peer entity. The result is shown in Figure 6.3, and it can be seen that both S-RELEASE exchanges now complete without loss.

We said above that what has been described is the basic mechanism. A natural extension is to change the meaning of the messages slightly so that the S-RELEASE request/indication says 'I think we have finished, do you?', with

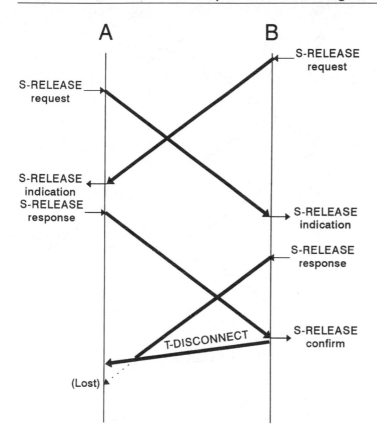

Figure 6.2 *Collision of S-RELEASE.*

the S-RELEASE response/confirm saying 'Yes, we have, please disconnect', or 'No, I would like to continue, please ignore this exchange'. This is called the **negotiated release** mechanism. In the non-collision case, the only problem is knowing what semantics is intended (agreeing that S-RELEASE should be negotiated or non-negotiated). This is accomplished by agreeing a separate functional unit which uses the same messages as those of the kernel, but with the differing semantics, and the ability to say 'No' as well as 'Yes'.

In the collision case, however, life is now rather more complicated. Of course, one could forbid a 'No' response in the collision case, but the decision was taken to provide a token (the **release token**) to control the issuance of an S-RELEASE if the negotiated release functional unit was in use, preventing collisions from occurring. (Solving the above-mentioned defect in the non-negotiated case by applying token control there too was considered, but rejected as being too much of a change from the original Standard.)

The S-RELEASE primitives are an important feature of the Session Layer. Almost every Application Layer standard in OSI has a normal termination using S-RELEASE (usually non-negotiated).

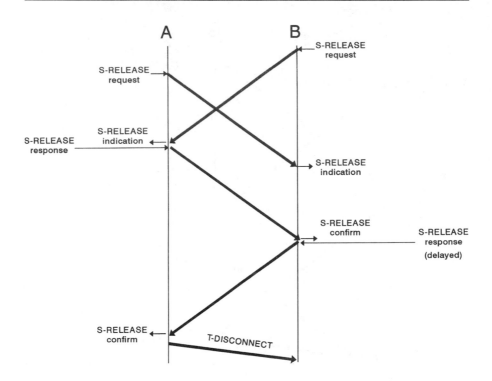

Figure 6.3 *Resolution of S-RELEASE collisions.*

The alert reader will have a lot of questions bubbling up. For example, if an S-RELEASE request has been issued, exactly what can you then do? We have said you cannot issue S-DATA requests, but can you, for example, issue an S-U-ABORT request? We would expect the answer to be 'Yes', and indeed it is. In general, however, the issuing of a service primitive puts the service into a new **state**, in which the set of permitted events (primitives you can validly issue and primitives you might receive) is reduced. A detailed specification of what events produce transitions to what states, and what events can occur in particular states, is hard to do in ordinary English, and the Session Protocol Standard contains 26 pages of **State Tables** that provide a clear and precise specification of these issues. The curious reader is invited to postulate some questions and to seek their answer by inspection of the State Tables in the Session Standards.

Note that what we are really talking about is what an application designer needs to be concerned with: we are not talking about where in implementation code particular checks are performed. Saying that, in a certain state, only certain primitives can be issued is a strong statement constraining what a legal application protocol design can specify. Saying that, in a certain state, certain primitives can be received is more like tutorial information, saying that, in this state, no other primitives need be considered by the application protocol designer.

State Tables are used in almost all OSI standards, but their use in the Session Layer is perhaps the most important because of the very large number of collision cases and disrupting services that can occur in this layer, and have to be very carefully treated if bugs are not to be present in the standards. Dialogue control and separation issues are very much about the interaction of events occurring approximately simultaneously at the two ends. Token control helps, but many cases have to be addressed by careful enumeration of what can occur, and specification of the appropriate response to ensure a coherent service. It is the difficulty of getting this sort of thing correct that is the major justification for a separate layer which concentrates on solving these problems in a general way for use by all application designers.

6.5   Minor and major synchronization

6.5.1   Introduction

The problem to be solved here has already been described. We want to provide mechanisms which will enable an application designer to specify simply and easily the checkpointing of the state of the distributed application in a way that is not affected by messages in transit. This requires a sort of synchronization of the activities of both ends, and a clear separation of the dialogues (message exchanges) before and after the synchronization point (the point at which the application designer can specify checkpointing). So we are concerned with synchronization, and/or dialogue separation.

6.5.2   Minor synchronization

Figure 6.4 shows a clear dialogue separation in a one-way flow of normal data (no use of expedited) achieved by the simple means of inserting a synchronization message into the one-way flow. This is perfectly adequate for many applications, where the application designer would specify checkpointing by application A when it issues the S-SYNC-MINOR (as the service primitive is called) request, and checkpointing by application B when it receives the S-SYNC-MINOR indication. (It is important here to note that the Session Layer in no way specifies checkpointing – it has no such concept; all it provides is an exchange of messages that provide synchronization and dialogue separation.)

If synchronization points are to be useful, it is desirable to be able to identify them later, and for this purpose the Session Layer serially numbers each synchronization point that is established, and delivers the number as a parameter of the appropriate service primitives.

Again we must consider what it means if minor synchronization primitives collide. From one point of view, this is a nonsense, for their use is in relation to a one-way flow of data, so having them issued only by the sender is clearly sensible. This leads us to the view that the ownership of the data token would be a sensible way to control the issuing of minor synchronization point requests,

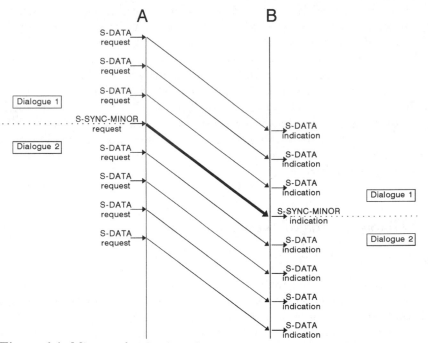

Figure 6.4 *Minor synchronization points.*

preventing collisions of such messages and hence potential problems with the numbering of the synchronization points. This would be a good solution if use of the session connection could switch from time to time between two-way simultaneous use and two-way alternate use, but as was pointed out earlier, the decision on these modes (and hence the existence of the data token) is made once and for all when the session connection is first established. There is therefore a separate and distinct token controlling the issue of minor synchronization primitives, and hence preventing their collision.

It would be wrong to leave this discussion with the impression that the S-SYNC-MINOR exchange can only be used for checkpointing, or must be used for checkpointing. The application designer is in full control. If the exchange provided by S-SYNC-MINOR is useful (and it is a pretty simple exchange) to carry some other application semantics, that is not ruled out. An example of this is presented in the discussion of FTAM (section 10.4).

6.5.3   Major synchronization

Now let us consider the somewhat harder problem. We want to provide a similar dialogue separation and potential for checkpointing in an arbitrarily complicated dialogue with two-way flow of data and the occasional use of expedited data in both directions. And we want to do this in a reasonably efficient manner, without too many round-trip times.

There are obviously other special cases of dialogue patterns that could be considered (for example, one-way with occasional use of expedited in the same direction), but these are not nearly as common as the case addressed by minor synchronization, and it seems inappropriate to do more than address that very common simple case plus the most general dialogue possible.

Suppose then, in a general dialogue, that application A decides it is time to checkpoint, and seeks to establish a synchronization point. An S-SYNC-MAJOR request is issued, and travels on normal T-DATA to application B. Application A stops sending. Clearly the issue of the S-SYNC-MAJOR request cannot be the synchronization point (the point of dialogue separation), because as shown in Figure 6.5, there are still messages originated as part of dialogue one that are on their way to A. On the other hand, the issuing of the S-SYNC-MAJOR indication to application B could well form the point of dialogue separation (the synchronization point) between dialogue one and dialogue two. Let us try to make that work. At this point then, if the application designer so determines, application B checkpoints its state, and then initiates dialogue two by issuing an S-SYNC-MAJOR response which is delivered to application A as an S-SYNC-MAJOR confirm, establishing the major synchronization point at A and enabling A to checkpoint its state at this point and then continue with dialogue two. This is shown in Figure 6.6. Does this work?

It is clear that it almost does. All requests or responses issued by A in dialogue one, whether they use transport expedited or transport normal data, will be delivered to B in dialogue one. Equally, anything issued by A in dialogue two is delivered to B in dialogue two. Anything issued by B in dialogue one is delivered to A in dialogue one, and any normal data issued by B in dialogue two is delivered to A in dialogue two. But ... whoops! ... anything issued by B in dialogue two which is carried on the transport expedited path may get delivered to application A in dialogue one, as shown in Figure 6.7. We have a bust protocol design. Back to the drawing-board.

The root of the problem is that A cannot distinguish between M1 and M2 in the figure, and we need to 'send a ferret down the expedited tunnel' to flush out the rabbits and hold up the others – in other words, to mark the division between M1 and M2. This transmission is not visible in the service, but the protocol message is called the **PREPARE** message. The rule for the session protocol machine is that any material carried on the expedited channel prior to the arrival of the ferret will be processed and result in indications to the application in the normal way, but once the ferret has arrived, nothing else is processed until the second ferret (represented by the message carrying the S-SYNC-MAJOR response/confirm) comes out of the normal data tunnel (Figure 6.8). Material in the expedited tunnel is only processed and delivered to the application when (and immediately after) the S-SYNC-MAJOR confirm has been issued. Thus we have now achieved our clear dialogue separation, and checkpointing can take place at the synchronization points if the application designer so specifies. The PREPARE message is often described as 'protecting dialogue two'. It ensures a clean start to that dialogue, preventing messages properly part of that dialogue from 'leaking' into dialogue one.

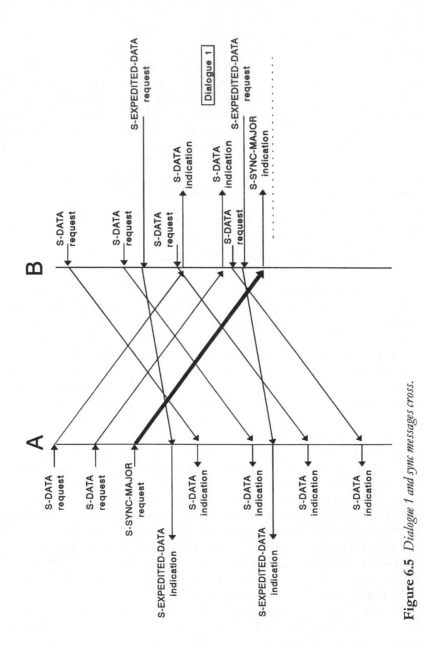

Figure 6.5 *Dialogue 1 and sync messages cross.*

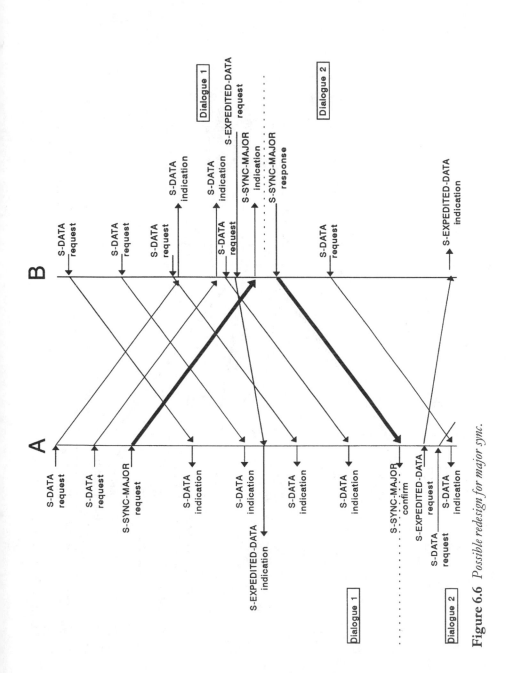

Figure 6.6 *Possible redesign for major sync.*

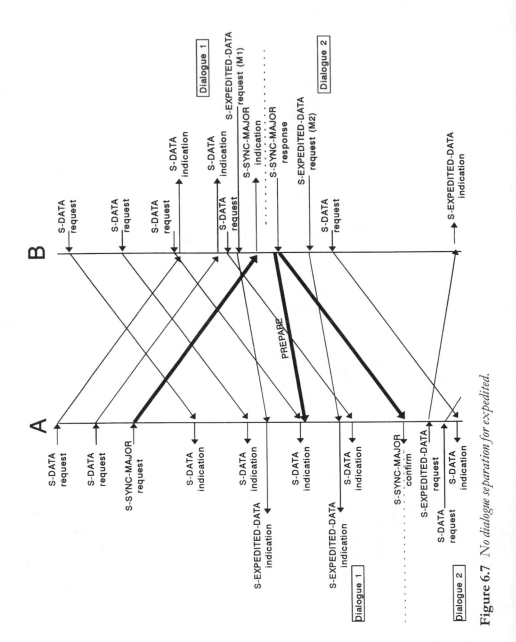

Figure 6.7 *No dialogue separation for expedited.*

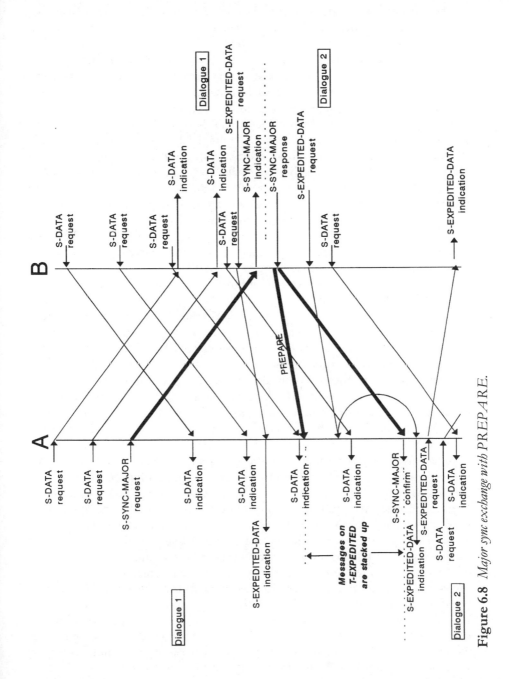

Figure 6.8 *Major sync exchange with PREPARE.*

The major synchronization handshake is efficient and effective apart from one minor(?) problem. Any use of expedited data in any of the protocols providing it (X.25 level 3, Transport protocols) imposes a round-trip delay before further expedited data can be sent; this is effectively the flow-control mechanism preventing overrun on the expedited path, where there is no explicit flow control. This is not normally a problem, as a series of expedited transmissions in quick succession is not what the service is intended to support.

However, as was pointed out earlier, the TP4 protocol not only delays any subsequent expedited data until earlier expedited has been acknowledged, it also delays the transmission of any normal data until the expedited has been acknowledged. Thus the effective handshake for S-SYNC-MAJOR looks like Figure 6.9 if TP4 is in use (but only if TP4 is in use), with the start of dialogue two transmissions by application B being delayed by the Transport Layer by a full round-trip time after the checkpoint. If use of this service is infrequent, there is no problem, but if it is used to mark the beginning and end of short dialogues in support of transaction processing, then the problem can become an issue, with those who ardently believe in use of TP4 strenuously opposing any use of the session major synchronization function. This will be discussed further when CCR and TP are discussed in Chapter 9.

Another point to discuss is collision of two attempts at major synchronization. As the reader will be expecting, this is handled by yet another token, the **major/activity token**. (It has this name because it also serves to control the issue of the 'activity' primitives described below.)

There is one further issue to consider in relation to synchronization points. It is all very well for an application design to propose checkpointing and issue the appropriate session primitives, but it is often highly desirable for both parties to know reasonably quickly that the other party has indeed secured the checkpoint data, so that earlier checkpoint data can be deleted from disc. In the case of a major synchronization, application A issues the service primitive, and the synchronization point (and hence any associated application procedures such as checkpointing) occurs at B prior to the response/confirm. Thus A knows that B has performed the appropriate procedures, as specified by the application designer, when the S-SYNC-MAJOR confirm is received. Moreover, A is not allowed to transmit (by the rules of the Session Layer) in dialogue two until the S-SYNC-MAJOR confirm has been received. It is a simple step for an application designer to require checkpointing before such transmissions, and hence the arrival at application B of data in dialogue two can be used as a signal that the application procedures associated with the major synchronization handshake have been completed. The application designer could then specify or allow the deletion of earlier checkpoint data. If this were not considered appropriate, it would be perfectly possible for the application designer, assuming all tokens were with application A, to require application A to issue an S-SYNC-MINOR request when checkpointing for the major synchronization point had been completed.

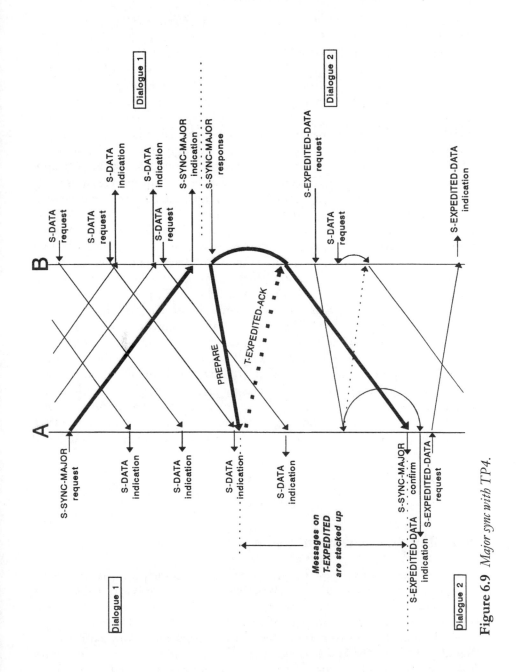

Figure 6.9 *Major sync with TP4.*

6.5.4 Confirmation of minor synchronization

In the case of S-SYNC-MINOR the situation is not so clear. There is only a one-way flow of messages and no 'blocking'. As soon as the S-SYNC-MINOR request is issued by application A, it can be immediately followed by further S-DATA requests, and application B is not transmitting anyway. Moreover, if A has control (has all the tokens), but in particular has the minor synchronization token, then B cannot be told to respond with a minor sync when checkpointing is complete without passing the token and producing potential confusion over confirmation of a sync point or the request to establish a new one. There are many ways of overcoming this problem, but in recognition of it, the S-SYNC-MINOR service primitive has been made what is usually called **optionally confirmed**. That is, the Session Layer allows, but does not require, a response/confirm to occur. If such a confirmation is indeed used, the pattern of exchanges is as shown in Figure 6.10. It is for the application designer to specify whether and when such a confirmation is to be issued, and the associated application semantics (there are no session semantics). The Session Layer provides one other widget on this particular tool: there is a yes/no parameter on the S-SYNC-MINOR request/indication that allows the application to indicate whether confirmation is wanted or not. Again, like many parameters in the Session Service, there are no Session Layer semantics associated with it. An application designer may choose to be perverse, and require confirmation if the parameter is set to 'No' and no confirmation if it is set to 'Yes'. Parameters of this sort, where the name appears to imply some semantics but there is in fact no Session Layer requirement, are usually the result of naming fields in messages (and providing parameters in the corresponding service primitive) in a way that fits the Teletex usage. The field is present, and named according to Teletex usage, but the Teletex application rules are not imported into the Session Standards, and other application designers may use these fields in totally different ways if they so wish.

6.6 Resynchronization

It will frequently be the case that recovery back to some previous checkpoint takes place after a complete system or application crash. In this case the session connection is lost, and a new session connection has to be established for any recovery operation. There are parameters on the S-CONNECT primitive to specify a **Session Connection Identifer** and an **Initial Synchronization Point Serial Number**. The Session Layer places no semantics or restrictions on the use of the Session Connection Identifier, although it is described as four fields: Calling SS-user Reference, Called SS-user Reference, Common Reference, and Additional Reference Information, reflecting the way it is used in Teletex. It can, if appropriate, be used to identify earlier session connections which failed,

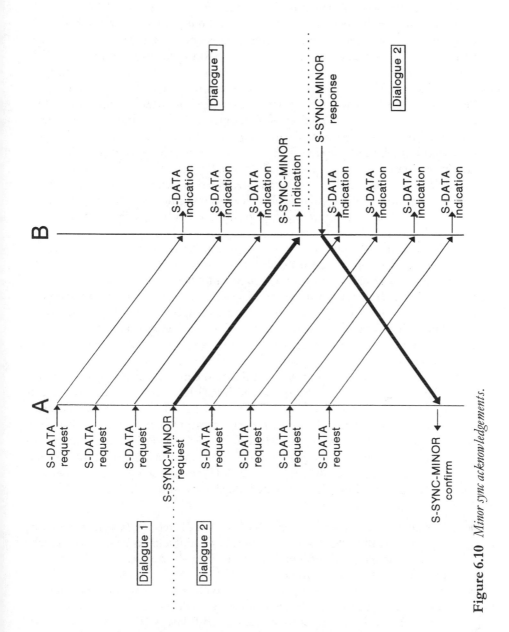

Figure 6.10 *Minor sync acknowledgements.*

and the Initial Synchronization Point Serial Number can be interpreted, if the application designer so specifies, as the identification of the checkpoint taken at that synchronization point in that old connection.

It can, however, happen that one or other of the applications detects that some problem has arisen even when the connection is intact. Perhaps flow is blocked and is not getting cleared. Perhaps (see exception reporting, section 6.10) the session protocol identifies a problem – perhaps it has been passed a token it already has – which it reports to the application. It can then be desirable to have a tool available that will bypass flow control, clear out the connection (a disorderly and truncated termination of dialogue one), with a clean start to a new dialogue, probably following reloading from some identified checkpoint (synchronization point). Again, the Session Layer does not talk about reloading checkpoint data, but what it does provide is an S-RESYNCHRONIZE request, indication, response and confirm that provides disorderly (potential loss of data) termination of dialogue one and a clean start (similar to major sync) to dialogue two, with identification of a sync point number 'to which resynchronization is taking place'.

If resynchronization was closely tied to checkpointing, it would be reasonable for the entire state of the session connection (in particular, the positions of all tokens) to be restored to the position they had when the identified sync point was established. But that is not the case. Checkpointing is a matter for the application designer, who may indeed preserve as part of the checkpoint information the position of tokens, and the Session Layer merely allows tokens to be repositioned, using exactly the same handshake as is used at the start of a connection, when resynchronization takes place.

The basic resync exchange is very similar to the major sync exchange, and in particular the clean start to dialogue two with the PREPARE message to protect it is identical. The difference, however, lies in the need to bypass flow control and discard any data left in dialogue one (**purging** the connection of dialogue one), in both directions. This involves a further PREPARE message, this time issued by the Session Layer supporting the application that initiated the resync. The initial handshake is as shown in Figure 6.11, and the rules for each protocol machine are given below (the complete handshake is shown in Figure 6.12).

- Application A issues an S-RESYNCHRONIZE request (with a parameter saying what the sync point serial number variable is to be set to – which can be interpreted, if the application designer so specifies, as a checkpoint number), and stops sending data.
- The corresponding message is transmitted by the session implementation supporting application A as transport normal data or queued for transmission if flow is blocked. At the same time, a PREPARE message is sent as transport expedited data, bypassing flow control, and telling application B to start purging, as described below.

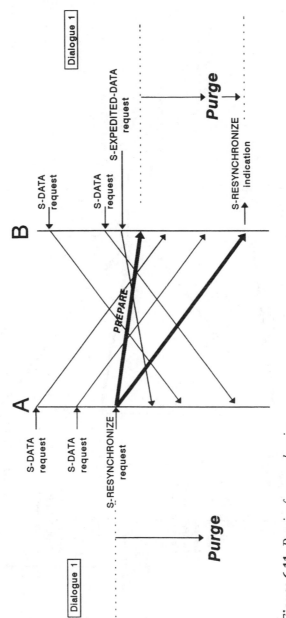

Figure 6.11 *Purging for resynchronize.*

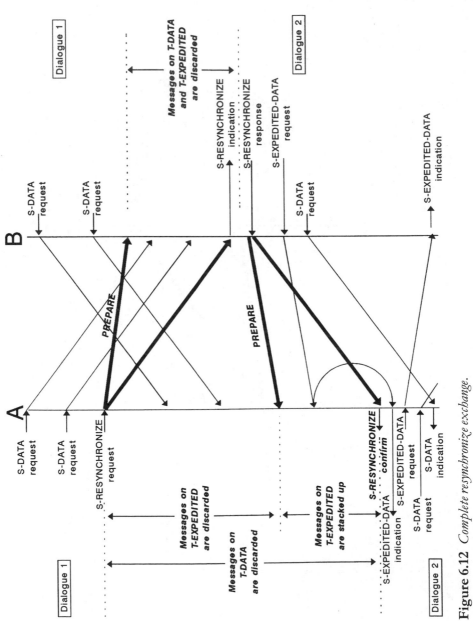

Figure 6.12 *Complete resynchronize exchange.*

- The session implementation supporting application A also begins reading and discarding (purging) everything waiting on the transport normal and expedited paths, thus freeing the flow in the reverse direction if it was blocked.

- When the session implementation supporting application B receives the PREPARE, it also begins to purge (read and discard) anything on the transport normal data path until it recognizes the message supporting the S-RESYNCHRONIZE request. At this stage the corresponding indication is issued to application B, which, assuming that is what the application designer said, reloads from the specified checkpoint, and returns an S-RESYNCHRONIZE response.

- The S-RESYNCHRONIZE response is mapped by the session implementation supporting application B into a normal data transfer and an expedited data PREPARE message, functioning exactly as for major sync.

- When the Session Layer supporting application A gets the PREPARE, it stops purging expedited data and instead stacks it up; it continues to purge normal data until the message signalling the S-RESYNCHRONIZE response appears, then it issues an S-RESYNCHRONIZE confirm to application A, signalling completion of the resychronization and the start of dialogue two.

There are a number of questions that will be bubbling up in the reader's mind, and these are dealt with below.

6.6.1   What about buffers in the upper layers?

We have implicitly assumed in the above discussion that there is no buffering between the Session Layer functionality and the application layer functionality in the implementation. Suppose, however, that the session, presentation and application are implemented as independent processes communicating via buffered messages with back-pressure flow control between these processes.

Even if the S-RESYNCHRONIZE indication can bypass these buffers and signal to the application, we have to make sure that any messages in the buffers are cleared out as the S-RESYNCHRONIZE indication and confirm primitives are passed up (or we need to pass up the PREPARE to cause the application to read and discard). Thus the 'purge' associated with resynchronization has to be recognized and implemented at all layers above the Session Layer.

Most implementors have recognized these issues, and it is now 'conventional wisdom' that independent implementations of the three upper layers is not a good approach. Rather session, presentation and application functionality are probably best bundled into a single process.

None of this discussion is, of course, the concern of the standards, relating purely to implementation architecture. It does, however, serve to make the point that the layering in the seven-layer model (and particularly the service primitive 'interface') is a useful and convenient tool for defining clearly the bits to be sent up and down the line. It is not, and was never intended to be, a prescription for an implementation architecture.

6.6.2 What about a blocked expedited flow?

Another question that is often asked is: 'Does the application have access to the transport expedited flow? If so, suppose that has got blocked and the PREPARE cannot get through?' Taking these in turn, there is indeed an S-EXPEDITED request and indication primitive that maps quite simply onto transport expedited. Moreover, if application A is sending S-EXPEDITED requests faster (even allowing for a round-trip time – which may be short – between each message) than they can be handled by the application, then either expedited data has to be discarded, or the expedited acknowledgement has to be delayed (preventing a following PREPARE message on the expedited flow). However, provided the application is not failing completely to process the expedited data, the blockage should hopefully clear in a finite time, and, provided there is little or no buffering on the expedited path from one session implementation to the other, there will be no noticeable delay on the resynchronization even if a delayed acknowledgement policy for S-EXPEDITED is implemented.

It would seem at first sight that discard of expedited would violate the Standards, but it is at least arguable that such action (in the case of overload), if accompanied by an S-P-EXCEPTION-REPORT indication (a session primitive described in section 6.10) to both applications, would be a perfectly conforming implementation, and would prevent blockage of the resynchronization procedures. It would also be possible to accept the delaying of expedited acknowledgements for some time-out period linked to the needs of the actual application, but this would require a close link between the transport layer's issuing of expedited acknowledgements and the application implementation.

The only internationally standardized OSI Application Layer protocol currently (1995) specifying the issue of S-EXPEDITED requests is the Virtual Terminal protocol (discussed in section 10.5), and it is only for implementations of that protocol that this issue has to be carefully considered.

This discussion, interesting as it may be, goes beyond the scope of this book. It has hopefully served to illustrate the importance of considering the complete implementation of all layers in relation to an application, and to reinforce the point that the existence of International Standards does not eliminate the need for intelligent planning of implementations.

6.6.3 What about TP0 and TP4?

The reader will remember that transport expedited is not available if TP0 is in use. Thus there can be no PREPARE message, thus making both the major sync and the resync procedures much simpler, and indeed the resync will then be incapable of bypassing flow control if flow is completely blocked.

For implementations expecting TP0 to be used, and where the application designer has indeed made use of resync, it is important to design the total implementation so that there is minimal buffering anywhere in the path between the two applications, and so that there is some intelligence in or above the Session Layer that will ensure that normal data flow is not blocked for an indefinite period. If this were done in the Session Layer, it could again be handled by an S-P-EXCEPTION indication and discard on a long-term blockage. If handled in a higher layer, then the only available exception signal would be an ABORT, and this could perfectly well be issued by an implementation issuing a resync and getting no reply, so little is gained.

The TP4 situation is somewhat different. Here expedited is available, but introduces a round-trip delay. While this is a problem in the case of major sync for applications that might issue this primitive fairly often, it is not considered a problem for resync. By its very nature (disorderly termination of dialogue one, lost messages), it represents an exceptional situation that cannot be expected to occur frequently, so a round-trip delay is not a big issue.

6.6.4   What about collision of resynchronization handshakes?

We might expect yet another token to control the issue of S-RESYNCHRO-NIZE requests and hence to prevent collisions of this handshake. In fact, this is not the case. Remember that resync is a way of getting out of messes, and that it is important that it should not be blocked unnecessarily, so token control in this case is not appropriate.

The procedures for the handshake have been fully worked out to take account of collisions between two sequences. It makes the procedures significantly more complicated than presented here, and is best summarized by saying that the procedures of the resync quoting the earliest sync point number (or that from the connection initiator if they are equal) completes much as described above, and the procedures for the other attempt are abandoned.

In fact, these collision procedures give rise to an interesting sequence of permitted exchanges. If application A issues an S-RESYNCHRONIZE request quoting sync point number 8, say, then application B (on receipt of the corresponding indication), instead of replying with an S-RESYNCHRONIZE response quoting 8, is permitted to reply with another S-RESYNCHRONIZE request quoting any earlier number (7, say). A can reply to this with a resync request quoting 5, say, and so on until (in principle), a request is made to resync to the start of the connection. This then has to be accepted.

This sequence can be important when a minor synchronization is 'destroyed' by a following and colliding resync. Consider Figure 6.13: application A has issued an S-SYNC-MINOR request which establishes at A the sync point with serial number 20, say, and shortly after, for whatever reason, issues an S-RESYNCHRONIZE request proposing a resynchronize back to sync point 20. Unfortunately, the S-SYNC-MINOR indication is never issued, because the PREPARE for the resync overtakes it and the Session Layer commences

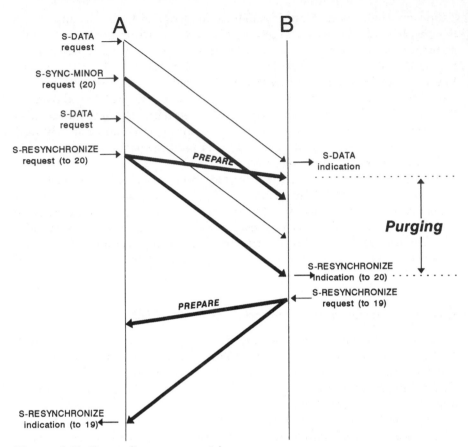

Figure 6.13 *Responding to a resync with a resync.*

purging. (The terminology used in standards work is to say that resynchronize is a disrupting service, in this case disrupting the minor synchronize service, preventing the completion of the S-SYNC-MINOR request/indication sequence.) When the S-RESYNCHRONIZE indication is eventually issued to the application, requesting resynchronization to sync point 20, application B has no knowledge of such a sync point, and can only respond with an S-RESYNCHRONIZE to an earlier sync point (19, say), which A can then accept.

6.6.5   What can be done while waiting for resynchronize to complete?

In the description of the resynchronize and the major sync sequences we said that 'Application A stops sending normal and expedited data'. The detailed description of these services specifies precisely what can be done while waiting for these sequences to complete, and the interested reader is invited, as an exercise, to examine the State Tables in the Session Service Standard, and to list the request primitives that can be issued between the issue of an S-RESYN-CHRONIZE request and receipt of the corresponding S-RESYNCHRONIZE confirm. A similar exercise can be conducted for the S-SYNC-MAJOR sequence. It will be observed that in all circumstances an S-U-ABORT is permitted, to abruptly terminate the session connection, but that little else is permitted.

6.7   Flavours of resynchronize

In the earliest work on the Session Standards, there were only two 'flavours' of S-RESYNCHRONIZE (a third was added later, and is described at the end of this section). The 'flavours' are identified by parameters in the service and proto-col. One case was called **resynchronize restart**, and one was called **resynchronize abandon**. In the case of restart, an earlier sync point number is quoted, and a chain of successive resyncs with decreasing sync point number can occur, or a resync abandon can be issued. (Similarly, a resync abandon can be issued if a resync restart is pending but not completed.) A resync abandon request/indica-tion cannot be disrupted (except by an abort), and has to be answered by a resync response/confirm. The synchronization serial number variable after completion of the resync abandon is set higher than any used so far in this connection. Thus the implied semantics of restart is 'going back to an earlier sync point', while that of abandon is 'getting a clean start'. Again, however, the reader will perceive that all that is really happening is the setting of a variable used to identify future synchronization points.

The Session Standards do put one further restriction on resync restart. It is not permitted to quote a sync point earlier than the latest major sync, the view being that major dialogue separation is created by major syncs, and that resyncs operate within that dialogue. Although major sync as such is not used in Teletex, the philosophy of a major sync-like division that one never goes back beyond is present there, and is reflected in the provision here.

Shortly before the finalization of the Session Standard, because of a request from the FTAM (File, Transfer, Access and Management) group, another fla-vour of resync called resync set was introduced. In the case of resync set, any arbi-trary sync point number is quoted on both the request/indication and the response/confirm. It is the one quoted on the response/confirm that determines the setting of the sync point serial number variable, and it is for the application designer to determine how these numbers are used, and what they mean.

This completes the rather lengthy discussion of resynchronization. In its full glory it is quite a complex set of services, and for further detail the Session Service Standard should be read.

6.8 Bypassing token control for data transfer

As with so much in networking, the moment controls are put in place, there are reasons for allowing them to be bypassed. This is also true of token control of data transfer. Two arguments were presented, again quite late in the development of the Session Standards, for being able to send (a small amount of) data 'in violation of the turn', that is, when not possessing the data token.

The first point comes from the possible use of the data token in support of data transfer to and from terminals. Two types of handling for dumb terminals could be identified in the early 1980s. In the first case, output from the host and input from the keyboard were both permitted to travel across the network simultaneously, and any contention for use of the screen was solved by some simple merging process, or by the human user voluntarily refraining from typing at certain times. If this communication was being supported by the OSI stack, this would correspond to two-way simultaneous use of session, with no data token. The second type of handling involved the concept of 'keyboard locked'. The keyboard was either unlocked, when the human user could type, and what was typed appeared on the screen and was transmitted to the host, or was locked, preventing typing, and the host transmitted material to the screen. If this communication was supported by OSI, this communication would correspond to two-way alternate use of session, with the presence or absence of the data token at the terminal end controlling the keyboard lock.

In practice, however, such systems usually had a single line at the bottom of the screen displaying 'system status', and the host could transmit data to that bottom line even if the keyboard was unlocked (the data token was with the terminal end). Thus we have our first example of a possible requirement to be able to transmit small amounts of data in violation of the turn. Of course, it might be possible to use expedited data, which is not affected by the data token, for this purpose, but the possible overtaking of normal data is not desirable, and the amount of user data available in the S-EXPEDITED-DATA request and indication, once transport and session headers have been taken out of the 32 octets available in the Network Service, is a maximum of only 14 octets, which is not really enough.

The second argument came from the group defining standards for the Presentation Layer. At this time their protocol was in a very early stage of development, but it seemed clear that the Presentation Layer would provide primitives in its service which should be invocable by an application (to invoke services specific to that layer) even if that application did not have the data token – services unconnected with the transfer of data. But the support of such services would probably involve the Presentation Protocol machines in the exchange (perhaps the two-way simultaneous exchange) of some data to carry out the service, and such an exchange would be prevented if the application had selected the two-way alternate functional unit. One option might have been for the Presentation Layer to 'track' the position of the data token, and to use S-TOKEN-GIVE requests, unknown to the application, to enable the Presentation Layer exchange of messages, and to reposition the token correctly at the end of that exchange. This looked not merely complicated, but in some sense a violation of the partitioning of functions into layers. The Presentation Layer should have no concern with tokens.

It could be argued that this latter point (and earlier ones about the problem of purging buffers on a resync because session primitives were not issued directly to the application) was clear support for the view that the architectural model was wrong, and that the Presentation Layer should have been positioned below the Session Layer. It was, however, much too late in the day for any such arguments to be seriously advanced, and other solutions had to be found.

The response was to introduce a new pair of service primitives: S-TYPED-DATA request/indication, permitting the transfer of a different 'type' of data over the session connection. This other type of data would not be subject to token control. As far as the service is concerned, S-TYPED-DATA is identical to S-DATA apart from the lack of token control: it carries unlimited user data, goes on the transport normal flow, and hence is subject to normal flow control, does not involve an end-to-end round-trip for each transmission, and so on. As far as the service is concerned, it looks a bit like the use of the Q-bit in X.25, providing two different 'colours' of data message, red and blue. In the protocol, however, there are a number of differences. S-DATA can be subject to segmentation in the Session Layer, and concatenation of messages supporting S-DATA and other session primitives (particularly token passing) within a single T-DATA transmission is permitted. Neither of these 'optimization' features are available with S-TYPED-DATA, so at the protocol level it is not quite like the Q-bit of X.25, which is literally a single on/off bit in normal data messages.

It would appear at first sight that the S-TYPED-DATA primitives should be made available only in two-way alternate mode (only when there is a data token). However, this would have involved the Presentation Layer in having two different protocol specifications in terms of the mapping of messages to Session Service primitives: in TWS operation, messages would map to S-TYPED-DATA, and in TWA operation, messages would map to S-DATA. This was considered somewhat undesirable, so S-TYPED-DATA was made available as a normal part of the Session Service, available in both TWA and TWS operation, and selected as a separate functional unit. (Note that while this is not part of the Session Kernel Function unit, when the OSI Presentation Service is the user of the Session Service, it is a mandatory part of the provision if required to support the presentation protocol.)

6.9 Activities

Remarkably little has been said above about Teletex, given the historical introduction. It is here that this is rectified. The Teletex exchange was concerned with the delivery of documents typed in on a Teletex machine, or being sent for printing by a Teletex machine. The transmission of such documents was an independent activity that the Teletex system engaged in, and the session connection was a sequence of such activities.

Normal operation was two-way alternate as far as the bulk data transfer was concerned – documents were going one way or the other, but a single connection could support both directions of transfer in sequence. The connection began with the exchange of **capability data**, designed to determine the capabilities of the Teletex machine to handle documents that might be sent to it or originate from it. It looked at such issues as whether it could print in 'landscape' format (a page on its side) or 'portrait' format (a page in an upright position), and the character repertoire it could handle (Teletex included not just the Latin alphabet, but Japanese as well as an optional feature). This was a two-way exchange, and in order to provide support for the exchange, S-CAPABILITY-DATA request/indication/response/confirm primitives were introduced into the Session Service. (These are there to enable the Teletex specification to be rewritten using the Session Services, but as noted earlier, this has never actually been done, and X.400 – the nearest one gets to that exercise – chose not to issue S-CAPABILITY-DATA requests. Thus there are no Internationally Standardized protocols today that make any reference to S-CAPABILITY-DATA.)

Having exchanged capability data, the end with control (holding all the tokens) started an activity. (There was a protocol message saying this was what it was doing, and it allowed the activity to be named and the initial value of the sync point serial number variable to be set for this activity.) This was a one-way unconfirmed exchange. To support it, we have the S-ACTIVITY-START request/indication. The Teletex system then transferred a document as a one-way flow, with checkpointing within it if it was large, and then ended the activity with a two-way exchange that was effectively a major synchronization point, on completion of which checkpoint data for checkpoints established during the activity could be discarded. (Here you see the philosophy of not being able to resynchronize to points earlier than major synchronization points.) As well as being able to have an orderly termination of an activity, it was also possible to discard the activity (abandon the transfer, again with release of any checkpoint data established, and with deletion of any partially received material), or interrupt the activity. In the latter case, checkpoint data would be retained, and at a later date the activity could be resumed from some checkpoint. Both interruption and discard were equivalent in their effect on the dialogue to resynchronization: they produced a disorderly termination of dialogue one (the activity being discarded/interrupted) and a protected start for the following activity.

To support these messages, we get S-ACTIVITY-END, S-ACTIVITY-DISCARD and S-ACTIVITY-INTERRUPT, all as confirmed services (request, indication, response, confirm), and S-ACTIVITY-RESUME as an unconfirmed service (request and indication), in addition to the S-ACTIVITY-START request/indication mentioned above.

S-ACTIVITY-RESUME has three additional parameters over S-ACTIVITY-START, called **Old Activity Identifier**, **Old Session Connection Identifier** and **Initial Synchronization Point Serial Number**. As usual, the Session Layer places no semantics on the first two, and merely uses the third to initialize the sync point serial number variable. The names derive from the use Teletex makes of these fields.

The synchronization point establishment is clearly the same as the minor synchronization concept coming from ECMA, and the Teletex message was used to support both, with no doubling of service primitives. The 'activity end' is effectively the same as a major synchronization, and both the 'activity discard' and the 'activity interrupt' are the same as resynchronization, except that chaining of request/indication sequences does not, of course, occur. Moreover, we need token control on 'activity interrupt' and 'activity discard' to ensure that collisions do not occur due to their more-or-less simultaneous issue by both of the communicating partners. In the end, it became clear that the simplest solution was indeed the addition of these extra primitives. It is, however, important for the reader to recognize that, in the session specification, the exchange of messages, the use of PREPARE, the purging of dialogue one and the stacking up of transport expedited to protect dialogue two occur for activity end, discard and interrupt in exactly the same way as for the major sync and resync exchanges. There is nothing new to understand.

Token control is used to prevent collisions of activity primitive exchanges, and in fact the same token was used for controlling major sync and for controlling the issuing of activity primitives, hence the name **major/activity token**.

Some readers may have seen tutorial text in which the PREPARE message is not shown on activity interrupt and activity discard. Why? Follow the tortuous route: Teletex involves TP0; TP0 does not support T-EXPEDITED-DATA; PREPARE is carried on T-EXPEDITED-DATA; therefore PREPARE will not be issued in many actual instances of use of session activity. (Note that CCITT Recommendation X.400 insists on the use of TP0, although the corresponding ISO standard does not. If other classes of transport protocol are in use, however, then a line monitor will indeed see a PREPARE message associated with activity termination.

It is now important to disentangle the Teletex semantics from the Session Layer semantics (the latter being by far the most important for the OSI application designer and the reader of this book). The above description has so far very much mixed both together. First, there are no restrictions in the Session Layer on the use of S-ACTIVITY-START or S-ACTIVITY-RESUME to commence an activity. There are two extra parameters on the resume primitives, but otherwise their effects are identical. No constraints are placed on the use of the activity identifier, the old activity identifier or the old sync point serial number fields. If application designers wish to use these primitives and fields in the same way as Teletex, they can of course do so. But if they want to be perverse and use S-ACTIVITY-RESUME to start 'new' activities, and S-ACTIVITY-START to resume interrupted ones, they can equally do so. In the same way, interrupting or discarding an activity is absolutely identical in terms of any effect on the Session Layer: they both produce disorderly termination of the activity. Secondly, note that most tutorials show the application that initiates an activity as the one that terminates it. This is not a restriction imposed by the Session Layer: the major/activity token can be passed during an activity, enabling termination of the activity by the other application.

So ... coming from the ECMA stable we have the concept of a session connection consisting of a series of dialogues separated by major synchronization points, with minor synchronization points placed between them, and with resync as the only mechanism for disorderly termination of a dialogue and a clean start to a new one. Coming from the CCITT stable, we have the concept of a session connection consisting of a series of activities which are begun and terminated (with an orderly end or a disorderly interrupt or discard), with minor synchronization points placed within them, and with the only data exchange outside activities being the exchange of capability data. Before reading further, readers are invited to put themselves in the role of the committee in 1984, and to come up with a sensible merger of these two approaches!

The first point to reinforce (discussed in section 6.1) was the decision to 'build' the session facilities from a series of functional units. These are listed below in the discussion on connection establishment, but critically, there is an **activity functional unit**. Application designers determine which functional units are needed to support their applications, and agreement on these functional units is made when the session connection is established. In particular, the activity functional unit will have been selected or not. While it might be unusual to select both the major synchronization functional unit and the activity functional unit, we do not wish to prohibit such selection. Let us assume that any combination of the functional units can be selected, and in the discussion below that all functional units (apart from the activity functional unit) have been selected.

If the activity functional unit is not selected, then the session connection is used in the 'pure' ECMA manner (Figure 6.14) – there are a series of dialogue units separated by major synchronization points, with minor synchronization points between them, and with resynchronization at any time. There is no use of capability data or of activity primitives.

On the other hand, if the activity functional unit is selected (Figure 6.15), then each activity looks rather like a 'pure ECMA' connection, with major and minor synchronization points and resynchronization within it, and with only capability data transfer and the passing of tokens before an activity commences and between activities.

There was some discussion on the use of S-DATA in the activity case. In 'pure' Teletex, this is never issued outside of activities, but the decision was taken to permit this (and typed data and expedited data transmission) as well as capability data between activities. In the event, this produced a number of later problems, particularly for the Session Layer, as an S-DATA request can be issued outside an activity by one application, with the corresponding S-DATA indication within an activity because the data transfer crossed with an activity start coming from the other end. In the late 1980s, there was some discussion on

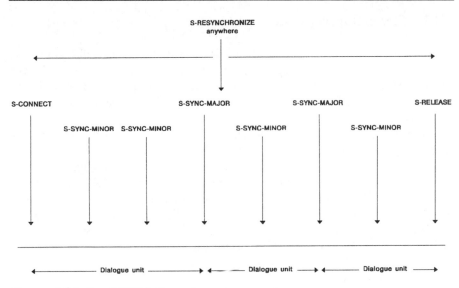

Figure 6.14 *Pure 'ECMA' use of a session connection.*

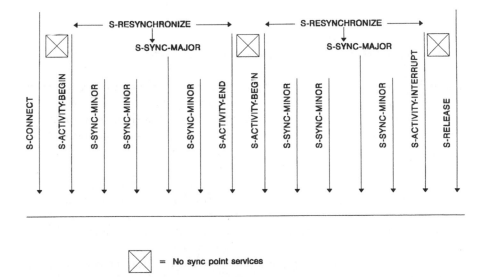

☒ = No sync point services

Figure 6.15 *Full session sync services in use.*

whether to reverse the decision to allow S-DATA requests outside activities, or whether to make S-ACTIVITY-START and S-ACTIVITY-RESUME into confirmed services to help to address this problem, but this was never done, and application designers who choose to allow data transfer outside activities (when the activity functional unit is selected) have to be aware that they are responsible for handling any problems that might arise from this collision case.

6.10 Exception reports

We have already briefly mentioned the S-P-EXCEPTION-REPORT indication as a means, if the exception reporting functional unit has been selected by the application, by which the Session Layer can inform the application of problems detected within the Session Layer implementation without having to abort the connection.

The Session Service also provides the ability for higher layers, including the application itself, to make such signals, through the provision of an S-U-EXCEPTION-REPORT request/indication. The session rules specify that if either of these primitives is issued, then the only permitted actions by the applications are the issuing of an S-RESYNCHRONIZE or the aborting of the connection with an S-U-ABORT. Typically, an application designer selecting this functional unit will specify that the response to an upcoming S-P-EXCEPTION-REPORT indication will be a resynchronize in some specified circumstances, and an abort in other circumstances. Note, however, that if an application designer does specify use of this functional unit, then the application specification is not complete unless the handling of this indication at any point in the connection is properly specified.

6.11 Negotiation and connection establishment issues

The S-CONNECT request/indication and response/confirm primitives are supported by transmission using T-DATA request/indication primitives. They carry a number of parameters that are used to ensure that the two implementations are in agreement on the facilities available on the session connection and on the initial state in terms of the value of the sync point serial number variable and the position of tokens.

The session describes the establishment of this agreement as **negotiation**, as one end proposes in the request/indication, and the other end determines anything left optional. While the application layer designer could in principle, given a suitable protocol design, leave the offer and the response as an implementation-dependent choice constrained only by the session rules, it is more common to find the exchange completely determined by the specification of the application.

One case where some element of implementation-dependent choice is permitted is in the use of the resynchronize functional unit in FTAM (File Transfer, Access and Management). FTAM defines a protocol that is capable of operating with or without this functional unit, so an implementation A initiating a connection to support FTAM transfers will propose use of this functional unit if and only if it can support this within its FTAM implementation. Similarly, if use is proposed by A, the responding implementation B will accept the proposal if and only if it can support its use within its FTAM implementation.

Functional unit	Associated services
Kernel	S-CONNECT, S-DATA, S-RELEASE, S-U-ABORT, S-P-ABORT
Negotiated release	S-RELEASE, S-TOKEN-GIVE, S-TOKEN-PLEASE
Half duplex	S-TOKEN-GIVE, S-TOKEN-PLEASE
Duplex	None
Expedited data	S-EXPEDITED-DATA
Typed data	S-TYPED-DATA
Capability data	S-CAPABILITY-DATA
Minor synchronize	S-SYNC-MINOR, S-TOKEN-GIVE, S-TOKEN-PLEASE
Symmetric synchronize	S-SYNC-MINOR
Major synchronize	S-SYNC-MAJOR, S-TOKEN-GIVE, S-TOKEN-PLEASE
Resynchronize	S-RESYNCHRONIZE
Exceptions	S-U-EXCEPTION-REPORT, S-P-EXCEPTION-REPORT
Activity management	S-ACTIVITY-START, -RESUME, -INTERRUPT, -DISCARD, -END, S-TOKEN-GIVE, S-TOKEN-PLEASE, S-CONTROL-GIVE

Figure 6.16 *Session functional units and primitives.*

The full list of session functional units and the service primitives that their selection permits is given in Figure 6.16. Note that the kernel functional unit is not negotiable: the associated service primitives are always available. Use of the remaining functional units and the associated service primitives is negotiated. (The reader is cautioned that this list is taken from the version of ISO 8326, the Session Service Definition, dated 1990, and that standards undergo an ongoing process of update and revision. The latest version should be consulted for any serious use.)

The S-CONNECT request/indication contains a bit-map notionally identifying the functional units needed by the application. Before transmitting the corresponding message, the Session Layer implementation notionally removes from the bit-map the bits corresponding to any functional units that it cannot support, and passes the message across. (I said 'notionally' here, because the only thing that is visible on the line is the actual functional units proposed by the total implementation, and OSI standards do not constrain or specify internal implementation architectures – a point made frequently in earlier text.) In the receiving system, the bit-map is again reduced according to the capability of that Session Layer implementation before the S-CONNECT indication is issued. Finally, the responding application may make further reductions before the bit-map is passed (unchanged) through the two Session Layer implementations to the initiating application, thus ensuring common agreement by all parties on what has been selected for use.

The existence of particular tokens is determined by the selection of functional units. Thus selection of the two-way alternate functional unit means that the data token exists. Selection of the minor synchronization functional unit means that the minor synchronize token exists, and so on. Whenever the bit-map contains a proposal or confirmation for a particular functional unit, the positioning of any corresponding token is also addressed. In the request/indication, the token is positioned as 'my side', 'your side', or 'you choose'. In the response/confirm, the final resolution of the last case is made.

The value to be used for the first synchronization point to be established on the connection (the initial synchronization point serial number) is also determined in the exchange. The initiator of the connection proposes a value (in the range 0 to 999 999), and the acceptor determines the final value as this or some lower value.

Another 'negotiation' in the protocol (not visible in the service) supporting the S-CONNECT primitive is the version of the session protocol in use. All International Standards are subject to revision, and where such revision changes bits on the line or procedures, it is important to be able to identify which version of a protocol specification is to be used on a connection. Thus negotiation (the initiator provides a bit-map of the versions supported, the responder selects) of the version to be used is an important aspect of ensuring interworking.

Finally, it should be noted that the S-CONNECT primitives all carry user data. In the first version of the Session Standards this was up to 512 octets, which leads into the discussion below.

6.12   Lengths of user data fields

Around the time that the Session Standards were stabilizing, there was discussion within the OSI architecture group about 'piggy-backing' of connection establishment. The reader will have noted that both the Network and the Transport Service provide user data (128 octets) on their CONNECT primitives, but that the layer above (Transport and Network) makes no use of this to carry connection establishment messages. T-CONNECT is carried in N-DATA and S-CONNECT is carried in T-DATA. If this were carried to the extreme, we would have about five round trips before an application could begin to do useful work: one to establish the network connection, followed by one to establish the transport connection, followed by one to establish the session connection, followed by one to establish the presentation connection, probably followed by one to negotiate the initial state of the application. This is clearly not acceptable.

The discussion concluded that there were good reasons, in terms of multiplexing and re-use, for avoiding 'piggy-backing' in the lower layers, but that it was desirable to carry as a single T-DATA request/indication the S-CONNECT request/indication with (in its user data parameter) an embedded P-CONNECT request/indication with (in its user data parameter) embedded messages for any necessary application request/indication exchange. The corresponding reply from the other end-system would contain the S-CONNECT response/confirm with (in its user data parameter) an embedded P-CONNECT response/confirm with (in its user data parameter) embedded messages for any necessary application response/confirm exchange. Of course, we have to ensure that either connections in all layers are accepted or connections in all layers are refused, prohibiting mixed situations, but otherwise there are no problems from this piggy-backing of the upper layer exchanges.

This approach not only allows a reduction of round trips – it confers the more important advantage that what is notionally the Session Layer response can be conditioned by the application being supported. Thus in the case of FTAM use of the resynchronize functional unit being proposed, the session implementation may be capable of supporting that for the X.400 application, but not for the FTAM application (for reasons of implementation architecture and product bundling). It is therefore desirable to be able to ascertain, before the session connection is accepted, which application is going to use it. This is achieved by the piggy- backing.

There is, however, one problem, which surfaced into a major 'row' in about 1986. It was resolved by a special week-long meeting of experts from the session and presentation layers and the major applications which were being standardized in Helsinki. The meeting discussed a number of issues of common concern in the upper layers, but the primary problem being addressed was the length of the user data parameter of the S-CONNECT primitives.

There were two primary arguments coming from the presentation and application groups. The first argument related directly to the fact that messages from the presentation layer and potentially a number of application standards that were to use the session connection all had to be fitted into the 512 octets of the S-CONNECT user data parameter. The Presentation Layer Standards were by now sufficiently close to completion that it was apparent that the length of messages they might require was potentially unlimited, but highly dependent on the needs of the applications that were to use the connection. It was also apparent that as new applications were developed in the future, predicting now the likely size of initialization messages such an unknown application might need to exchange was very hard. Thus determining a 'sensible' partitioning of any fixed length field between the different groups was not possible. With one voice the users of the session service said 'We have to have a user data parameter of unlimited length. Please!'

The second argument requires an understanding of the functions of the Presentation Layer, presented briefly in earlier text, and discussed more fully in the next chapter. The important point, however, is that in the OSI architecture, application designers do not determine the bit-pattern (and hence the length) of their messages. The actual encoding of the information exchange is a matter for the Presentation Layer, and could be extremely verbose or extremely compact. It could even vary according to the relative bandwidth of the network and CPU power of the communicating systems. (At one extreme, spending CPU cycles on heavy compression could be sensible, at the other extreme it would not be.) This makes working with a fixed length almost impossible. Application designers literally do not know whether the information flow they are specifying can be fitted into 512 octets or not.

The Session Layer experts countered with two arguments of their own. First, that the standardization process had been completed for the Session Standards, and that a number of implementations were already out in the field. Making a change now would be disruptive, and could lose OSI credibility. Secondly, it really is irresponsible to transmit large amounts of data in the S-CONNECT, where there is no provision for checkpointing within the large transmission. Said the session experts 'OK – just maybe 512 octets is not enough. But surely a fixed length of 64K octets would be ample to meet any practical need?' The users replied 'WE WANT UNLIMITED USER DATA. WE WANT UNLIMITED USER DATA.' And at the end of the week, the agreement was indeed unlimited user data, not just on the S-CONNECT, but, to avoid any further problems, on all the Session Service primitives.

This change was promulgated in International Standards as a formal new version of the Session Protocol, making Session the first of the main OSI standards to introduce a second version, and to test out the effectiveness of version negotiation. In practice, however, implementors very quickly got the message that version 2 was where all the action was going to be, and there are few, if any, version 1 implementations in use today. On the other hand, it is probably true that all messages sent in anger so far are less than 512 octets in length.

7

The encoding question

7.1 Introduction to Presentation Layer concepts

Again we require something of a mind-shift in looking at the Presentation Layer, compared with either the Transport or the Session Layers. In the Transport Layer we saw a very simple set of service primitives, supported by a number of different protocols, with the only effect of using one or other of these being on the quality of the resulting service. In the Session Layer, we saw a lot of added value through the provision of a whole set of largely independent service primitives, each supported by its own piece of protocol. In the Presentation Layer, by contrast, we see only one new (confirmed) service, the P-ALTER-CONTEXT request/indication, response/confirm, supported by protocol, with all other actions related simply to transformation of user data parameters on primitives closely paralleling those of the Session Layer.

The reader may wish to review section 2.4.6, which identifies the concerns of the Presentation Layer, and the reasons for permitting a varying representation of data in different instances of communication.

The P-ALTER-CONTEXT service primitives are concerned with negotiating the representation to be used, but all other P-service primitives are a simple reflection of the S-service primitives. For every S-service primitive in the Session Layer, there is a P-service primitive with an identical set of parameters (for example P-SYNC-MAJOR). The rules for when these P-primitives can be issued are precisely those of the session service, and the protocol supporting these service primitives is in almost all cases a simple and direct mapping between the P-service and S-service primitives, in both directions. What then is the added value?

The critical difference is in the nature of the user data parameter of each of the primitives. In the Session Service, the user data parameter of each service primitive is a string of octets of unlimited size – remember?). Specifying its value is a matter of clearly specifying the value of these octets. In the Presentation Service, however, the user data parameter is pure information, divorced of any representation. The presentation protocol machine generates an appropriate (agreed by negotiation) octet string for the Session Service to carry this information during transfer, and decodes a received octet string to produce pure information on receipt, for passing up in the Presentation Service primitive.

This can be a hard concept to grasp, particularly for those who view layering as an implementation architecture. It is clearly rather hard to pass pure information divorced of representation in a real implementation interface, and people sometimes say that 'The Presentation Layer maps from a local representation to an agreed transfer representation', because that is what some piece of code somewhere in the implementation will actually be doing. It is, however, an inappropriate model as it would imply that application layer standards specify values in some local representation – clearly a nonsense. Local representations of information are part of the implementation, and have no visibility in standards work.

7.2 Abstract and transfer syntaxes

The reader will be asking 'But what is pure information, and how does an application layer designer specify a value for pure information?' This is quite a hard question to answer.

It can help to clear the mind to consider some aspects of information theory. If a set of known values are to be transmitted, with each one being transmitted at random (no dependencies on what was last transmitted), and the probability of transmission of a particular value is known, then the (probably) optimal encoding for transmission uses a number of bits for each value which is inversely related to the probability of its transmission. Thus if one value occurs very often, that would be represented by a single zero bit, say, and all other values would be represented by a pattern starting with a one bit. Values that occurred very infrequently would be represented by a bit-pattern containing a great many more bits, depending on the total number of values in the set.

Thus we see that the focus is on **values** as a set of things that need to be represented by an arbitrary but unambiguous string of bits. Any piece of information to be transferred is either identical to some other piece of information (indistinguishable from it), in which case it is the same value, or differs in some aspect, in which case it is a different value. We are not here concerned with looking at internal structure. A piece of information consisting of a list of six integers has values that we can represent on paper as, for example $\{39, -26, 5, 78, 81, 0\}$, which is one single value of this information, and $\{39, -26, 5, 79, 81, 0\}$ is another single value. There is no concept that this second value might be considered nearer to the first than, for example, $\{1023, 87, 234, -456, 56, 9\}$: that depends on looking inside the single value, something we do not necessarily wish to do.

For any particular protocol design, it is at least possible to consider the theoretical set of all possible values of the information it wants to send in the user data of presentation service primitives. This may be an infinite set of values, like those specified above, but it none the less must be a well-defined set of values if the protocol is well specified.

We talk about the set of **presentation data values** for this application protocol as this collection of values, and we give a name to this collection. We call it the **abstract syntax** of the protocol. So application protocol designers specify their abstract syntax in some way – formal notation, ordinary English, whatever.

An abstract syntax then is a collection of presentation data values (sometimes just called **data values**, and sometimes just called **values**, or **abstract values**) to be transferred by the Presentation Layer in the operation of some particular protocol.

In order for the presentation protocol machine to convert such abstract values into bits for the Session Layer to transfer, it is necessary to have associated with this abstract syntax (this collection of presentation data values) a set of bit-strings. This set of bit-strings is called a **transfer syntax for this abstract syntax**. A transfer syntax (set of bit-strings) for an abstract syntax has the following properties.

- For each (presentation) data value in the abstract syntax there is one or more bit-strings in the transfer syntax associated with that value.
- Each bit-string in the transfer syntax is distinct, and has precisely one abstract value associated with it.

In other words, the transfer syntax provides bit-strings that unambiguously, but not necessarily uniquely, represent the abstract values (presentation data values) in the abstract syntax with which it is associated. Where there is more than one bit-string in the transfer syntax associated with some particular abstract value, then it is an implementation option which one to use in any particular transfer. If a transfer syntax has a single bit-string for each abstract value, we call it a **canonical transfer syntax**. (The importance of canonical transfer syntaxes is discussed in section 8.2.6, but relates to security issues.)

The reader should at this stage note that there are two further potential requirements that are not a requirement on a well-formed transfer syntax. First, the bit-patterns representing an abstract value are not required to be a multiple of eight bits, they can be any length, and secondly they are not required to be self-delimiting. The precise meaning of this latter point is discussed below, but both features impose requirements on the design of the presentation protocol which the reader may wish to think about.

In order to support the concept of differing representations of presentation data values and Presentation Layer negotiation of the representation, we need two additional features.

- We need to recognize that any particular abstract syntax may have more than one defined transfer syntax associated with it, providing alternative means of encoding (representing) the abstract values.
- We need a means of identifying abstract syntaxes and transfer syntaxes with names (identifiers) that can be used to refer to them in the presentation protocol negotiation of which transfer syntax to use.

It is important that the name-space for naming abstract and transfer syntaxes should permit allocation of identifiers by any group likely to be defining OSI application layer protocols, and by any computer vendor or other implementor that wants to define vendor-specific transfer syntaxes (optimized for communication between that vendor's implementations). This requirement was satisfied by work within the group charged with standardizing a notation which could be used for abstract syntax definition. This form of name is called **an ASN.1 OBJECT IDENTIFIER**, and it is discussed more fully in Chapter 8 on

ASN.1 (Abstract Syntax Notation One). Its use is much wider than the simple naming of abstract and transfer syntaxes, which is why it is called an object identifier rather than a syntax identifier, but its use to identify unambiguously abstract and transfer syntaxes is the only concern in this chapter.

7.3   Data transfer requirements placed on the Presentation Layer

It might be assumed that, for any particular presentation connection, there will be a single abstract syntax in use, corresponding to the application protocol running over that connection. However, there are two reasons why this approach proved too simplistic and limiting.

- Any particular group defining a protocol may find it convenient to group some of their values into one abstract syntax, and some into another. Thus for example, in the case of FTAM (File, Transfer, Access and Management), there are values to be transmitted which are part of the main protocol, saying things like 'open file x', 'write to it', and so on. There are also values to be transmitted which are the values to be stored in some particular type of file (for example, lines of characters from some defined repertoire for a simple character file). Clearly it makes sense to define an abstract syntax for the main protocol, and separate abstract syntaxes for each type of file that we might be concerned with. Depending on how many files are open, and what type they are, there may be a need to transfer values from several abstract syntaxes (an arbitrary number) in a fairly random sequence within a single presentation connection.
- The concept of Application Service Elements (discussed in Chapter 9) recognizes that the total information transfer to completely support an application may be made up of parts defined by a number of different groups, each defining an Application Service Element, and hence each with an information exchange requirement. It avoids a large number of potential liaison problems in ensuring unambiguous transfer syntaxes if each of these groups can operate independently and define separate abstract syntaxes, with values from the abstract syntaxes of any of the Application Service Elements in use being transferred over the presentation connection.

There are two other complications to consider:

- Application Service Elements frequently define a protocol as the transmission of presentation data values that have holes in them. This is actually just the normal situation with layering. The Application Service Element provides some form of carrier service, and other Application Service Elements provide their own presentation data values to fill in the holes. The question of holes (often called black holes) is discussed more fully later, but for the present all that matters is to recognize that, early in its development, the Presentation Layer recognized the concept that a presentation data value might have embedded within it presentation data values from some other abstract syntax (to arbitrary depth).

- It can happen for some applications that the same abstract syntax (the same set of abstract values) is used in two different circumstances which require to be distinguished, and which perhaps require different encodings. Let us look at the FTAM example again. Suppose we have set up monitoring (to some log file) of the main protocol exchanges in some instance of use of FTAM. This file will contain a series of values from the main FTAM abstract syntax, but it is clearly important, if this file is later accessed using FTAM, that such values are not confused with values forming the main FTAM protocol (designed to open, write, read, files etc.) in this particular communication. Moreover, it might be desirable under some circumstances (for example, where implementations from the same vendor are communicating) for the transfer syntax for these values when they are values in the log file to be a vendor-specific one closely related to the way they are stored on disk, while the transfer syntax for these values when they form part of the main FTAM protocol exchange might be some internationally standardized or more highly optimized transfer syntax, but anyway, different. These considerations give rise to the concept of a presentation context.

A **presentation context** is defined as an association between an abstract syntax and an associated transfer syntax. In other words, it is a set of presentation data values (those in the abstract syntax) for which a transfer syntax has been agreed, and which represents an instance of use of an abstract syntax on some presentation connection. To fulfil the requirements discussed above, we recognize that any one given abstract syntax may have multiple instances of use (multiple presentation contexts, with the same or with different transfer syntaxes), and that the basic unit of data transfer should be the transmission of a presentation data value from some identified presentation context. At any point in time on a connection, a potentially unlimited number of presentation contexts will have been agreed for use (defined), and values from any of these contexts can be transferred. This set of presentation contexts is called the **defined context set** (DCS).

So ... with these concepts in place, what are the main requirements to be placed on the Presentation Layer? First, it should support the attempt by an application to define a new presentation context for some named abstract syntax, negotiating the transfer syntax to be used for that presentation context. (It may also be useful to allow deletion of contexts from the defined context set.) Secondly, it should support the transfer (in the user data parameter of each Presentation Service primitive) of a list of presentation data values, each one potentially from a different presentation context in the defined context set, and possibly containing embedded presentation data values from some other presentation context. Thirdly, it must define an appropriate protocol to support that transfer.

The second requirement is simply met by defining the user data parameter of each Presentation Service primitive in precisely that way: as an ordered list of presentation data values from any presentation context in the defined set (defined at the time the Presentation Service primitive is issued). The alert reader, however, will already have some alarm bells beginning to ring. It is clearly rather important that any changes to the defined context set are managed in such a way that if a presentation data value from some context is present on a request or response service primitive, then that context must still be part of the defined context set when the message reaches the remote system, and the corresponding indication or confirm is issued. This begins to look a bit like the dialogue separation requirement of session, and one solution could have been to require that all changes to the defined context set coincide with a major synchronization. That solution, however, is clearly not acceptable, given the possible use of activities without major synchronization, and the concerns discussed earlier (section 6.5.3) about the efficiency of major synchronization when using TP4. The problem will be discussed when the negotiation of contexts (the first requirement above) and the supporting protocol (the third requirement above) are discussed below.

Another problem relates to embedded presentation values. It can be the case that a presentation data value (at the outer level, say) carrying an embedded presentation data value is relayed with little understanding of its form or transfer syntax by the relay system. This requires some care in the way in which embedded values are handled, and introduces the concept of a relay-safe transfer syntax, which is discussed more fully in Chapter 8.

7.4   Establishing the defined context set by negotiation

In the simplest case, all contexts to be used on a connection will be negotiated and agreed as part of the initial exchange of messages that are piggy-backed on the S-CONNECT exchange as described earlier (section 6.12). There will be no additions or deletions to that set of contexts during the lifetime of the connection, and the concerns about encoded data crossing with or overtaking changes to the defined context set do not arise. This is part of the kernel presentation functional unit. The ability to add to the defined context set and delete contexts during a connection using the P-ALTER-CONTEXT service primitives is part of what is called the context management functional unit, and as for the Session Layer, its availability is negotiated at the time the connection is established.

To establish contexts at connection establishment time, the procedure is as shown in Figure 7.1. Notionally, all concern with the transfer syntax is a Presentation Layer matter (the application designer does not specify transfer syntaxes), so the P-CONNECT request carries only, as far as presentation context negotiation is concerned, an ordered list of abstract syntax names for which presentation contexts are to be established. It does not mention the transfer syntax to be used.

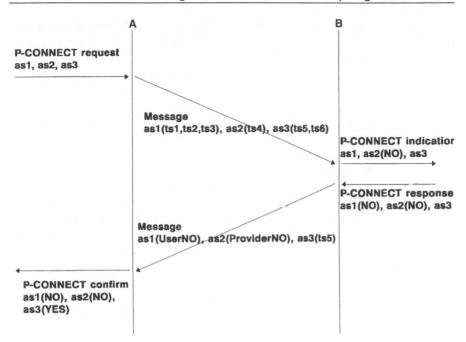

Figure 7.1 *Establishing contexts on P-CONNECT.*

Despite this formal position as far as the model and the service definition are concerned, agreement was reached in the middle 1980s, but nowhere documented in any standard, that application designers were free to specify static conformance requirements for transfer syntaxes (that is, the ones that all implementations had to support), and many Application Layer standards do indeed specify mandatory implementation of transfer syntaxes produced using the so-called ASN.1 Basic Encoding Rules (discussed in section 8.1.7) in order to ensure interworking for those applications.

When the P-CONNECT request is issued, the presentation layer then notionally forms the message supporting the P-CONNECT (and which forms the user data parameter of the S-CONNECT that is to be issued). That message contains *inter alia* a data structure consisting of the list of abstract syntax names, with each one having associated with it a list of one or more transfer syntax names that are being offered as candidates for agreement to support that abstract syntax.

We said 'notionally' again, for implementation structure is not constrained by OSI standards, nor is it visible on the line. All that matters is that the total implementation, with full knowledge of the use that is to be made of each presentation context, offers one or more transfer syntaxes for each required presentation context. Note also that, to support the establishment of multiple contexts for the same abstract syntax, the list of abstract syntax names is an ordered list, and the same abstract syntax name may appear more than once.

Clearly, an implementation will not offer transfer syntaxes that it does not support, but there is no requirement that it should offer all those that it does support, if other information makes it inappropriate to do so.

On receipt of the S-CONNECT indication carrying this message, the presentation layer notionally flags as not available (rather than removing) any abstract syntax in the list for which there is no offered transfer syntax that it can support and then issues a P-CONNECT indication to the application layer containing the list. (The question of identification of the application to which this is notionally addressed – FTAM, X.400, or whatever – is discussed in a later section.)

The application then determines which contexts are to be established by further flagging items in the list as not established before returning the list on the P-CONNECT response. The protocol machine now adds precisely one transfer syntax name for each context which is to be established, and returns (as user data of the S-CONNECT response) a message which informs the originating implementation of the contexts that have been established, and the list of which contexts have been established and which have not is passed up to the application. For those not accepted, there is an error code that determines whether the context was refused by the provider (and if so whether this was because there were too many in the DCS, no offered transfer syntax was supported, or the abstract syntax was not supported) or by the user.

There is thus a limited form of negotiation available to the application designer: it is possible, for example, to specify that an attempt be made to establish a presentation context for each of a number of abstract syntaxes, and to specify that the receiving application should choose one of these for establishment and reject the rest. More commonly, however, each presentation context in the list will be accepted, and the negotiation is entirely confined to establishing (within the presentation layer) the transfer syntax to be used for each one.

The message actually carries with each presentation context proposed for definition an odd-numbered integer value (the reason for using only odd-numbered values is given in section 7.5.5 in the discussion on collisions). This value forms the **presentation context identifier** and is associated with bit-patterns transmitted later to identify the presentation context of the presentation data value they represent (and hence specifying how to map them into an abstract value).

7.5 The supporting protocol

7.5.1 Generating the Session Service user data parameter

The Presentation Service user data parameter contains an ordered list of presentation data values, each being a value from the defined context set. The encoding of that value into a bit-string is well defined by the well-formed transfer syntax associated with the presentation context. Moreover, we assume that the handling of embedded presentation data values is the responsibility of the designer of transfer syntaxes supporting such structures, and no direct support is provided in the Presentation Layer protocol. (Again, further discussion on this issue appears in Chapter 8.)

Now the bit-pattern defined by the transfer syntax has three deficiencies in terms of simple mapping to the Session Service.

- It is not a multiple of eight bits, and the Session Service user data parameters are all required to be octet strings (a requirement which reflects the requirements of X.25 and hence of the Network Service and Transport Service).
- It is only unambiguous in relation to other bit-strings in the same presentation context. The same bit-string can (and frequently will) appear in several transfer syntaxes (presentation contexts) with totally different abstract values (typically from different abstract syntaxes).
- It is not self-delimiting.

Let us address the last point first, as it has only recently become clearly understood in standards work.

A transfer syntax may be 'hand-crafted' – manual design of the bit-patterns in it – but it is far more common for it to be defined by the specification of general-purpose encoding rules that can be applied to any abstract syntax that has been specified using some defined notation with which the encoding rules are associated. We say that the notation defines a **type** (or data type, or data structure, or abstract type) whose set of values forms and defines the set of abstract values in the abstract syntax. In this case, the encoding rules may have been designed so that, without any knowledge of the type used to define the abstract syntax, the end of each bit-pattern can be determined using only a knowledge of the encoding rules themselves. Such encoding rules were considered in the past to produce **self-delimiting encodings**, but it is important here to note that such encodings are only 'self-delimiting' if the process trying to delimit them does indeed have full knowledge of the applicable encoding rules. It is also important to note that the process of finding the end may be very simple (some sort of length count at the head of the encoding), or could be arbitrarily complicated, but still theoretically possible using only knowledge of the encoding rules. The next step along the sliding scale to not being self-delimiting is where the end cannot be determined from encoding rules alone, but requires a knowledge of the type used to define the abstract syntax (full knowledge of the abstract and transfer syntaxes). Thus, for example, the length of each bit-string in the transfer syntax may be the same provided the set of abstract values is the set of values of a fixed length character string, but not otherwise. Going further along the spectrum, we might have a transfer syntax (for example, the simple ASCII encoding of a variable length character string, with no length count or delimiter) such that, if the encodings of two different values are concatenated, a receiver has no way of determining where the boundary lies, and ambiguity would arise in the decoding process.

This discussion has been intended to bring out the point that self-delimiting is an ill-defined term, but as a minimum requires knowledge of some specific encoding rules. It was, in retrospect, unfortunate that throughout the 1980s a single notation (ASN.1) and one single set of encoding rules (Basic Encoding Rules) were almost universally used in the definition of abstract and transfer syntaxes, and that the Basic Encoding Rules did indeed provide relatively easy determination of the end of an encoding without knowledge of the type used to define the abstract syntax. Thus the idea of a self-delimiting transfer syntax, as a fundamental property of a transfer syntax, gained credence.

Again, the ASN.1 Basic Encoding Rules always produced bit-strings that were a multiple of eight bits – again a property of the transfer syntax that a process decoding it would only know by having knowledge of those Basic Encoding Rules. This led to the concept of **an octet-aligned transfer syntax**, but this suffers from similar problems to the concept of self-delimiting. 'Octet-aligned' can be given meaning in relation to a specific transfer syntax (every value is a multiple of eight bits), but an encoding rule may produce an octet-aligned transfer syntax for some abstract syntaxes and not for others.

The protocol defined in the Presentation Layer is itself specified using the ASN.1 notation and applying the Basic Encoding Rules. It is thus not inappropriate to assume a knowledge of these encoding rules within all implementations, and to optimize for the self-delimiting and octet-aligned nature of these encodings. A not-yet-resolved (1995) defect report on the Presentation Layer protocol points out that the text currently uses these two terms, which are, as discussed earlier, hard to define, and optimizes in cases where a receiver may not have enough knowledge of a transfer syntax to determine the end of an encoding, or even to determine if it is octet-aligned. The proposed resolution of the defect is to avoid use of these terms, and to optimize specifically and only for transfer syntaxes defined using the Basic Encoding Rules, which have strong properties, and which it can be assumed are universally implemented.

The reader may be asking 'How can an implementation determine from a transfer syntax OBJECT IDENTIFIER that it has been generated using the ASN.1 Basic Encoding Rules?' The answer is that such transfer syntaxes are all identified by the same OBJECT IDENTIFIER: assigned to the Basic Encoding Rules. (Remember that a transfer syntax OBJECT IDENTIFIER only really needs to be unambiguous within the scope of an abstract syntax OBJECT IDENTIFER, so this approach gives no problems.) Thus basing Presentation Layer protocol optimization on the use of this OBJECT IDENTIFIER is valid.

With that preamble then, what is the general form of the mapping from a list of presentation data values to the Session Service user data parameter?

In the general case, each presentation data value is mapped to a bit-string using the negotiated transfer syntax. That bit-string is then made octet-aligned and self-delimiting by wrapping length and bit counts around it, and the presentation context identifier (an integer, also made self-delimiting by wrapping a length count round it) is added to the head of it. These encodings for each presentation data value in the list are then appended to each other, and the whole sequence has a further length count placed in front of it, producing the set of octets that forms the Session Service user data. There are clearly interesting design (encoding) issues within the Presentation Layer about the form of length counts to handle arbitrarily large lengths. These were actually resolved by using the ASN.1 notation to define a data structure to handle the general case, a slightly simplified form of which is:

```
SEQUENCE OF SEQUENCE
    {context-id INTEGER,
     encoding BIT STRING}
```

and then applying the Basic Encoding Rules to that. (The meaning of the above piece of ASN.1 should be clear to the reader from what has gone before, but a more detailed treatment appears below.) Note that the concepts of abstract and (negotiated) transfer syntax only apply to things above the Presentation Service. The use of ASN.1 and its Basic Encoding Rules in the Presentation Layer protocol is nothing more than a convenient shorthand for defining a fixed bit-pattern for the protocol.

There are clearly significant overheads in this process if every presentation data value in the user data parameter is from the same presentation context, and has a transfer syntax obtained by applying the ASN.1 Basic Encoding Rules (already self-delimiting – given knowledge of these encoding rules – and octet-aligned). In this case, there is an optimization that permits a presentation context id to be encoded, followed by a count of presentation data values from that context, followed by the transfer syntax encoding (self-delimiting and octet-aligned) of a series of presentation data values from that presentation context, followed, if necessary, by further sequences of this sort. Note that in this case, the end of the resulting Session Service user data parameter can only be determined by a receiver using the lower layer delimitation mechanisms (which fundamentally rest on the bit-stuffing of the Data Link Layer), and cannot be determined from any encoding produced by the Presentation Layer.

The reader should observe two points.

- The process of mapping is broadly simple: map to the transfer syntax bit-pattern, wrap it round to make it a self-delimiting octet string, add the presentation context identifier, repeat for the next presentation data value, and wrap the entire list up and pass to the Session Layer.
- The actual mechanisms and encodings when optimizations that are considered desirable are applied become quite complex.

7.5.2 Support for negotiation

Negotiation of presentation contexts has been broadly described above. Again, an ASN.1 data structure is defined and the Basic Encoding Rules applied to determine the messages. The structure used to propose new presentation contexts is

```
SEQUENCE OF SEQUENCE
  {context-id INTEGER,
  abstract-syntax OBJECT IDENTIFIER,
  transfer-syntaxes SEQUENCE OF
                    OBJECT IDENTIFIER}
```

with the reply being a similar message but with a single transfer syntax. During a connection, this message is carried on the Session Service primitive designed to meet this need, the S-TYPED-DATA primitive, and is supported in the Presentation Service by the P-ALTER-CONTEXT request/indication response/confirm (the only new Presentation Service primitives). (The actual message used is slightly more complicated than that shown above, because a presentation context can also be deleted, and a proposed deletion can be refused.) A new presentation context is added to the defined context set at the responding end when the P-ALTER-CONTEXT response primitive is issued, and becomes available for use for presentation data values on that primitive or on later primitives. It is added to the defined context set at the initiating end when the P-ALTER-CONTEXT confirm primitive is issued.

The above messages also form part of the Presentation Layer protocol supporting the P-CONNECT service primitives (and mapping into the user data of the S-CONNECT service primitives) to establish an initial defined context set.

The alert reader should have spotted a small problem here. We said that the P-CONNECT primitives could also carry presentation data values to support the (perhaps negotiated) initialization of the application. Like any other P-service primitive, the P-CONNECT primitives have a user data parameter that is a list of presentation data values. But at the time the P-CONNECT request is issued, there is nothing in the defined context set, and an agreed transfer syntax for these values is not available. For the P-CONNECT request and the P-ALTER-CONTEXT request only, the presentation data values are permitted to be from a context which is proposed for addition to the defined context set, rather than being restricted to ones that are already in that set. But what transfer syntax should be used to transfer such values?

The Presentation Layer protocol permits such values to be transferred using **multiple encodings**, potentially one for every transfer syntax proposed for the corresponding presentation context, tagged with the transfer syntax identifier for that encoding.

Of course, there is still no guarantee that such values can be successfully decoded by a receiving implementation. There has been a lot of discussion of this 'data unreadable' problem within the standards community. In particular, the Presentation Service goes to great lengths to avoid the transfer of data that cannot be decoded. In this case, however, there is no option if we want to allow application data on this exchange. The application designer should assume that a presentation data value is delivered up, but it may not be possible to handle it in a way that requires it to be recognized and distinguished from other presentation data values in that abstract syntax. The modelling aspects of this situation have, however, never been properly resolved.

With this multiple encoding of an arbitrarily long list of presentation data values on the P-CONNECT primitives, the reader should now readily understand why the users of the Session Service said with one voice 'WE WANT UNLIMITED USER DATA!'

7.5.3   Collisions

The reader may have hoped that we had left collision case problems in the Session Layer, but regrettably this is not so.

If there is no use of P-ALTER-CONTEXT (context definition only on P-CONNECT), then there are indeed no collision problems to be resolved and the Presentation Layer has no additional complicating features. In the presentation kernel functional unit, P-ALTER-CONTEXT is not available. This exchange becomes available if the presentation context management functional unit is agreed for use (using a negotiation on the P-CONNECT similar to that of S-CONNECT negotiation).

The first problem that arises is shown in Figure 7.2. In this case, we have contexts with identifiers 1, 3 and 5 already defined, and both sides now propose the addition of a context with an identifier of 2, but for different abstract syntaxes. Clearly this cannot be allowed to happen. The resolution is blindingly

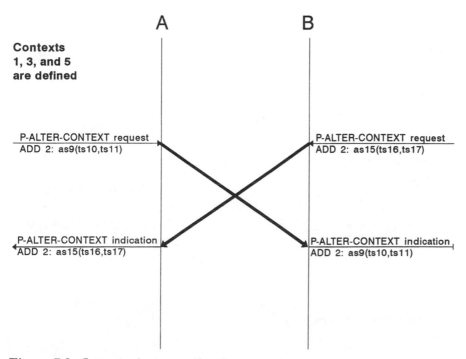

Figure 7.2 *Contention for context identifier 2.*

simple: the implementation that initiates a connection (where the P-CONNECT request is issued) only ever proposes the establishment (on the P-CONNECT request or on a P-ALTER-CONTEXT request) of presentation contexts with identifiers which are odd numbers, and the peer implementation (where the P-CONNECT indication is issued) only ever proposes the establishment (on a P-ALTER-CONTEXT request) of presentation contexts with identifiers which are even numbers. Thus the colliding P-ALTER-CONTEXT primitives can now be processed wholly independently, and make their own independent contribution to the defined context set.

If we look at proposed deletions, we need to determine when actual removal from the defined context set (preventing use of that context for any subsequent presentation data value) is to occur, and we see some further problems. If we delete on the issuing of the P-ALTER-CONTEXT request, then the collision case in Figure 7.3 can occur, while if we delete only when the confirm is issued the collision case in Figure 7.4 can occur. This is resolved by deleting when the confirm is issued, but forbidding the use of contexts proposed for deletion between the issuing of the request and the arrival of the confirm.

The above collision cases were easy to resolve. A much more serious and interesting problem arises when a P-ALTER-CONTEXT exchange is disrupted by the purging effect of a session resync. Figure 7.5 shows what can happen. Following the resync, we have a defined context set at application A which contains context 4, and one at application B which certainly cannot because the response/confirm exchange (carried on S-TYPED-DATA) saying which

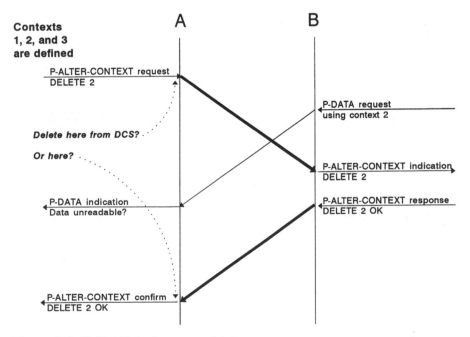

Figure 7.3 *P-DATA after context deletion.*

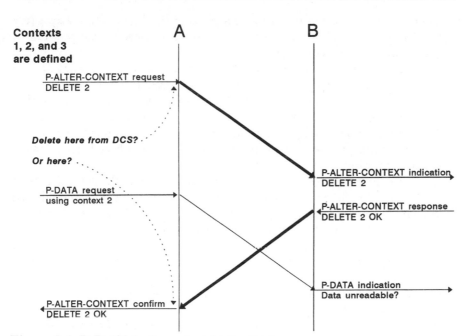

Figure 7.4 *P-DATA after context deletion (bis).*

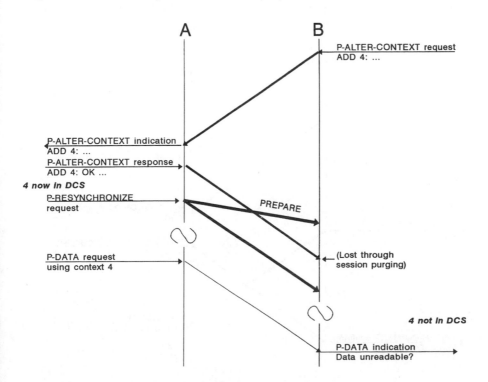

Figure 7.5 *Resync destroying P-ALTER-CONTEXT.*

transfer syntax has been selected never arrived at the Presentation Layer (the S-TYPED-DATA indication did not get issued) because of the purging of dialogue one in the Session Layer.

This raises an interesting philosophical question. If session resynchronization occurs, what should happen to the defined context set? If you believe strongly that 'restart from a checkpoint' should be the (only) semantics an application can apply to a session resync, then it would be natural to want to have the defined context set restored to what it was at the time the checkpoint was taken, that is, the time the corresponding synchronization point was established. This is called **context restoration**.

Of course, if we are to do this, we need to make sure that the defined context set is indeed always in a consistent state at such a time. For sync points established by S-SYNC-MAJOR there is no problem – session dialogue separation prevents a P-ALTER-CONTEXT exchange spanning the dialogue boundary. In the case of S-SYNC-MINOR, however, dialogue separation is only achieved for a one-way flow, and the collision case shown in Figure 7.6 can in principle occur. Again, this can easily be resolved by forbidding the issue of a P-SYNC-MINOR if a P-ALTER-CONTEXT exchange is outstanding and we really want to make context restoration possible.

But do we? The reader will be aware that the checkpoint/back-up semantics is not built into the Session Layer. Resynchronization does nothing more than terminate dialogue one (disorderly) with a clean start to dialogue two, and with

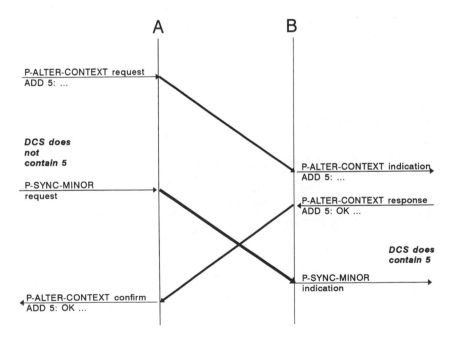

Figure 7.6 *Minor sync and alter context collision.*

the sync point serial number variable set to an agreed value. It is for the application designer to associate checkpoint/back-up semantics with this, or not to do so. What then should the Presentation Layer assume?

There was considerable disagreement among experts on what was appropriate. On the one hand, the checkpoint/back-up semantics is an obvious one for some applications to want, so providing context restoration as part of the Presentation Layer specifications looked attractive. Moreover, because, notionally, in the model, the knowledge of the transfer syntax used for a presentation context is encapsulated within the Presentation Layer, it is not possible within the terms of that model for an Application Layer checkpoint to record and later restore such data. This is more a debating point than a real problem: as was stated earlier, the total implementation is what matters, and checkpointing and restoring what is notionally Presentation Layer data is clearly possible. None the less, this discussion adds strength to the view that context restoration should be provided.

Another problem is that clearly something has to be done. The collision problem shown in Figure 7.5 is a very real one. We just cannot go on operating with different defined context sets.

This was one of the secondary, but important, issues at the upper layers meeting in Helsinki that resolved the Session Service user data problem. There gradually emerged a fairly clear consensus that many application designers did not want context restoration to be automatically applied, but rather wanted defined context sets to be unaffected by a resync in the non-collision cases which will be the most common. So the rule mentioned earlier was invoked: 'Your job is to produce standards: if you can't agree, make it optional'. The **context restoration functional unit** was introduced. If not selected, then the defined context set would not be affected by resync (or by S-ACTIVITY-INTERRUPT and S-ACTIVITY-DISCARD) – provided the collision case can be resolved. If selected, then provided the resync was quoting a sync point number established during this presentation connection (remember the existence of resync SET), the defined context set would be reset to that which obtained when the sync point was established. The context restoration functional unit clearly only makes sense if the context management functional unit has been selected, since it is only in the latter case that the defined context set can change between the establishment of a sync point and a later resync, and such a restriction was included in the P-CONNECT negotiation.

That still leaves the problem of resolving the collision case. Discussion went on for about 12 months. There was consideration of a third exchange after the P-ALTER-CONTEXT response/confirm (Figure 7.7) which would have the effect of disallowing a resync until it had been received. There was consideration of a new Session Service primitive exchange that would provide protection against a later resync using a PREPARE message, in precisely the same way that the second half of the major sync and resync exchanges obtained protection for the start of dialogue two. But in the end, the solution was again blindingly simple: if context restoration is not selected, then whenever an S-RESYN-CHRONIZE request is issued, the user data contains not just the mapping of

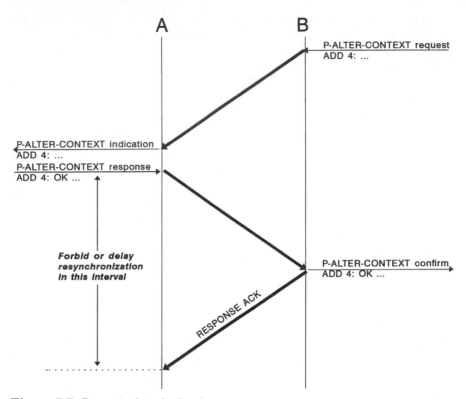

Figure 7.7 *Protecting by a third exchange.*

the presentation data values on the P-RESYNCHRONIZE request, but also a complete statement (giving the presentation context identifier, the abstract syntax identifier and the transfer syntax identifier) of what the defined context set is at the end issuing the resynchronize request. Thus while the P-ALTER-CONTEXT exchange can still be disrupted, we still achieve a consistent defined context set at both ends following the resynchronize request/indication exchange. Of course, we have in the same way to carry this message on the S-ACTIVITY-INTERRUPT and S-ACTIVITY-DISCARD exchanges, but that poses no additional problems.

In fact, it did not prove possible to completely solve the collision problems if both the context restoration and the activity functional units are selected, and 'data unreadable' situations can occur in this case. However, it is believed that no application designer has so far chosen to use these options. Indeed, despite all the work that went into providing for it, no application designer for an international standard has chosen to use the context restoration functional unit at all!

The above discussion has hopefully served not only to identify to the reader the tools provided by the Presentation Layer that an application designer has available, but also to develop further awareness of the problems which can arise from the purging effect of the S-RESYNCHRONIZE exchange, and which may affect an application designer's own protocol.

7.5.4 And what about Teletex?

We have seen the pressures for Teletex compatibility in the Transport and Session Layers. What about the Presentation Layer?

The Presentation Layer Standards came somewhat later, and now the issue had changed. X.400 (1984) had been published, with the X.410 Recommendation containing all the interaction with the lower layers. This, as mentioned earlier, made direct reference to the issue and receipt of Session Layer services (in a way that was believed to produce Teletex compatibility in terms of the bits on the line). Thus the pressure on the Presentation Layer was not described in terms of Teletex, but rather in terms of being able to specify X.400 (1988) in terms of the issue and receipt of P-service primitives, again with no change to the bits on the line compared with X.400 (1984). This was quite a tall order and, if anything, was harder than the task that had faced Transport and Session. In the event it proved possible only by the lucky accident that back in 1982 ASN.1 had assigned the same universal class tag value to both the SEQUENCE construction and to the SEQUENCE OF construction.

Two things had to be done to accommodate X.410. The first was to introduce the concept of a default presentation context determined by prior agreement. In the case of X.410, this of course meant the X.410 protocol and the ASN.1 Basic Encoding Rules! The second was to introduce a parameter into the P-CONNECT primitives called **Mode**, with values 'X.410-1984-mode' and 'normal'. The former value modified the behaviour of the presentation protocol (following the P-CONNECT exchange) to be effectively a null layer. Once again, the desired political objectives were achieved, and X.400 (1988) did indeed proudly boast that it was now a respectable application sitting on top of the Presentation Layer. The X.400 text did, however, have to consider the setting of the 'Mode' parameter. How to get backwards compatibility and yet permit a movement into the future?

As frequently happens in such difficult areas, the CCITT experts and the ISO experts disagreed. The texts say how to run X.400 with the parameter set in both ways (such differing implementations, of course, not being able to interwork), but which to support (or both) is left as an implementation option.

7.6 Connectionless presentation services and protocol and related issues

As with the other layers, the connectionless Presentation Service is very simple: just a P-UNITDATA request and indication. There is, however, some significant added value. The exchange carries a list of presentation data values which are treated in a very similar manner to the list on the P-CONNECT request/indication primitives. The message carries, for each presentation data value in the list, the abstract syntax identifier for the presentation data value, followed by a set of multiple encodings, each carrying a transfer syntax identifier.

This focuses attention on the problems of negotiation of an agreed transfer syntax when the communication is essentially a one-way flow. This problem does not just occur with connectionless communication. Consider an electronic mail (X.400) message carrying a spreadsheet or some form of image. The precise encoding of the spreadsheet data, or the image format to be used, is a transfer syntax issue, and some negotiation could be desirable. But X.400 is both a relaying and a broadcasting application, and negotiation in a P-CONNECT is clearly not useful. Similarly, selection of a good transfer syntax for storing a file on a general-purpose file server (which can perhaps in the general case only store the file but cannot transform from one transfer syntax representation to another, and where the file is to be retrieved later by multiple other systems) poses the same relay and broadcast problems. All these cases might benefit from the 'multiple encodings' used for the P-CONNECT and P-UNITDATA primitives, although such an approach is not currently employed by either FTAM or X.400.

Another approach to negotiation in the relay and connectionless cases, but with less applicability where there is a broadcast element, is to have a potential recipient lodge, in some form of world-wide directory such as that provided by X.500, the transfer syntaxes it supports for each abstract syntax that it supports, and to let the sender of the data select from this list. The use of X.500 is, however, not yet sufficiently mature and the problem of negotiating transfer syntaxes is not yet serious enough for these approaches to have been developed.

8
Writing it all down

Discussion of ASN.1 is included at this point in the text as the notation is effectively part of the interface between the Application Layer and the Presentation Layer. It is a definitional notation used by application designers which invokes algorithms (encoding rules) that are effectively part of the Presentation Layer.

The text cannot hope in the space available for ASN.1 discussions to provide a complete tutorial on the use of the notation, and the reader is referred to other texts or to the Standard if serious work is to be done using ASN.1, either as a reader of published specifications or as an application designer using ASN.1. The aim here is to present the major features and principles of ASN.1 and its encoding rules, with some discussion of conceptually difficult areas and remaining problems and issues (as of 1995).

In the second part of this chapter, there is discussion of new work related to ASN.1. This discussion is based on the Draft International Standard text, and while it is hoped that much of what is presented will remain valid, the reader is cautioned to check later text as it emerges from the standardization process.

8.1   ASN.1 in the 1980s

8.1.1   History

The idea of providing support for application designers by providing a notation for defining data structures, a defined (machine-independent) encoding for those data structures, and tools to produce such encodings from local representations of data in programming languages was an important one, and is normally credited to the Xerox Courier Specification, part of the XNS protocol suite.

In early 1980 there was recognition within the CCITT group that defining the X.400 (electronic mail) protocol would involve some very complicated data structures, and that notational support for this activity was essential. A language was needed with about the power of normal high-level programming languages for defining repetitive and optional structures using a number of primitive data types. But it needed to be supported by an algorithm, later called encoding rules, which would determine the bit-pattern representation during transfer for any data structure, no matter how large or complex, that could be written down using the language. The Xerox Courier Specification provided important input, and the notation was developed into CCITT Recommendation X.409 – part of the X.400(1984) series.

At that time, most groups developing Application Layer standards in ISO had identified a similar problem: the protocols they were developing were just getting too complicated for hand-crafting the bit-patterns. Here, however, the problem was exacerbated by the strong emergence of the Presentation Layer concept of separating abstract and transfer syntax definition (these concepts were accepted much later by CCITT/ITU-T workers), which required some sort of notation to glue together the two definitions. No such notation was emerging. Some groups tried using variants of BNF (Backus–Naur Form), a notation originally developed to help programming language designers to precisely specify the syntax of their programming languages. It had the necessary power, but there was no *de facto* standardization of the notation, and of course no agreed and application-independent encoding rule specification.

When drafts of X.409 were passed to ISO, they were greeted with open arms, and the acceptance of this notation as the way to define OSI Application Layer protocols was almost (and unusually) immediate and universal. The text did, however, undergo an important change. X.409 was written as a single specification, with a series of paragraphs each of which first presented a language construct, then presented the algorithm defining the encodings related to that language construct. For ISO purposes, with the concept of a clear separation of transfer syntax definition (with potentially multiple transfer syntaxes for any given abstract syntax), these two aspects needed to be clearly separated in separate documents. X.409 was therefore rewritten as ISO 8824 and ISO 8825.

ISO 8824 was called **Abstract Syntax Notation One**, reflecting recognition that there could well be other notations for abstract syntax definition, and ISO 8825 was called **Basic Encoding Rules**, reflecting recognition that other encoding rules could indeed exist. At this time the abbreviation for the notation was ASN1. But it was amazing how often it got mistyped as ANS1 and then misread as ANSI – the abbreviation for the American National Standards Institute! The Americans said 'Look, we know it is not the same abbreviation, and confusion should not occur, but in fact we are getting confusion. Would it be possible to find another name?' The resolution of the discussion was the introduction of the 'dot' into the abbreviation, so we now have 'ASN.1', and nobody ever mistypes it as ANSI! (ANS.1 is the nearest you get.) The abbreviation for the encoding rules was BER, which provided no problems.

There was, of course, some reluctance on the part of CCITT to adopt completely new text from ISO because of fears that technical changes might have been introduced, but in the end (about 1985/86) CCITT agreed to work with common text based on the ISO drafts, and eventually published such text in the 1988 Recommendations as X.208 (ASN.1) and X.209 (BER), withdrawing X.409. The move into the X.200 series – general OSI infrastructure – reflected the universal view that ASN.1 was nothing to do with X.400 as such, but was a general tool for all OSI application designers to use.

A number of additions were made to ASN.1 during the 1980s, the most important of which was the OBJECT IDENTIFIER data type used to carry the names of abstract and transfer syntaxes (and many other types of conceptual object needing names in OSI), but there were no major additions to the concepts introduced in X.409. By contrast, a significant number of new concepts were introduced into the work that was finally approved as Recommendations and Standards in the autumn of 1994. These are discussed in the next section.

8.1.2 Overview of the notation

Readers who are already largely familiar with ASN.1 should skip this section – it is about the 'What?' and not the 'Why?' – but it would be wrong not to include at least this overview for readers who have never met ASN.1 before.

The best way to understand any language or notation is to read a few examples of it, and these are readily obtainable from any of the OSI Application Layer standards. Figures 8.1 and 8.2 are often-quoted examples originally developed by this author. They are fictitious, designed only to illustrate features.

The first point to note is that an ASN.1 data type is built up from primitive data types (INTEGER, REAL, BOOLEAN, NULL) using three main construction mechanisms: repetition (SEQUENCE OF and SET OF), alternatives (CHOICE) and lists of fields (SEQUENCE and SET). Once an ASN.1 data type has been defined, it can be used in the definition of other ASN.1 data types exactly as if

```
PersonnelRecord ::= SET
 {         Name,
  title       GraphicString,
  division  CHOICE
   {marketing   [0] SEQUENCE
      {Sector,
       Country},
    research    [1] CHOICE
      {product-based [0] NULL,
       basic         [1] NULL},
    production [2] SEQUENCE
      {Product-line,
       Country    }              }

  etc.
```

Figure 8.1 *An ASN.1 date type definition.*

```
Trade-message3 ::= SEQUENCE
  {invoice-no     INTEGER,
   name           GraphicString,
   details        SEQUENCE OF
                  SEQUENCE
          {part-no  INTEGER,
           quantity  INTEGER},
   charge         REAL,
   authenticator Security-Type}

Security-Type ::= SET
   {    ...
        ...
        ...    }
```

Figure 8.2 *An ASN.1 data type definition (bis).*

it were a primitive data type, and such types can be defined before use or after, thus permitting forward references. Indeed, mutually recursive data structures are permitted. Combined with CHOICE, such recursively defined data structures can still have finite representations for some of their values. In Figure 8.1, Name, Sector, Country and Product-line are the names of data types defined before or after the definition presented in the figure. Equally, the definition of these data types could have been included in-line in the definitions in the figure.

The second point to note is that for the SEQUENCE construction, each field is listed as a field-name (beginning with a lower-case letter – ASN.1 is case sensitive), which plays no part in defining the actual bits on the line followed by the name of a primitive type or defined data structure which determines the form of the field. Fields are seperated by commas.

A complete list of the ASN.1 primitive types in the version of ISO 8824 dated 1990 is given in Figure 8.3.

There are a small number of points to make here to help the reader understand the ASN.1 in the figures or in standards. More substantive points are addressed in the next part of this chapter.

The NULL data type is typically used in a CHOICE to identify an element where all that matters is that that particular CHOICE is occurring, with no additional information to be provided or needed. The text in square braces (for example, '[0]' in the figure) is called a **tag** and is discussed more fully below.

ASN.1 has the concept of a **module** within which definitions can be grouped, from which they can be exported, and into which they can be imported. Modules

BOOLEAN

INTEGER

ENUMERATED

REAL

BIT STRING

OCTET STRING

NULL

OBJECT IDENTIFIER

Character String types:	NumericString, PrintableString, TeletexString, VideotexString, VisibleString, IA5String GraphicString, GeneralString
Useful types:	GeneralizedTime, UTCTime, EXTERNAL, OBJECT DESCRIPTOR

Figure 8.3 *ASN.1 primitive types (1990).*

are identified by an ASN.1 OBJECT IDENTIFIER value (although early definitions did not contain these), and strictly speaking anyone who wants to use ASN.1 needs a part of the object identifier name-space – see discussion in section 8.1.4. If one looks at the connectivity of modules obtained by export and import links, it includes almost all the ASN.1 modules defined in any Application Layer standard – there is use in almost every standard of some importation or exportation of ASN.1 definitions from/to some other standard.

The difference between SEQUENCE and SET is in the order of transmission of the fields: for SEQUENCE, a sender is required to transmit them in the order listed in the notation; for SET, the order of transmission is an implementation option for the sender. This could, of course, be regarded as an encoding issue that the application designer should not be concerned with, and which has no place in the notation. Indeed, in order to provide canonical encodings (encodings with no options), this freedom is removed in some encoding rules and SET then becomes synonymous with SEQUENCE.

INTEGER fields in ASN.1 are not constrained to 16-bit or 32-bit integers. Rather, they are indefinitely large. An important addition round about 1988 was the introduction of a subtype notation, most commonly used to subtype integers, but applicable to any ASN.1 type. This notation in its full glory is quite complex, and enables a new type to be defined as any subset of the values of any given type. The notation is enclosed in round brackets, and is most commonly used in the following way:

```
Month::=INTEGER (1..12)
Day::=INTEGER (1..31)
Daily-temperatures::=SEQUENCE SIZE (31) OF INTEGER
Name::=PrintableString (SIZE (1..20))
```

8.1.3   The ASN.1 value notation

The fields in a SEQUENCE or SET can be marked OPTIONAL, in which case they may be present or absent in a message, but the application designer needs to state what it means if they are absent. (ASN.1 uses the term **element** rather than 'field'.) Alternatively, they can be marked DEFAULT, followed by a value for the data type of the element. For example, INTEGER DEFAULT 3 states that if the element is missing, the meaning is exactly the same as if it were present with the value 3, and the application designer need add no further text. It is important to recognize here that ASN.1 allows default values not just for primitive fields like INTEGER and BOOLEAN, but also for any arbitrarily complicated data type that can be defined using ASN.1. In this it goes further than most typical programming languages. Equally, just as complicated types can either be written down within an enclosing definition or be defined separately and referenced, so complicated values can be written down after the DEFAULT keyword or can be defined separately and referenced.

The value notation was originally designed specifically to support the DEFAULT keyword, but it has found applications within the English text of application standards to identify special cases, in tutorials to identify values being transmitted, in the notation for defining subtypes of a type, and latterly in the newly introduced information object concept (Section 8.1.4). In the case of OBJECT IDENTIFIERs, there are many, many more instances of the value notation (to assign object identifier values to modules, abstract syntaxes, transfer syntaxes, and so on) than there are instances of use of the words OBJECT IDENTIFIER for type definition. As with the type notation, the value notation is fairly obvious and easily understood. Further discussion here is not appropriate.

8.1.4   The OBJECT IDENTIFIER data type

Provision in the notation for a data type to carry unambiguous identification of objects (the OBJECT IDENTIFIER data type) would not be very useful unless enough additional text was produced to determine how values of this type got assigned to objects that needed identifying, and how such values could be encoded. This led the ASN.1 group into the definition of a structure of **registration authorities** to support this need and hence, arguably, into activity that went outside of the group's defined scope – that of defining a notation for data structure definition.

(The reader may be unfamiliar with many of the objects and standards mentioned in this paragraph. They are here for illustration and no attempt is made to describe them in detail. In some cases they will be discussed further later in the text.) There are a number of mechanisms in use in OSI and related standards for unambiguous naming of objects, with a variety of properties and requiring a variety of organizational structures (registration authorities) for the allocation of parts of the name-space. There have been some discussions about trying to rationalize the provision of naming formats in OSI to some minimum necessary number, but this has not come to fruition. Thus communications-related standards such as SGML (Standard Generalized Markup Language) and EDIFACT (Electronic Data Interchange for Finance, Administration, Commerce and Transport) and CDIF (CASE Data Interchange Format) all define their own naming structures with properties very similar to ASN.1 object identifiers. There are also separate naming and addressing structures used for X.500 Distinguished Names, X.400 Originator/Recipient Names, and Network Service Access Point addresses. None the less, the range of objects for which ASN.1 object identifiers have been specified as the naming mechanism is large: abstract and transfer syntaxes, ASN.1 modules, Application Contexts, Application Entity Titles, ROSE Operations, X.500 attributes (the component parts of X.500 Distinguished Names), X.400 Extended body Parts, FTAM Document Types and Constraint Sets, Terminal Profiles, RPC Interface types, and Managed Objects and their attributes.

The ASN.1 object identifier name-space was built on similar principles to the name-space used for allocating Network Service Access Point (NSAP) addresses, but with the important distinction that NSAP addresses had of necessity to have a relatively short maximum length while ASN.1 object identifier values are normally carried in Application Layer protocols where length is not too much of an issue and indefinite length can be accepted. None the less, common to both is the principle of a world-wide unambiguous name designed so that almost anybody could relatively easily obtain a part of the name-space for allocation to objects that they wished to identify. (Readers might care to consider at the end of this section how they personally – in their business capacity – might most easily obtain a part of the object identifier name-space for their own part of their organization's use.)

Another important issue which arose in the definition of the ASN.1 object identifier was whether the identifiers should be relatively terse and numeric (efficient in transfer, but relatively unfriendly for human use), or whether they should contain character parts (or be exclusively character-oriented, making them more verbose but more human-friendly).

The decision for ASN.1 names was to make them terse and numeric, while the later decision for X.500 Distinguished Names was to provide for a much greater use of character information. In fact, X.500 names consist of a series of **attributes**, each attribute having a value which is typically, but not necessarily, a character string. A value of the name during transfer is defined as the value of an ASN.1 data structure which is a sequence of items, each item in the sequence itself being a pair of items, the first an ASN.1 object identifier that identifies a defined attribute, and the second the value of an ASN.1 type determined when the attribute was defined.

At the same time as the decision was taken to introduce the OBJECT IDENTIFIER data type to carry world-wide unambiguous terse names, the OBJECT DESCRIPTOR data type was introduced to carry a user-friendly name that would be likely to be world-wide unambiguous, but was not guaranteed so to be. In fact, it was simply a character string, with no allocation of name-space and no restrictions (other than the application of common sense) on the strings that are allocated by different groups. The idea was that whenever an object identifier value was allocated to identify an object unambiguously, an object descriptor value would be allocated at the same time to provide user-friendly but not necessarily unambiguous identification. A protocol designer providing fields to identify objects would typically provide a field of type OBJECT IDENTIFIER, but would then choose whether to accompany this with a field of type OBJECT DESCRIPTOR, either mandatorily present or present at the option of the sender (use of the keyword OPTIONAL). What has happened in practice is that application designers have chosen with almost no exceptions to provide only a field for carrying the OBJECT IDENTIFIER, and one often finds allocations of object identifier values to defined objects with no corresponding object descriptor value allocated. Thus object descriptors can be regarded largely as a historical relic.

What then does the OBJECT IDENTIFIER name-space look like? It is based on an **object identifier tree** which is a structure with a root node, arcs beneath that to other nodes, with arcs beneath them, and so on. Each node is assigned to some responsible body that allocates arcs and nodes beneath it. The body ensures that all the arcs beneath its node are numbered sequentially starting from zero (names – lower case – can also optionally be assigned to an arc), and that each node beneath it is either assigned to some responsible body (or retained for further use by the body itself) or is assigned to name some **information object**. 'Information object' is the term used for things that are named by object identifiers, and reflects the fact that usually the 'thing' being named is some definition or piece of information, such as an abstract syntax definition. Thus information objects being named by object identifiers are all associated with some leaf node of the tree. The object identifier name of an information object is a list of integer values which are the values of the arcs, taken in order, from the root of the tree to the leaf node assigned to name the information object. Thus a typical object identifier could be written as

{1 0 8571 2 1}

and is encoded for transfer as specified in the ASN.1 Encoding Rules. The top parts of the tree are allocated and assigned numbers and names within the ASN.1 Standard (Figures 8.4, 8.5 and 8.6). In computer communications, the names of arcs play no part, but in writing down object identifier values for human consumption it is permitted and normal to use the names instead of the numbers for those arcs allocated in the ASN.1 Standard. For other arcs, either just the number is given, or the name is given with the number in brackets. Thus the above example would more usually be written as:

{iso standard 8571 abstract-syntaxes(2) ftam-pci(1)}

and is an object identifier allocated in the FTAM Standard (ISO 8571) to name the abstract syntax of their main protocol messages.

Figure 8.4 shows the top three arcs, assigned for CCITT/ITU-T use, ISO use and allocation by joint ISO and CCITT/ITU-T decision. Beneath the 'joint' arc, we have about 20 arcs allocated so far for areas of joint ISO and CCITT/ITU-T standardization. Thus all object identifiers used in the X.400 series of Recommendations begin

{joint-iso-ccitt mhs-motis(6) ...}

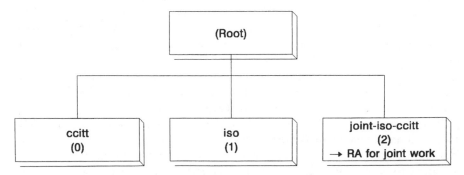

Figure 8.4 *Top arcs of object identifier tree.*

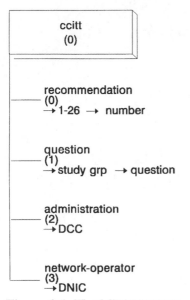

ccitt
(0)

recommendation
(0)
→ 1-26 → number

question
(1)
→ study grp → question

administration
(2)
→ DCC

network-operator
(3)
→ DNIC

Figure 8.5 *The CCITT/ITU-T branch of the tree.*

Note the problems that this use of 'ccitt' causes when the name of CCITT was changed to ITU-T. (At the time of writing, the top arc is still labelled 'joint-iso-ccitt', but the text says that the responsibility for further allocation lies with ITU-T.)

Figure 8.5 shows the arcs beneath the ccitt arc, providing some name-space for the writers of CCITT/ITU-T Recommendations (where the work is not joint with ISO), for PTTs, and for RPOAs (private telephone operators). The Recommendation arc has 26 arcs beneath it, numbered 1 to 26 and corresponding to the letters A to Z. Beneath each of these there is an arc for every CCITT/ITU-T Recommendation, numbered with the number of the Recommendation. Thus, should they require it, the writers of Recommendation G.432 could allocate object identifiers beginning

{ccitt recommendation g(7) 432 ...}

Figure 8.6 shows the arcs beneath the ISO arc, providing in a similar way name-space for the writers of ISO standards (where the work is not joint with CCITT/ITU-T). Importantly, there are also two further arcs, one giving name-space to national bodies, such as BSI in the UK and ANSI in the USA, using the Standard ISO 3166 which allocates three-digit numeric codes to countries, and one giving name-space through an existing ISO registration authority which will allocate to international organizations an **International Code Designator** (ICD), a four-digit numeric code. In the case of the UK, BSI has set up mechanisms for the allocation of object identifiers to anybody in the UK

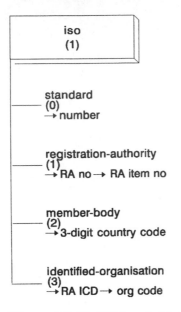

Figure 8.6 *The ISO branch of the tree.*

needing some name-space, beneath the national-body arc. ECMA has obtained an International Code Designator and is prepared to allocate beneath that to its members. At least two major computer vendors are known to have obtained their own ICD. Rather interestingly, the US Government chose not to allocate under national-body, but rather sought and obtained a pair of ICDs, one for civil and one for military use, and is allocating under those.

In general then, it should be relatively easy for any organization within the UK and the USA to get some object identifier name-space. In other countries similar developments are occurring at varying paces.

None the less, there still remains some concern that getting object identifier name-space to the lowest levels may prove difficult. Thus in theory, if a lowly computer bureau user made use of the Distributed Transaction Processing (DTP or TP) protocol through an operating system interface to Cobol programs written to communicate between two machines, he/she would need some object identifier space to identify the resulting syntaxes and procedures being employed: the user has, in fact, defined a protocol. There was, and still is, concern that this could inhibit the use of the TP Standard, and text has been included in these Standards to provide object identifiers sufficient for use in these circumstances.

8.1.5 Encoding the ASN.1 REAL data type

Rather more discussion of the Basic Encoding Rules in general occurs below, but here we mention briefly the encoding of the REAL data type. (Readers who have never undertaken assembler language programming and are unfamiliar with floating point number formats in computer hardware may want to skip this section.) The following discussion gives the 'Why?' of the representation of REAL, and the reasoning that lay behind the text in the Standard, but the reader could be forgiven for thinking that there is over-much concern with assembler-level efficiency for present-day tastes. REAL was not present in X.409, being added in about 1986.

There are few difficulties in the definition of the set of abstract values the type contains. Formally, it is the set of real numbers that can be expressed as M times B to the power E where M and E are finite positive or negative integers and B is 2 or 10, plus other specified values (see below). These sets do, of course, overlap, but do not include values such as one-third or PI, although they contain values arbitrarily close to these real numbers. There was some discussion at the time about making provision for the precise identification of 'special' values like PI, e, etc., and the encoding of REAL has hooks for extensions to support this, but such extensions have never been progressed. The only 'other specified values' referred to above that are included in the encoding (and hence in the abstract value set) of REAL are PLUS-INFINITY and MINUS-INFINITY.

The encoding for the B=10 set of values was determined by reference to an existing ISO standard, and is essentially a binary-coded-decimal encoding common to Cobol systems. The B=2 case corresponds to normal floating point hardware units, and is rather more interesting. The requirements of such an encoding differ significantly from standardization of floating point formats for almost any other purpose. In particular, efficiency or numerical accuracy in the performance of arithmetic operations is not an issue. The dominating factor has to be the question 'How efficient can the code be that has to transform from existing actual floating point hardware formats to and from the transfer representation?' Thus the existence of an IEEE standard for floating point arithmetic units has little relevance. While this may well be a highly appropriate standard for new hardware systems or software emulation to adopt, it is a long way from being easy to transform into and out of unless your existing system is already an IEEE floating point unit. In 1986, and still today, there was/is no sign that floating point units that conform to the IEEE Standard will be the only ones in existence in the foreseeable future. Thus the IEEE Standard does not satisfy the requirements.

Let us take an example of what has to be considered. A format using a one's complement mantissa or a two's complement mantissa or a sign and magnitude mantissa could be adopted. It is clear that if sign and magnitude is adopted for transfer, real systems with any of these approaches could very simply use the floating point unit to determine the sign and negate negative values to provide data for a sign and magnitude representation. On the other hand, producing a one's complement or two's complement representation from a floating point unit that uses sign and magnitude is a much more lengthy and difficult job. Thus the answer is clear: sign and magnitude is right for transfer.

A similar consideration led to the introduction into the transfer format of an extra field not found in any real floating point architecture. The transfer consists of five fields packed into octets:

S   The sign of the number (+1 or −1)
M   The mantissa, a positive integer of unlimited length
B   The exponent base (2, 8, 16, reserved)
E   The exponent, a two's complement integer of size one octet or two octets or three octets, or with a length field of one octet encoding the length of the exponent
F   A scaling field of two bits.

The value represented is S multiplied by M times B to the power E, multiplied by two to the power F. Why this last provision? If a floating point unit is asked to dump its accumulator into a set of main memory octets for transfer, the exponent will appear somewhere in the set (sometimes at the start, sometimes at the end), but is always short enough to be easily manipulated by register arithmetic and so is no problem. On the other hand, the mantissa will also appear somewhere in the set of octets, usually at either the beginning or the end, and there will be an implied decimal point somewhere within the mantissa encoding. The mantissa will often be too big to manipulate easily with register arithmetic, so shifting it should be avoided. It is a simple (fixed) subtraction from the exponent to move the implied decimal point to the end of the mantissa, and hence to transmit the mantissa as an integer. The problem is, however, that we would like to use the octets containing the mantissa as the octets to be used to transfer M, zeroing any bits in those octets that are before the start of the mantissa, or between the end of the mantissa and the end of these octets. The decimal point needs to be positioned by subtracting, a fixed value from the exponent, at the end of these octets. The problem is that for a single unit subtraction from the exponent, the implied decimal point moves one bit position if B=2, two bit positions if B=4, three bit positions if B=8, and a full four bit position if B=16. Thus the nearest we may be able to get to positioning it where we want it is to a position which is zero to three bits away. Zero to three can be encoded as two bits, and the provision of F is precisely to allow this value to be represented in transfer. Reconstituting the floating point number (in a different hardware representation) on receipt by multiplying by 2 to the power F is a simple table look-up and floating point multiply, and poses no efficiency problems.

The text in an informative annexe in the Standard encourages the transmission of the mantissa without shifting, even if this implies the transmission of additional zero bits at the end of it, giving the implication of a higher precision in the original format than was actually present. This has been (and continues to be) criticized by one ISO national body, with repeated inputs requesting that the annexe be changed and text added to make it clear that low order zero bits should not be transmitted, even if this would mean shifting the mantissa. The text, however, remains as described above.

8.1.6   The ASN.1 macro notation

An interesting (?) feature of ASN.1 is its macro notation. In 1982, when an early draft of X.409 was presented to ISO experts, it looked very similar to what it is now: a notation for defining abstract syntaxes, that is, sets of abstract values; in other words, a notation for defining data types (plus the encoding rules). In the next version, however, its nature suddenly dramatically changed with the introduction of a major new piece of syntax with no associated encoding rules into the language, purporting to allow the definition of 'operations'. The reason was simple. X.409 was never seen by CCITT workers as simply a language for defining data structures. It was seen as a language providing notational support for the whole of the X.400 work, whatever that might imply. Data structure definition for protocol messages was an important part of that, but was not the whole requirement.

The additional requirement came from a piece of work which later became known as ROSE (Remote Operations Service Element), and which was originally published in CCITT Recommendation X.410. (Like ASN.1, it was later moved to the X.200 series as part of the mainstream OSI infrastructure.) The new syntax, hard-wired into the X.409 text, introduced notation that allowed an ASN.1 user to write things such as that shown in Figure 8.7.

The ROSE specification provided a general carrier mechanism to invoke an operation on a remote system, and to return a normal result or an error code from that system. Each operation required to have associated with it an integer value identifying the operation (in later years this was changed to an object identifier value), an ASN.1 data type to carry the arguments of the operation, another ASN.1 data type to carry back the (normal) results of the operation, and a series of possible error codes, each of which again had associated with it an ASN.1 data type to carry parameters associated with the error code.

The ROSE group did not define any actual operations. That was for the users of ROSE (the mainstream X.400 workers) to do, but they did want a simple and defined notation to be specified that would let such other workers define operations to be invoked using ROSE. The syntax of Figure 8.7 was designed to provide precisely that.

When ISO experts saw the new text, there was immediate and fairly widespread opposition. Part of it stemmed from a lack of understanding. What had

```
look-up OPERATION
        ARGUMENT SEQUENCE
                {name   PrintableString,
                 where DatabaseID       }
        RESULT   AddressingInfo
        ERRORS   {UnknownDatabase,
                  NameNotFound    }
        ::= 3
```

Figure 8.7 *Addition of the OPERATION notation.*

defining operations to do with a notation for abstract syntax definition? Fairly clearly, given that there were no associated encoding rules, nothing! (Except that the extended notation had old ASN.1 data structure definitions for arguments, results, and error parameters of operations as the major part of any use of the extended notation.) Part of the problem was the differing perception of the scope of X.409, but part of the problem was a very real concern that if the notation was extended to allow the definition of 'operations', simply because they needed data types to be defined as part of their definition, then what else might there be a need to extend the notation for? What was its real scope and bounds? This proved a perceptive objection with hindsight.

At one point, it looked as if there would be separate ISO and CCITT standards, one without the 'operations' syntax, and one with, but then CCITT withdrew the proposal to add this new syntax, and instead proposed a general-purpose macro notation such as most self-respecting programming languages possess. This was hard to resist: the macro notation text was hard to understand, but it appeared to introduce no new concepts; and it was late in the day with the 1984 Recommendations nearing finalization. The macro notation proposal was accepted. In fact, it is wrong to equate the ASN.1 macro notation with any conventional macro notation in programming languages, which is usually largely an intelligent textual substitution tool. The ASN.1 macro notation purported to allow a user to define a new syntax for the definition of ASN.1 types and values. The new syntax could be anything the user wished. The full power of BNF (Backus–Naur Form), the notation often used to define programming languages, was made available to the ASN.1 macro definer. Thus it was (and is) possible to define an ASN.1 'macro' which would allow a piece of syntax identical to Fortran, Cobol, Pascal, or C to be legally inserted in the middle of an ASN.1 module as the purported new notation for an ASN.1 type or value. It was a very powerful (and dangerous – syntax that is arbitrarily hard to parse, or even downright ambiguous, could easily be defined) tool whose capabilities have never been even nearly fully exploited in any actual use.

When defining a macro, the definer gave it a name (OPERATION, for example!) and specified the new syntax for type definition and the new syntax for value definition. Thereafter, the keyword OPERATION, followed by the new type syntax, could be used anywhere a normal ASN.1 type definition could be written, and the corresponding new value syntax could be written anywhere a value of that type could appear (for example, after DEFAULT). Unfortunately, the nature of the macro definition mechanism made the actual type being defined by the new type notation dependent on the parsing of a value using the new value notation. As type notation can and does frequently appear in ASN.1 with no corresponding value notation, this was clearly something of a flaw!

The important point, however, from the point of view of ROSE, was that the general form of value assignment in (old) ASN.1 looked like Figure 8.8. By introducing the macro notation concept and defining an OPERATION macro and an ERROR macro, this immediately allows the syntax:

look-up-operation OPERATION ⟨new type syntax⟩
      ::= ⟨new value syntax⟩

which, surprise, surprise (with an appropriate definition of the new type syntax and the new value syntax in the OPERATION macro) is just the syntax proposed for addition to ASN.1 in order to support the ROSE requirement for a notation to define operations!

For a couple of years, the macro notation was thought by many to be a curiosity which happened to satisfy the needs of ROSE, but which was best swept under the carpet and forgotten about. But then, round about 1986, there was suddenly an explosion of macro definitions. Just about every group of CCITT experts defining OSI protocols realized that they had a need for a notation (which would usually, but not always, include some real ASN.1 type or value definitions) to define something, and that the ASN.1 macro notation provided them with a fairly formal way of specifying that notation. But there was little or no semantic underpinning in the ASN.1 text. The macro notation began to be called a chimera – an apparently formal way of saying something, but with any semantic underpinning resting on English language text provided by the users (often absent), and with serious flaws in terms of possible ambiguity. About this time tools began to appear giving good support for the implementation of protocols specified using ASN.1, but because of the lack of any real semantics beneath use of the macro notation, these tools found it hard to support macros other than by treating the syntax defined by macros such as the ROSE OPERATION macro as a wired-in part of ASN.1 – precisely what had been proposed in 1983!

The upshot in the late 1980s was considerable opposition in some quarters to the definition of new macros, and to a desire to replace all current macro uses. This had the unfortunate result that a number of new pieces of notation involving ASN.1 types and values, such as the GDMO – Generic Definition of Managed Objects notation, were defined using ordinary English, rather than by the more formal (at least in terms of syntax) definition of an ASN.1 macro notation. It did, however, result in a long close look at just what the real user requirement was: what macros were actually being used for. The result was the introduction of a simple parameterization into the ASN.1 notation, together

```
name-being-assigned   ASN.1-type  ::=  value-being-assigned


     e.g.


     int1   INTEGER  ::=  3


     real   REAL     ::=  {37, 10, -1}
```

Figure 8.8 *General form of value assignment.*

with the introduction of the information object class concept and associated syntax. These are described under the 'new work' section below (section 8.2.4).

8.1.7 Principles of the Basic Encoding Rules

It would require a full book on ASN.1 (and such texts do exist) to completely cover the Basic Encoding Rules. None the less, the new work can only be properly understood if some of its more interesting features are presented.

The first point relates to extensibility of protocols. From the very beginnings of the ASN.1 work there was recognition that the separation of encoding rules from abstract syntax definition presented pitfalls for the unwary in moving from version one of a protocol to version two of that same protocol, and that such movements would be common, particularly in the early days of OSI standards development.

Suppose the abstract syntax for version one is defined as the values of some type, and the abstract syntax for version two as the values of a type containing precisely the same set of values, with the same semantics, but with some additional values. This can happen, for example, if some element in a SEQUENCE, or even an outer-level type, is changed into a CHOICE of that element or type and some other type, or if new OPTIONAL elements are added to a SET or SEQUENCE. In this case, a user new to the work might expect that the encoding for those values that were common to version one and version two (values where the version one CHOICE is taken, or the additional OPTIONAL elements are omitted) would be the same. Moreover, there can be clear implementation advantages if a version two system can interwork with a version one system merely by avoiding sending values that are in version two only, without having to have two different encodings for version one values – one for use when talking to version one systems, and one for use when talking to version two systems.

Some serious thought about the possible design of encodings will soon enable the reader to understand that the above properties are in no way either automatic or even natural in the design of encoding rules. They require to be carefully designed in, and generally carry a quite high cost in the transmission of redundant information. The design principles of PER (Packed Encoding Rules) – developed in the early 1990s and discussed below in section 8.2.6 – by contrast provide for much less verbose encodings, but lose most of these extensibility provisions.

In order to provide support for such extensibility provisions, BER is a somewhat verbose protocol. It adopts a so-called TLV (Type, Length, Value) approach to encoding in which every element (field) of the encoding carries some type information, some length information, then the value of that element. Where the element is itself structured, then the Value part of the element is itself a series of embedded TLV components, to whatever depth is necessary. This has some important consequences. First, it means that if some element in version one of a protocol is replaced in version two by a CHOICE of that element and some other element of a different type, the encoding for values in version two that were present in version one can be unchanged: no specific bits are needed to say which CHOICE has been taken, as all elements are self-identifying whether in a CHOICE or not. Secondly, the existence of lengths at all levels of nesting means that if, in version two, additional optional elements are added at the end of a sequence it again retains the level one encoding. Even if the elements are not optional, a level one system can still detect the presence of added but unknown elements and ignore them. The addition of new types anywhere in a SET construct has similar properties. Another property that this approach provides for BER is that an incoming bit-stream can be parsed into a tree structure of elements and embedded elements without any knowledge of the actual ASN.1 type to which it relates. As a special case of this, the end of the encoding can be determined without any knowledge of the type. The widespread assumption that BER was the encoding for ASN.1, and the strong properties of BER with regard to extensibility, led to (often hidden) assumptions about extensibility properties that were only made explicit by the new work in the early 1990s.

The second main point relates to the general structure of the encoding. The encoding for a type that is a SEQUENCE of a number of other types is constructed by concatenating the complete encodings of the component types and putting a T and an L at the head. This is not a representation of data structures commonly used for high-level language data structures, particularly if the size of the inner elements depends on the actual value represented. In such cases it would be more common for the outer level structure to be an array of pointers, each pointing to the structure representing one of the elements, and probably using dynamic memory management to permit changes to variable length components. Thus the task of transforming a common internal representation to a BER representation can be a CPU-consuming task.

8.1.8   ASN.1 tags and extensibility

One of the (unfortunate?) consequences of trying to ensure that level two encodings were the same as level one encodings when new values were added to the abstract syntax was the presence in the ASN.1 notation of **tags**. If the encoding is to be a TLV style, the T has to be determined. Moreover, if the T is to be used to distinguish the elements in a SET (transmitted in a random order), or the chosen alternative in a CHOICE, then it has to be different for all such elements and all such alternatives. But suppose the user wants a CHOICE to be a choice of two INTEGER values (with different semantics). If the encoding of a CHOICE is to be nothing more than the encoding of the chosen alternative (in order to allow elements in version one to be turned into CHOICEs in version two), then there will be nothing to distinguish the two INTEGER encodings, and we have to forbid CHOICEs where the alternatives are the same type. Similarly we have to forbid SET elements in which the elements are the same type. (Note that these restrictions do not arise if we allow the encoding algorithm to assign the T, or treat SET like SEQUENCE and identify chosen items in some other way.) The restrictions are, of course, unacceptable, so we need to refine the concept of a type, allowing the user to specify the T part of an element independently of the actual type of that element. This produced the tag concept, which has no counterpart in high-level language data structure definition, and is the hardest part of the ASN.1 notation for a beginner to understand. Using this concept, the T part of the encoding is constructed from a tag that is formally part of the type being defined. Tags consist of a **class** (universal, application-specific, context-specific, and private) and a **number** (an integer), providing a simple structure to the tag name-space. For primitive types the tag is assigned in the ASN.1 standard from the universal class. In fact, just two classes, universal and one other, would have sufficed, but at the time this work was done the concept of presentation contexts was not well developed, and it looked as if ASN.1 tags might have to be used to separate messages with the same encoding produced by different application designers. A user of the notation can override the tag on any type which is defined by specifying a new tag, in square brackets, as a class name (context- specific has a null name) and a number. Thus:

```
[UNIVERSAL 29] (only allowed in the ASN.1 Standard)
[APPLICATION 32]
[PRIVATE 45]
[6]
```

are all tag values that can be put in front of a type reference to change its tag, and hence the T value used when it is encoded. The rules are then fairly simple. All alternatives of a CHOICE and all elements of a SET are required to have distinct tags. In practice, as a matter of common style, the user normally (in version one) simply adds tags [0], [1], [2] in turn to every alternative of a CHOICE and to every element of a SET. In version two, however, he/she is careful to retain these tags, and to add new elements with different tags, even if it breaks that pretty sequence, because he/she knows that changing the tag will change the encoding. If tags were hidden and automatically assigned, they would be different in version two from version one.

In fact the Basic Encoding Rules provided two options when a tag was added to some type. In the first option, both tags were included in the encoding, making it possible, from the tags present (the innermost being a universal class tag), to identify the type of a primitive element (integer, boolean or real) without any knowledge of the type definition. Thus a line monitor, with no knowledge of the protocol involved, could in principle produce a pretty display with integer values as integer values and boolean values saying TRUE or FALSE, for example. However, there would be more octets on the line than are really needed. All that really need be encoded is the outermost type (the one most recently added by the user to prevent ambiguity). Both options were available in 1984, but the wrong default was chosen.

If all tags were to be encoded, making the type of the element explicitly identified by a universal tag in the encoding, then the square bracket notation was used as shown above. If, however, the application designer wanted only one tag to be transmitted, then it was necessary to write, for example:

[6] IMPLICIT INTEGER

Of course, that is what everybody wanted, and specifications produced in 1984 were littered with the word IMPLICIT, much reducing readability of ASN.1 by a beginning user.

In 1988, it became possible to change the default by saying in the module heading IMPLICIT TAGS so that simple use of a tag produces that one tag only and the word EXPLICIT has to be included if implicit tagging is not wanted. This has been widely taken up, and the word IMPLICIT is now hardly ever seen with tags on current specifications.

In the work of the early 1990s, a further step was taken, partly as the result of developing encoding rules where extensibility is not a concern and user assigned tags are completely ignored in the encoding. The words AUTOMATIC TAGS can be included in the module heading, and in this case (if BER is in use), the tags are automatically generated and the user need not include them. Of course the extensibility properties are now lost, but as stated above, this is less of a concern now than in previous years, and the gain is a data structure definition that looks much more like what one is used to in high-level language definition, and that is much more readily understandable by someone new to the work.

8.2   Developments in ASN.1 in the early 1990s

The text in this section is based on the International Standards finally ratified in 1994 for the major extensions to ASN.1 that were developed in the early 1990s. There are four main parts:

* a general discussion of the problem of 'holes';
* a discussion of the ASN.1 support for 'holes' from 1982 to 1990;
* the macro replacement work (relating also to holes, but going beyond simple holes);
* the character abstract syntax concept.

While this text does not provide a complete treatment of all the new work in the early 1990s, it covers all the major items that an application designer might wish to use, and all the conceptually difficult areas.

8.2.1   Black holes and all that – general discussion

The whole concept of layering in the bottom six layers is based on doing part of the total job by defining exchange of information in messages, leaving a 'hole', typically called a **user data parameter**, to be filled in by the next layer. That next layer defined the message to go in the hole, but again left a hole in its own material, and so on. The architecture of the Application Layer (discussed in more detail in the next chapter) continues this approach. We do not talk about any further layers, but we do have many protocols which define messages with 'holes' in them for other protocol designers to fill in. The difference, however, is in the nature of the holes. In the lower layers, up to and including the Session Layer, most messages were defined with a single hole that would carry a transparent octet string (user data). In the Presentation Layer, there are arbitrarily many independent holes in each message, each hole being capable of holding a presentation data value. We have already briefly mentioned that the Presentation Layer model recognizes that some of those presentation data values may contain other presentation data values embedded within them, thus recognizing the concept of a hole in a presentation data value to be filled by values from some other, perhaps arbitrary, abstract syntax.

When we come to real application standards, the ability to define data structures with 'holes' in them is critically dependent on the abstract syntax notation in use and the support for 'holes' in any associated encoding rules. If the 'hole' is to carry values from any abstract syntax, then attention must be paid (in the encoding rules supporting the 'hole') to the same sort of questions that the presentation protocol had to address: how to carry a collection of arbitrary bit-strings, each of which may not be self-delimiting and may not be octet-aligned, and how to identify the abstract and transfer syntaxes to be used to interpret those bit-strings? And what optimizations are sensible for special cases of octet alignment, use of the same abstract and transfer syntaxes, or whatever? The discussion of the presentation protocol should have convinced the reader that such issues are non-trivial, and require careful design. In this section we are concentrating on the support for 'holes' provided by ASN.1 and its encoding rules.

It is important here to distinguish clearly between the embedding of material at the abstract level, where 'hole' is a good term, and the way encodings might operate. A hole at the abstract level could be supported by a 'hole' in the bit-pattern of the encoding, embedding the encoding of the inner material in the encoding of the outer. For some approaches to encoding, this would be a very natural approach. Alternatively, the hole at the abstract level could equally well be supported by encodings that carry the encoding of the contents of a hole after the bit-pattern representing the container value. The way encodings operate is not constrained.

It is also important at this stage to point out that a piece of communication is not fully defined until all holes have been filled in. Moreover, where a protocol leaves a hole, it is essential to have some way of identifying what is in that hole in an instance of communication. In the case of the lower layers, the contents of the hole in a pure OSI stack will be the next layer of OSI protocol (with its user data). If other protocols, such as TCP/IP protocols, were to be carried above a partial OSI stack, then some means is needed to identify to a receiving implementation the actual protocol being carried.

There are in general three mechanisms used to do this in the lower layers.

- Carry in each layer an explicit protocol identifier for the protocol in the layer above. This is the Xerox and TCP/IP approach in many layers, and has been used by other protocol suites. It is not used in OSI.

- Carry in the layer filling in the hole, in some standardized way, a protocol identifier. This is the approach in the Application Layer of OSI (Chapter 9). In some ways it is merely a different way of describing the first approach.
- Ensure that the varying contenders for filling in a hole can be distinguished by their early octets. This is the approach that has been taken in the Network Layer for determining what fills the Data Link Layer user data. Again, it is almost just another way of describing the second case above.
- Use any available addressing mechanisms so that the contents of one or more holes relate to either the sending or the receiving address chosen.

The last case is the ultimate fall-back, but suffers from the fact that the values used to identify protocols A and B (say) are not universally defined, but will vary from receiver (typically) to receiver. The TCP/IP concept of 'a well-known port' is a variant on this theme that attempts to make the addressing information used for particular protocols consistent across all systems.

In the Application Layer, there are the holes in the presentation layer to worry about, but also the possible holes in presentation data values to be filled by further presentation data values that may themselves have further holes. In this case, the contents of individual holes in presentation data values may be identified by the containing material, but the fall-back provision, which also determines the contents of the holes in the Presentation Layer, is the carriage within the Association Control Service Element (ACSE) (discussed in Chapter 9) of an **application-context** value: an ASN.1 object identifier. This object identifier references a specification that provides any additional information needed to define completely the contents of any undefined holes and the total behaviour of the application over the presentation connection.

The ASN.1 Standards have changed considerably from 1982 to 1994 in the provision of mechanisms to support 'holes'. In order to understand these developments we will define (for the purposes of this text – the terms are not used in the ISO standards) two types of hole, and then go on in the next section to look at the mechanisms ASN.1 provides for their support. The first type of hole we will call **the ASN.1 data type hole**, and the second the **presentation data value hole**.

An ASN.1 data type hole is characterized by the provision of a hole which can only be filled by a data type defined using ASN.1. The group defining the container does not define an abstract syntax (the ASN.1 type is incomplete). Rather, when a user group defines the container contents, it is the (now complete) ASN.1 data type (container plus contents) that is used to define an abstract syntax. Thus there may be many different abstract syntaxes defined with the same outer container (one for each contents), but the fact that they have the same container is not visible beyond the pure ASN.1 notation level. The encoding rules applied to the contents are of necessity the same as those applied to the container. A typical example of this type of hole is the ROSE Standard, discussed briefly earlier and in more detail below. ROSE defines ASN.1 data types to be used to invoke remote operations, but they have holes in them to carry information related to the actual operations needed for some application. ROSE does not define any abstract syntax, rather the users of ROSE define their operations (and hence the ASN.1 data types to fill the holes), and define and name an abstract syntax which consists of the values of the ROSE PDUs (Protocol Data Units) carrying their operations. Clearly some notational support is needed to link together the provision of a hole and the definition of material to fill it. As mentioned earlier, the macro notation has in the past been used to partially support this requirement, in the absence of anything designed for the task.

By contrast, a presentation data value hole represents the situation where the carrier is regarded as complete, even with the hole present, and an abstract syntax is defined for its messages. The ultimate contents of the hole can be from any other abstract syntax (perhaps not even defined using ASN.1), and can certainly have a different transfer syntax from that of the carrier. It now becomes necessary to have some way of identifying the abstract syntax used to fill these holes and the transfer syntax that has been applied to the material. A typical example of this type of hole is the X.400 electronic mail standard, which provides for the carriage of what is called **an extended body part** with the mail message. An extended body part might be something like a spreadsheet, a word processor file, an image file, a piece of animation, a piece of video, or a database file. Abstract and transfer syntax definitions, perhaps implicit by reference to some vendor's implementation, are needed if such material is to be carried. Again, some notational support is needed to identify such holes, but there is less need for linkage between the definer of the hole and the group filling it: anything for which an abstract and transfer syntax has been defined can fill it. (The perceptive reader will recognize the implementation and conformance problems this can raise.) It is easily said that 'anything can fill it', but what is an implementation actually expected to handle? For these sorts of hole, one expects to see a **Protocol Implementation Conformance Statement** (PICS) provided by an implementor using a standardized pro forma provided by the carrier group, with space on the pro forma to say, in the case of X.400, precisely what extended body parts are supported by the implementation.

8.2.2   ASN.1 support for holes

The history of ASN.1 hole handling, by both the ASN.1 group and by the users of ASN.1 (application designers), has unfortunately been an unhappy confusion of these two types of hole, and an only partial solution of the problems raised by holes. The distinction between the two types only began to be clearly recognized in the work of the early 1990s.

There is also another type of (less respectable) hole, introduced in a number of application standards, which we will call the OCTET STRING hole. In this case, the application designer specifies a field as an ASN.1 octet string for the purposes of defining his/her own abstract syntax, then proceeds to populate the field with the encoding of an ASN.1 type (perhaps defined by some other group) using some fixed encoding rule (usually BER, but sometimes BER followed by the application of some cryptographic algorithm). Use of this mechanism cannot be prevented by the Presentation Layer or by ASN.1, although text in the 1994 Standard deprecates this use of OCTET STRING, but clearly does not fit in any way with the spirit of the Presentation Layer. It prevents any form of transfer syntax negotiation, and fails to carry with the OCTET STRING either an abstract syntax or a transfer syntax identification. Equally, because a normal type is used to define the hole, there has never been, and probably never will be, any notational support in ASN.1 to link the container and the contents. Its use is to some extent a historical relic (Reliable Transfer Service Element and X.400 – discussed in section 9.3) from the days of protocols sitting directly on top of the Presentation Layer, and from the days before the concept of relay-safe encodings was properly understood, and it will not be discussed further in this book. The reader is, however, asked to avoid introducing such holes in any designs he/she becomes responsible for!

The earliest treatment of holes in ASN.1 (*circa* 1982) supported only the ASN.1 data type hole (and that in a very weak way), and preceded the entire concept of presentation data values that emerged *circa* 1985. The support took the form of an ASN.1 type called ANY. Describing an element of a SEQUENCE as ANY meant that someone, somewhere, would eventually say what went in the field. There was no means of identifying the actual content of the field, nor of cross-linking the field and a definition of possible contents. A typical use today (taken from X.500) would be an element of a SEQUENCE construct defined as:

```
bilateral-information ANY
```

In this case, it is assumed that two parties to a communication will mutually agree the specification of what goes in this ASN.1 data type hole when they are communicating using this protocol, and will use knowledge of the address of the corresponding party to determine what the contents are in an instance of communication. The use of address information as a protocol id has been discussed in principle earlier, and is not ideal, particularly if the same agreements are in place with a number of correspondents, or when one correspondent wishes on different occasions to use different material in the hole, but it is the ultimate fall-back when no other provision has been made for identifying material in a hole.

In the case of ANY, the 'hole' had to be filled with a type defined using ASN.1, and the Basic Encoding Rules specified quite simply that the encoding of an ANY (for embedding as a TLV component in the encoding of the enclosing type) was the encoding of the type that was chosen to fill it. It was really the robustness of the ASN.1 Basic Encoding Rules (the uniformly applied TLV concept) that made this simple approach work. Because the end of a BER encoding could (and can) be determined without knowledge of the type being encoded, ASN.1 data type holes could be skipped if necessary without affecting the ability to interpret the rest of the message. In particular, if identification of what was in the hole appeared in some later field of the message, there was still no problem in continuing the parse and locating that information.

Another problem with ANY was that, in the early days, it was often abused by being used to stand for 'for further study', or to identify that there would in due course be a further element of a sequence, but the application designers didn't yet know what it should be. If the ANY was marked OPTIONAL, then it could be argued that the protocol was actually implementable, because values where the ANY was omitted were well defined. But such uses frequently left the reader in doubt about whether there was, somewhere, some other standard that specified the ANY contents, or whether there would be a later specification that would remove the ANY. Such uses are less common today, as protocols have matured.

In about 1984, the problems with ANY were becoming recognized, and use of the raw ANY, or a **black hole** as it then became colloquially called, was deprecated in the ASN.1 Standard, and the construct 'ANY DEFINED BY field-name' was introduced. This was an attempt to try to ensure that, whenever an ANY was introduced, some other field 'near' to it (at any rate, in the same message) would contain some value (an integer or an object identifier) that would, by reference to some specification, determine the contents of the ANY field. This construct replaced ANY in a number of specifications, but the rather rigid definition of 'a field near to the ANY' restricted the take-up of this construct, and many protocols still contained a 'raw ANY' at the end of the 1980s. Moreover, while this notation did help to ensure that the ASN.1 data type filling the ANY field (and any associated semantics) was identified somewhere in the protocol, it did nothing to identify where the mapping of the integer or object identifier to the ASN.1 data type and its semantics could be found. Thus it was really only a partial solution.

At about the same time as the ANY DEFINED BY construct was introduced and the raw ANY was deprecated, another mechanism was introduced called the EXTERNAL type. This was the first attempt to provide notational support for a presentation data value (pdv) hole, although at this time the term pdv was not as current as it is now. The word EXTERNAL was used because the idea was that what went into the hole was external to the current specification, that is, external to the current abstract syntax. It could be a value from an abstract syntax defined using some notation other than ASN.1, and even if defined using ASN.1, it might be encoded with different encoding rules from the carrier.

The intent was very clear that this type should carry an embedded pdv, forming a presentation data value hole, but the technical terms which were emerging at about the same time to describe Presentation Layer concepts were generally not used in the definition of EXTERNAL. Indeed there was, and remains, a body of opinion that wishes to see minimal use within the ASN.1 Standard of OSI Presentation Layer concepts. It can be used as a means of defining data structures in the lower layers of OSI, or completely outside OSI, as well as by OSI application designers. This attitude can sometimes make a clear specification of its use in support of the Application Layer of OSI more difficult.

The early design of EXTERNAL envisaged that the Presentation Layer protocol would specify the message going into Session Service user data parameters as simply the BER encoding of

SEQUENCE OF EXTERNAL

and some tutorial texts still say that this is indeed the presentation protocol. In fact this definition never appeared as an actual standard, because if the presentation data values in the user data parameter of a P-service primitive were all BER encodings, and were all from the same presentation context (a common case), this data structure contains a lot of redundant information; in particular, the presentation context and the T and L of the EXTERNAL are repeated for every presentation data value in the list. So the presentation protocol actually abandoned ASN.1 for encoding the user data parameter and defined that part of its protocol in ordinary English, copying much of the text (with changes) from the ASN.1 definition of EXTERNAL.

There were mistakes made in the design of EXTERNAL. The presentation concepts and terms were still maturing, and it was not made clear that it carried an embedded pdv. Moreover, there were only three options provided for identifying what filled the hole, none of which was wholly satisfactory.

One option was to carry an integer which (in rather obscure text) was intended to be a presentation context identifier for a context in the defined context set on this connection at the time the message containing the EXTERNAL was transmitted/received. This was clearly not relay-safe, to use modern terminology (this issue is discussed further in section 8.2.3), and the X.400 Standards (in some cases by folklore and rumour, rather than explicit text) avoided this option, as relaying of material was fundamental to their operation.

The second option provided for EXTERNAL allowed the presentation context identifier to have with it a transfer syntax object identifier. This was to cover the case (on P-CONNECT or P-ALTER-CONTEXT) where a presentation context had been proposed, but the transfer syntax had not yet been agreed.

The third option provided for EXTERNAL was to carry a single ASN.1 object identifier that was intended to identify both the abstract and transfer syntax of the embedded value. This was, in retrospect, undoubtedly an error, and the EMBEDDED PDV construct in the 1994 Standard contains two object identifiers, quite straightforwardly specifying the abstract and transfer syntax of the encoding. (In order to provide backwards compatibility with EXTERNAL, however, the transfer syntax object identifier is optional.) Because the X.400 (electronic mail) use of EXTERNAL had to assume a fixed encoding of the contents of the EXTERNAL (no transfer syntax object identifier), static text was needed to determine the transfer syntax. Typically, if the contents of the EXTERNAL was ASN.1-defined at the abstract level, then one could either define use of BER, or one could define use of the encoding rule negotiated for the outer level encoding. Of course, in 1994, the two definitions would in practice give the same result, and text saying which was intended was often missing in uses of EXTERNAL. If, however, the contents of the EXTERNAL was not ASN.1-defined (an extended body part in X.400, for example) then a specific definition of transfer syntax had to be associated with the object identifier when one was assigned to identify a body part. If, for example, the body part was a Lotus-123 spreadsheet, or a dBase IV file, or a WordPerfect 5.1 file, then the object identifier assigned to the body part had to identify not just the abstract object, but some specific encoding (for example, that of MS-DOS) of the abstract object that was being carried. If a Mac encoding was wanted, then a further object identifier would have to be defined, and there would be no obvious link between the two. Thus the original EXTERNAL encouraged the use of a single identifier for the combination of abstract and transfer syntaxes, ignoring the concepts of the Presentation Layer. The 1994 Standard attempted to correct this situation before it was too late by including a pair of object identifiers in the EXTERNAL replacement (the EMBEDDED PDV construct), while allowing the transfer syntax object identifier to be omitted for backwards compatibility with the old EXTERNAL.

The main message of the Association Control Service Element (ACSE) is carried in the first presentation data value of the P-CONNECT request. Other application specifications contributing to the connection could have carried their messages on subsequent presentation data values of the P-CONNECT request, but in the early days of ACSE use, it was often regarded as almost another layer. In particular, it provided for embedded pdvs by having a user data parameter defined as:

        SEQUENCE OF EXTERNAL

and other application designers chose not to place their initialization exchange directly in the P-CONNECT presentation data values, but rather in one of the ACSE EXTERNAL fields, regarding themselves as the sole users of A-ASSOCI-ATE, and ACSE as the sole user of P-CONNECT.

We see then that the usage of EXTERNAL was (in the late 1980s) a bit of a mixture of simply filling in an ASN.1 data type hole and filling in a presentation data value hole.

In the 1994 specification, ANY was removed and EXTERNAL was deprecated. An EMBEDDED PDV type was provided to clearly and directly support the inclusion of presentation data values from arbitrary other abstract syntaxes, with identification of their transfer syntaxes, and a separate mechanism (information object classes) was introduced for handling ASN.1 data type holes, linking the container to the contents, and identifying the contents.

8.2.3 Relay-safe encoding

One of the problems with the handling of embedded pdvs relates to material that is being stored/relayed from one connection on to another, either in support of some relaying protocol like X.400 (electronic mail), or where material is deposited on a file-server and later collected. If the relaying/storing system knows enough about the material to convert it to 'pure information', and re-encode in a possibly different transfer syntax, then there is no problem. Frequently, however, we require a design which does not require such detailed knowledge on the part of the relay/storage system, which wishes to handle the material transparently with no capability to change the encoding. It is clear that end-to-end negotiation of transfer syntax using the presentation protocol to perform the negotiation of transfer syntax is not possible in relay/storage cases, but mechanisms based on prior knowledge or on use of X.500 can be used to select an appropriate encoding for the material that is being stored/relayed. It remains, therefore, to identify the material and its encoding in a reasonably efficient manner.

For an outer-level presentation data value (even if being relayed/stored), identification can be performed by establishing a presentation context to identify the abstract and transfer syntaxes, and transmitting the material in that context. The relaying/storage system merely needs to ensure that an equivalent presentation context (same abstract and transfer syntax) is established for forwarding/retrieval.

More commonly, the material being relayed will be an embedded pdv (A, say), and that embedded pdv may contain further embedded pdvs (B, say). It is the case of these further pdvs (B) that is particularly hard to handle using the presentation context. Suppose they were carried in an ASN.1 EMBEDDED PDV type, and that a presentation context was established for them, with the presentation context identifier in the encoding of the embedded pdv. What this means is that there are references from inside a pdv (A) (which is being relayed with no decoding and no understanding) to the external environment in which it was received (a presentation context on that connection). Such references are completely invisible to a system transparently relaying pdv A, and the only solution would be to establish an identical entire defined context set for forwarding/retrieval. This is not really feasible, and such an encoding is not **relay-safe**. We can define, then, a relay-safe encoding of a pdv as one such that any embedded pdvs, or pdvs embedded in them, make no references to presentation contexts established on this connection. In other words, the abstract and transfer syntax object identifiers of any embedded material must be explicitly present in the pdv being relayed (in the relay-safe encoding). Unfortunately, despite the relative compactness of the ASN.1 object identifiers, this can introduce unacceptable overheads if there are a lot of small embedded pdvs with the same abstract and transfer syntax, a situation which will arise quite frequently in handling character strings using the mechanisms provided in the 1994 Standard.

What is needed for efficient encoding is some indirect indexing mechanism, comparable to the establishment of a presentation context and use of the presentation context identifier, but with the table that is being indexed carried within the relay-safe encoding. This was provided in the ASN.1 encoding rule extensions and new encoding rules defined in the early 1990s. Thus for any particular style of encoding rule (see section 8.2.6), there is typically a basic version, a relay-safe version, and a version that is both relay-safe and canonical (no implementation options in the encoding).

If this approach is considered a little more, the reader will recognize that what is effectively happening is that some of the Presentation Layer functionality (definition of a presentation context) that was previously carried out at the connection level and applied to all pdvs on that connection is now being carried out at the level of a pdv, and applied to all the pdvs carried in that pdv (and so to any depth). For relay-safe encodings, the presentation connection merely sets up the environment for the outermost encodings. For embedded pdvs, the environment for their encoding is carried in the encoding of the immediately enclosing pdv. This can lead the reader to ask 'Have we moved to an architecture where the Presentation Layer is in some sense no longer a single layer, but is rather recursively introduced whenever embedded pdvs occur?' This will be discussed further in Chapter 9 when the Application Layer architecture is treated in detail.

8.2.4   Information object classes (macro replacement), etc.

Let us now return to the notational support needed to tie together the introduction of a hole and the definition of material to fill that (and precisely that) hole.

When the then current uses of macros was examined in the early 1990s, it became apparent that in most (not quite all) cases, they related to ASN.1 data type holes: quite frequently to raw ANYs, possibly to ANY DEFINED BY constructions, and sometimes to EXTERNALs which were being used to provide an ASN.1 data type hole and not to provide for an embedded pdv.

In many cases, there was a single ASN.1 data type hole, and an associated object identifier field to identify the type that was put in the hole. (This was the case where EXTERNAL was most often used, and where the 1994 INSTANCE OF ... construction was the appropriate replacement for the EXTERNAL.) The macro introduced a syntax that included the name of the class of objects being carried in the hole, and the specification of the ASN.1 type of the object and an associated ASN.1 object identifer to identify it. An example is given in Figure 8.9. Note that while the macro enabled an XYZ object to be specified and identified, the link to the actual EXTERNAL or ANY carrying that object was distinctly tenuous.

In other cases, there was a more complex situation, with a number of related holes to be filled, and additional information collected by the macro syntax that did not directly relate to the ASN.1 data types filling the holes, but rather selected some optional procedures or processes in the carrier protocol concerned with the handling of objects of this class. A good example here is the ROSE use of macros, where there is an ANY DEFINED BY field in the 'invoke' message which needs an ASN.1 type defining to carry the arguments of the operation, another in the 'return result' message which needs a type defining to carry the result of the operation, and another in the 'return error' message which needs ASN.1 types defining for each possible error return to carry parameters associated with a particular error. In addition, there needs to be an iden-

```
languages HEADING-EXTENSION
  VALUE SET OF Language
    ::=
      {joint-iso-ccitt mhs-motis(0)
       ipms(1) hex(3) id-hex-langs(7)}
```

Figure 8.9 *Notation defined by a simple macro.*

tifier assigned for the operation being defined, for each of the possible errors a set of operations might produce. ROSE also used the macro syntax to collect details of **linked operations**: operations Y1, Y2, ... which, as a result of system A invoking operation X at B, could be invoked by B at A. Operations Y1, Y2, ... are the linked operations for X. The complete definition of all the information that needed to be provided when defining an object from the class of objects called **ROSE operation** was provided by a single use of the OPERATION macro (which might reference the names of errors), and the complete definition of the information needed to define an object from the class of objects called **ROSE error** was provided by a single use of the ERROR macro. These macros provided all that was needed to complete a whole set of related holes, and to provide any additional semantics such as specification of the linked operations.

This approach worked quite well, and the ROSE-defined OPERATION and ERROR macros and their associated syntax were known and loved by many application designers, but it suffered from two problems: first, the link between the holes that were filled by the macro and the uses of the macro itself was tenuous, and in particular was informal and could not be supported by the growing body of ASN.1 tools that assisted in OSI Application Layer implementations; secondly, where a macro was used to identify a complete set of things that filled a hole (or holes), such as a set of ROSE errors and operations, there was nothing in the notation to relate these definitions to the set of values in some particular abstract syntax specification. Words were used like 'the abstract syntax is defined as the set of values of the ROSE data type, with the holes filled by the operations and errors defined in the body of this Standard'. Or more commonly, such words were not used, but merely implied. There was the further problem, identified earlier, that the macro approach gave complete freedom to designers to specify their own syntax for collecting the information needed to define an object from some class. This not merely led to dissimilar syntax defined by different groups for doing the same sort of thing (for example, separating lists of values by comma or by vertical bar), but also left the definer free to specify syntax that could be very hard to parse by a machine parser, and made the ASN.1 syntax completely open-ended.

The 1994 Standard removed the macro notation as a normative part of the Standard, leaving its definition as an informative annexe to enable readers to cope with historical material that still used macros.

The replacement provision addressed all the above problems, while retaining a syntax for defining objects of some specified class that could be tailored, within reasonable limits, by the group defining the information to be collected for that class of object.

The basic concept is of the **Information Object Class**, and defining such a class is equivalent to defining a macro. The definer determines the nature of the information that is to be collected, and, within rigidly defined limits, specifies the syntax to be used for collection. A model which proved helpful in the development of this work is a **table**, whose form (columns) is determined by the definition of the object class. Thus column 1 might be defined to hold an ASN.1 object identifier value to identify an operation, with column heading

```
OPERATION ::= CLASS
    {&ArgumentType  OPTIONAL,
     &ResultType    OPTIONAL,
     &Errors  ERROR OPTIONAL,
     &operationCode OBJECT IDENTIFIER UNIQUE}
WITH SYNTAX
    {[ARGUMENT &ArgumentType]
     [RESULT    &ResultType]
     [ERRORS    &Errors]
     CODE       &operationCode}
```

Figure 8.10 *Definition of the OPERATION class.*

'&id', column 2 might be defined to hold an ASN.1 type with column heading '&Arguments', column 3 likewise might be defined to hold an ASN.1 type with column heading '&Results', and column 4 a set of references to objects in the ERROR class (a separate table), with column heading '&Errors'. (The & symbol was introduced as the first symbol of a table heading to enable human users to clearly distinguish such a thing from an ASN.1 type or value reference.) Each row of the table then defines one object of the OPERATION's class. Figure 8.10 shows the way this information object class would be specified. Note the 'with syntax' clause that is used to define the way the information is to be collected. This allows only a very simple keyword/value approach to defining the collection syntax, with square brackets denoting optional parts of the syntax, but in fact proved sufficient for syntax defined in this way to be almost as user-friendly as that defined by a macro, but much easier to process. The corresponding definition using macros would have been as shown in Figure 8.11. No attempt will be made to talk the reader through that figure, and if it is totally incomprehensible, don't worry!

With that class definition, it is now possible to define objects of that class. Figure 8.12 shows two operations (rows of the table) being defined using the new

```
OPERATION MACRO ::=
  BEGIN
    TYPE NOTATION ::=
      Arguments
      Results
      Errors
    VALUE NOTATION ::=
      value(VALUE OBJECT IDENTIFIER)
    Arguments ::= empty | ARGUMENT type
    Results   ::= empty | RESULT    type
    Errors    ::= empty | ERROR
  END
```

Figure 8.11 *The equivalent macro definition.*

```
lookup OPERATION ::=
        {ARGUMENT VisibleString
         RESULT   Address-type
         ERRORS   {invalidName,
                   nameNotFound}
         CODE     {myOIDs 1}      }

insert OPERATION ::=
        {ARGUMENT SEQUENCE
                  {VisibleString,
                   Address-type }
         ERRORS   {directoryFull}
         CODE     {myOIDs 2}      }
```

Figure 8.12 *Definition of objects of class OPERATION.*

```
lookup OPERATION
        ARGUMENT VisibleString
        RESULT   Address-type
        ERRORS   {invalidName,
                  nameNotFound}
        ::= {myOIDs 1}

insert OPERATION
        ARGUMENT SEQUENCE
                 {VisibleString,
                  Address-type}
        ERRORS   {directoryFull}
        ::= {myOIDs 2}
```

Figure 8.13 *Equivalent notation using macros.*

notation, and Figure 8.13 shows the way they would have been defined using the macro definition. Note in particular that in the new work the new syntax is delimited by a pair of round brackets, whereas using the old macro notation, the only way the end of the new syntax could be found was by performing a parse as specified in the macro definition (which might, of course, appear much later in the material being processed, as ASN.1 allows forward references everywhere). Figure 8.14 shows an assignment that gives a collective name to the resulting table (the set of four operations we have defined here). This was not present in the use of macros.

```
My-ops OPERATION
        ::= {lookup, insert}
```

Figure 8.14 *Defining a table of OPERATIONs.*

```
ROSE-invoke ::= SEQUENCE
    {op-code    OPERATION,
     invoke-id INTEGER,
     argument  ANY DEFINED BY op-code}
```

Figure 8.15 *Definition of a pdv with a 'hole'.*

This has addressed the syntax issues, but what about tying the definition of a class to the holes it is associated with? How does one replace the ANY and ANY DEFINED BY constructs? Let us consider a simplification of the ROSE protocol. Figure 8.15 shows a simplified version of the ROSE invoke message as it appeared in the late 1980s. There was a tacit understanding, partially supported by text concerning macros, that the OPERATION keyword meant the OBJECT IDENTIFIER type, and was the operation identifier, and that the ANY carried the arguments data type defined for that operation. The first step is to identify these fields as containing values from columns of the OPERATION class table. This is shown in Figure 8.16, where it is now clear that this particular ANY and this particular OBJECT IDENTIFIER are determined by the definition of an OPERATION information object. Moreover, we can add what is called a **relational constraint** which specifies that the value in the 'identifier' field and the value in the 'argument' field have to be related by being values from the same row of the table 'My-ops' (Figure 8.17). The reader will appreciate how this has closed the loop, enabling a precise statement of how the hole is to be filled, and hence a precise statement of the abstract syntax.

There is just one problem with what has been presented so far: the definition in Figure 8.17 has to appear in the ROSE Standard, but My-ops and its associated definitions have to appear in the Standard produced by some ROSE user.

```
ROSE-invoke ::= SEQUENCE
    {op-code    OPERATION.&Operation-code,
     invoke-id INTEGER,
     argument  OPERATION.&Argument}
```

Figure 8.16 *Tying the hole and id together.*

```
ROSE-invoke ::= SEQUENCE
    {op-code    OPERATION.&Operation-code
               (My-ops),
     invoke-id INTEGER,
     argument  OPERATION.&Argument
               (My-ops{@op-code})          }
```

Figure 8.17 *Identifying a table.*

```
ROSE-invoke {OPs-Table OPERATION}   ::=   SEQUENCE
   {op-code    OPERATION.&Operation-code
               (OPs-Table),
    invoke-id INTEGER,
    argument   OPERATION.&Argument
               (OPs-Table{@op-code})      }
```

Figure 8.18 *Parameterizing the definition.*

Moreover, there will typically be multiple such definitions by different groups of ROSE users.

This is addressed by the **parameterization** of a piece of ASN.1 specification. Parameter substitution is relatively well understood in computer science, and is often what macros for text manipulation are actually all about. Any type, value or table which might be otherwise explicitly included as part of an ASN.1 specification can instead be represented by a parameter. In the case of ROSE discussed above, we parameterize the ROSE data type with a parameter that is a table (called Defining-Table) of information object class OPERATION as shown in Figure 8.18, and then in the user standards the data type used to define the abstract syntax for the user's application is defined by applying the actual parameter My-ops to the parameterized ROSE-invoke thus:

```
ROSE-Invoke { My-ops}
```

In fact, parameterization of ASN.1 specifications turned out to have two additional beneficial spin-offs. First, there were one or two uses of the existing macro notation where the macro was in fact being defined precisely for the purpose of parameterization and parameter substitution, so that such a feature was needed for the basic macro replacement work. Secondly, parameterization enables bounds (particularly bounds on integers, number of elements in a SEQUENCE OF, and so on) to be left as parameters in a base standard, and to be supplied later, perhaps with several variants for different environments. The actual parameters can be supplied at the time the abstract syntax is defined (in which case the protocol is tightly defined, but possibly with several abstract syntaxes for the different ranges of bounds), or can even be left as parameters of the abstract syntax, their implemented values being specified in the PICS (Protocol Implementation Conformance Statement) produced by an implementor, and/or required values can be referenced in procurement statements. This helps with what has long been a troublesome area in OSI. Implementations do have limits, but there is a reluctance to put these into the base standard, because that can unnecessarily tie the standard to current technological capability, and also because appropriate bounds and sizes are often heavily dependent on the environment in which a standard is used. On the other hand, clearly identifying where implementation variation might occur is obviously important. Parameterization serves all these purposes.

8.2.5 Character abstract syntaxes

Another troublesome area in the OSI work is that of character repertoires. If an international standard is being defined, it is clearly inappropriate to specify text fields as fields of characters from the Latin alphabet. Even within Europe, systems that supported only the ASCII or the EBCDIC character set (very common in the 1970s and 1980s) were incapable of covering any of the major languages apart from English. But implementing support for fields that can contain Japanese and Chinese and Greek and Urdu and Hebrew (to name but a few!) characters can be rather hard, depending on the precise definition of 'support'.

The problem is not entirely originated by ASN.1, and cannot be completely solved by ASN.1, but notational support in this area is needed. ASN.1 went through three main iterations in attempting to address this problem.

The earliest text (X.409 in 1984) had a limited range of character types defined covering basically a very limited character set, the ASCII character set, and (surprise, surprise – remember the Transport and Session and Presentation discussion?) the Teletex character set defined in CCITT Recommendation T.61 and the Videotext character set defined in T.100 and T.101. T.61 was interpreted in 1984 as allowing ASCII and Japanese, but other character repertoires were explicitly added to it progressively in the late 1980s and the early 1990s, and it now contains quite a broad range of character repertoires.

The first ISO standard for ASN.1 took a somewhat different approach to this area. There was in existence at that time (and still is) something called colloquially 'The International Register of Character Sets', or more correctly 'The International Register of Coded Character Sets to be used with Escape Sequences'. This was a collection of about 110 register entries, each listing the complete set of characters in some character repertoire, together with code to identify each repertoire, and an encoding for each character within it. For most of the entries the encoding structure used a single octet for each character, and the code tables had the same structure as those normally used to define ASCII (128 positions arranged in eight columns of 16 rows, with control characters in the first two columns and the delete character in the bottom right). Most, but not all, languages of the world were registered, so an arbitrary character could be encoded by using the ASCII 'ESC' (standing for 'escape') – present in that code position in all entries in the register – followed by the assigned codes to reference a register entry, followed by the encoding of the desired character or characters.

The ASN.1 work in 1985/86 took this register as its base. Existing character types, in particular TeletexString, were redefined to reference the register, and new types were added to enable the full generality of the register encoding to be used in a field.

Problems arose in the late 1980s from two sources. First, the character sets recognized in T.61 were greatly extended, giving pressure for a similar extension to the corresponding ASN.1 type, which was now defined not by reference to T.61 but by reference to the International Register, and hence was not automatically affected. Secondly, there was increasing recognition that, no matter what one meant by 'support', a field which was defined to carry any character from the International Register, which was continually being extended, was hard to support in an implementation. Thirdly, and most importantly, SC2 (Sub-Committee 2, the ISO group responsible for character set standards) had embarked on an ambitious programme to define a completely new structure for character set encoding which would accommodate in one structure all the languages of the world, with defined subsets for the most common requirements, such as the set of European languages. This used a coding structure based on two octet or four octet character encoding, was entitled 'Universal Coded Character Set', and was given the number ISO 10646 out of sympathy for ISO 646, the old and well-beloved standard that underlaid ASCII and the International Register. This work, after some quite serious controversy, came to a conclusion in 1992.

ASN.1 introduced a new data type called UniversalString, and married together the existing ASN.1 subtyping mechanisms with the defined subtypes of ISO 10646 to give good support for this new standard. It is now possible to specify a field in an ASN.1 type as carrying any specified combination of the defined subsets of ISO 10646, or even to define new subsets. The conformance statement of ISO 10646, reflected in the ASN.1 text, does however forbid use of ISO 10646 unless the implemented subset is specified. In ASN.1 use, this means that UniversalString is required to be subtyped, although the subtype specification could involve a parameter that is only determined by the PICS (the implementor), not by the base standard. This is the recommended way of using UniversalString in an OSI application design, and further reinforces the importance of the parameterisation mechanisms.

However, these discussions led to a much closer look at the whole question of appropriate character set support, with a strong liaison statement from the Remote Database Access (RDA) group that they required to be able to negotiate the character repertoire to be used as part of connection establishment, or even later.

The result of these discussions was the inclusion in the 1994 text of the CHARACTER STRING data type, supported by the new concepts of a **character abstract syntax** and a **character transfer syntax**. A character abstract syntax is largely synonymous with **character set** or **character repertoire**, and the **character transfer syntax** with the encoding of that character set. The important difference, however, is that use of these terms implies the allocation of ASN.1 object identifiers to identify the abstract syntax (repertoire) and the transfer syntax (encoding), and the ability either to name repertoires and encodings or to negotiate them by the definition of presentation contexts. This is a very powerful feature. It not only allows base standards to be written and implemented without placing early constraints on the character repertoires to be used, but it also makes ASN.1 (and hence the application designs using it) much less dependent than hitherto on the vagaries of character set standardization. All that is required if another new character set standard is produced is for that standard to allocate ASN.1 object identifiers for character abstract and transfer syntaxes, and it automatically becomes available as far as ASN.1 and application designs are concerned, although getting implementation support does, of course, remain another matter.

In fact, there are other SC2 character set standards in addition to ISO 646 and ISO 10646, which had previously been ignored by ASN.1. Support for these now merely (!) requires an addendum to them to define the appropriate character abstract and transfer syntaxes. A (normative) annexe to ISO 10646 performs this function for all the combinations of all the defined subsets of ISO 10646, and serves as an illustration for other standards. The definition is algorithmic, with a separate object identifier for all possible combinations of the defined subsets. Again, however, it will be the market-place that will decide which combinations people actually demand in procurement, and which implementors choose to support, but ASN.1 (and any Application Layer base standard using it) is off the hook.

8.2.6   Other encoding rules

A brief outline of the structure and approach of the Basic Encoding Rules was given earlier in this chapter, but it is appropriate here to give a brief mention of other encoding rules that emerged in the early 1990s.

The need for other encoding rules   Almost the whole of the Presentation Layer work is predicated on the idea of negotiating transfer syntaxes, and hence on there being multiple transfer syntaxes defined. During the whole of the 1980s, such negotiation was a nice theory, but never happened in practice. There was one, and one only, set of encoding rules for ASN.1 (the Basic Encoding Rules), and implementors were sufficiently busy producing standards that would interwork with other vendors that there was little interest in defining vendor-specific encodings which were close to local representations.

In the early 1990s, however, there was a growing interest in the question of the standardization of appropriate transfer syntaxes and the provision of better encoding rules.

There were a number of viewpoints. At the one extreme there were those that were horrified at the apparent verboseness of the TLV encoding of the Basic Encoding Rules where (apart from extensibility issues) the T part is largely overhead and the L part (given the presence of subtyping) is also frequently unnecessary. At the other extreme there are those that argue that the maximum overhead in BER for most uses is probably no more than 100% (twice as many octets as necessary), and probably in practice rarely more than 50%. What is a factor of two in octets? Factors of ten or more in line-speed come every few years, so .... Moreover, if there were a proliferation of encoding rules, open interworking could be prejudiced because not everybody would implement the same set. Another attitude recognized the importance of optimized transfer syntaxes, particularly for things like FTAM (File Transfer, Access and Management) Document Types, or ODA (Office Document Architecture) documents, or perhaps X.400 Body Parts, but questioned the value of better ASN.1 Encoding Rules: greater gains could, in this view, be obtained by hand-crafting some transfer syntaxes to optimize common cases for these sorts of transfer. In the middle were those that saw the importance of having a number of internationally standardized encoding rules for ASN.1, making appropriate trade-offs.

By 1992 there had emerged a recognition that at least one new set of encoding rules for ASN.1 was needed, and perhaps more. There were two dimensions to the problem.

One was the basic structure of an encoding, with three approaches being discussed: Basic Encoding Rules (already in place), Packed Encoding Rules – PER (optimized for bits on the line), and a set of LightWeight Encoding Rules – LWER (optimized for the CPU cycles needed for encoding and decoding). These are important concepts discussed extensively below.

The other dimension related to the need for special features in the encoding. Two of these special features were recognized, and could be considered with any of the three basic approaches to encoding.

The first has already been discussed at some length: making the encoding relay-safe. The only real issue here is whether one needs to provide a non-relay-safe version (apart from BER which has existed in a non-relay-safe fashion for some time). Perhaps it would be simpler if all encoding rules always produced relay-safe encodings? The counter argument is that if a particular character abstract and transfer syntax is used for embedded CHARACTER STRING data types in many small presentation data values in a connection, such as might occur in terminal or windows traffic, it is far more efficient to define an outer level presentation context once and for all and reference it as necessary from the embedded CHARACTER STRING encodings (which is not relay-safe) than to identify the character abstract and transfer syntax in every outer level pdv that is transmitted (which would be relay-safe).

The second special feature is the definition of a **canonical encoding**, that is, one for which all implementation options have been removed. Why is this needed? The recognition first came in the work on X.500 and X.400. They had a requirement to add an authenticator to an abstract value which would enable a recipient to detect whether that abstract value had been tampered with during transfer. The desire was to accept the Presentation Layer model that relaying systems might (but need not) change the actual encoding by decoding and re-encoding, but, of course, must faithfully relay the abstract value unchanged. Existing authenticator mechanisms had been developed to authenticate a bit-string, not an abstract value. (Typically such authenticators were produced by using some hashing of the octets in the bit-string into a few octets, and then encrypting these for transfer using a secret encryption key. Without knowing the encryption key, an agency tampering with the bit-string in transfer cannot generate a new correct authenticator for the modified bit-string.) One way to use such a mechanism to authenticate an abstract value is to determine a one-to-one mapping between abstract values and bit-strings, then to authenticate the corresponding bit-string. A one-to-one mapping between a bit-string and an abstract value is in fact nothing more than an encoding/decoding rule with no implementation options in the bit-pattern produced, or a canonical encoding rule. (The Directory work used the term **distinguished** encoding rule, which meant the same thing.) The way this is in theory used for authentication is first to encode using the canonical encoding rules, then to authenticate the resulting bit-string (which is then discarded) to provide an authenticator for the abstract value, then to transmit the abstract value and authenticator (involving encoding it and decoding at the receiving end), then to re-encode the abstract value using the canonical encoding rules to provide a bit-stream which can be checked against the authenticator. In principle, this involves double encoding at the sending end (once to get the canonical bit-string and once for transfer), and decoding and re-encoding at the receiving end (once to get the abstract value and once to get the canonical bit-string for authentication). Where, however, the canonical encoding is a strict subset of the encoding used for transfer, optimizations are possible in a real implementation which allow the encoding produced for authentication to be used for transmission, and the received bit-string to be used for authentication.

The important thing, therefore, is to ensure that for each of the main encoding approaches (BER, PER and LWER), there is a normal version, a relay-safe version, and a version that is both relay-safe and canonical.

What then are the main features of BER, PER and LWER? The following sections discuss each of these in turn.

Features of BER   BER has already been characterized as a TLV encoding. Each primitive type encodes into a TLV. Each constructed type encodes into a TLV with the TLVs of the elements in the V part. All T, L and V parts are a whole number of octets. The T part unambiguously identifies the element within the context in which it occurs, and is formed from the tags that the user has (if necessary) to assign in order to provide for a T part that is

- different for each element of a CHOICE;
- different for each element of a SET (transmitted in any order);
- different for each optional element and from any following mandatory element in any series of optional elements in a SEQUENCE (to enable the omission of items to be recognized).

The T part also contains one bit that identifies whether the V part is primitive or is a series of TLV fragments. The L part is always present, and determines the length of the element, either as an octet count or by indicating that it is a set of TLV triplets terminated by a zero octet. (The encoding of the T part, and in particular the reservation of the tag [UNIVERSAL 0], ensures that a zero octet can never appear as a valid T.) BER was designed before subtyping was introduced into the notation, and completely ignores any subtype information. Thus if an octet string is specified in the notation as always precisely eight characters long, this information is ignored, and the length field is still encoded. The encoding of lengths and of integers effectively poses no limit on the size of integers that can be supported (the encoding of the largest representable INTEGER value would take about 100 million years to transmit at 100 terabits per second). For most T parts, a single octet will be used. For L parts a single octet is used if the length is less than or equal to 127 octets. Thus the T and the L normally put a two-octet overhead on each element.

Features of PER PER takes a rather different approach from that taken by BER. The first point is that the T part is omitted from encodings, and any tags in the notation are completely ignored. Potential ambiguities are resolved as follows.

- A CHOICE is encoded by first encoding a **choice index** which identifies the chosen alternative by its position in the list in the notation.
- The SET construct is treated exactly like SEQUENCE: elements are transmitted in order.
- When a SET or SEQUENCE has OPTIONAL or DEFAULT elements, the encoding of each element is preceded by a bit map to identify which OPTIONAL or DEFAULT elements are present.

The second point is that PER takes full account of any subtyping information, and will omit length fields whenever possible. Moreover, integers that are subtyped into a range that potentially requires more than one octet, but never more than two (for example, (0..65 535)) are always encoded into precisely two octets with no length field. Parts of the encoding (lengths or primitive values) that require more than eight bits encode starting on an octet boundary, but elements that require less than an octet pack together in the minimum number of bits. Thus in BER SEQUENCE OF BOOLEAN, with 64 boolean values, would encode into an amazing 196 octets, while in PER it would encode into 9 octets, and SEQUENCE SIZE (64) OF BOOLEAN would require only 8 octets. A more realistic example might be SEQUENCE OF INTEGER (0..65535), which with 64 two-octet integer values in BER would encode into 259 octets. In PER, it would encode into 130 octets. The sequence

```
SEQUENCE
{first-field INTEGER (0..7),
second-field BOOLEAN,
third-field INTEGER (0..3)
fourth-field SEQUENCE
   {fourA BOOLEAN,
 fourB BOOLEAN} }
```

would encode into precisely one octet (BER would take 19), making it possible in some cases to retrofit a hand-crafted and heavily packed protocol with an ASN.1 definition and a PER encoding, although this was not a major design requirement for PER.

Features of LWER Turning now to LWER, we again find a major change of approach. The LWER work was still immature in 1994 amd was not included in the 1994 set of Standards. All that this text can do is to discuss the design approach and some of the problems. The idea of LWER arose from implementors of tools that support the easy implementation of protocol handlers for protocols defined using ASN.1. Such tools read in an ASN.1 type definition and map it into an in-core data structure (typically using the C language) which is capable of holding values of that type. The implementor of the protocol then writes a program to write to the in-core data structure to generate (in this local format) the value to be transmitted, then invokes a run-time routine provided by the tool to encode this value into (typically, in the early 1990s) BER, ready for transmission. The process is reversed on reception. The LWER encoding rules are based on the experiences of implementors of such tools to define, as a working design, a mapping of the value of any ASN.1 type into an indefinitely large memory, with dynamic memory allocation and with a known word-size (16 bits, 32 bits, or 64 bits). To give the flavour, a SEQUENCE of six elements maps into six words in memory. If the element is a boolean or an integer, the word holds the element. If the element is a variable length character string, the word holds a pointer to a block of memory containing the string (with a length count at its head). If the element is a SEQUENCE OF SEQUENCE (the SEQUENCE again being six elements), the word holds a pointer to a block of memory with an iteration count at its head, holding six words for each iteration, some of which may be integers or booleans, and some of which may be further pointers. The resulting structure is a strict tree. The encoding rules are then obtained by a simple tree-walking algorithm to transmit in a specified order the blocks of memory forming the value tree. In 1995 there are still a number of unresolved issues concerning the LWER encoding, and all that can be done in this text is to mention some of them. The reader who wishes to know more must obtain the latest OSI documents. The first issue relates to the word-size: clearly with the word-orientation of LWER we need at least three LWER encoding rule specifications, one based on a 16-bit word, one based on a 32-bit word, and (perhaps?) one based on a 64-bit word. Then there is the problem that, if one defines the octet order in memory such that a character string goes from low numbered octets to high numbered octets, we find that in some computer systems an integer has its most significant octet first (so-called **big-endian**), and in some systems it has it last (so-called **little-endian**). Does this mean we need six LWER encoding rules? And are there not some systems with word sizes greater than 16 where other permutations of the octets are needed to get the integer value? A more difficult problem arises with integer values that won't fit into the word size. Should the encoding rules (and the model in-core representation) be made more complicated to allow pointers to a longer block if the integer value exceeds the word size, or is it acceptable to say that these encoding rules have implicit size restrictions on INTEGER? Or should account be taken of subtyping? And what about length counts that exceed the word-size? And finally and similarly, how do we model pointers that cannot fit into the word-size, and more importantly how do we flatten the tree structure for transmission? Can we define the tree-walking in such a way that actual pointer values need not be transmitted, merely a flag saying this field is a non-null pointer? It is at this stage impossible to say more about the likely final form of LWER: it is even possible that these problems will cause LWER to be abandoned. Notice finally that LWER will be fast and efficient for encode/ decode provided it is used between two similar architectures (two 16-bit machines or two 32-bit machines, both big-endian). Its advantages would be rather less if the communicating machines have dissimilar architectures. The question arises whether there is a sufficiently large class of implementations that would benefit from LWER, or whether it would be better to encourage tool providers to obtain object identifiers and allocate them for their own formats, restricting the use of any particular LWER to interworking between implementations based on the same tool? Notice also that the number of octets on the line will be far higher than PER, and probably higher than BER, particularly for the 32-bit and 64-bit versions. Thus this protocol is only really applicable when bandwidth is not a major concern.

The pressure to develop PER and LWER arose partly from technical considerations, and partly because private organizations were known to be developing encoding rules with similar properties, so that international standardization was appropriate to prevent an explosion in the number of encoding rules in use in the world.

The technical considerations were based on a recognition of the various trade-offs necessary in designing a set of encoding rules. The dimensions listed below were identified as important for evaluating the quality of a set of encoding rules (in no particular order).

Bandwidth: A sensible reduction of bandwidth requirements compared with BER is desirable for heavily structured data, where the ASN.1 overhead can be large compared with the contents of the ASN.1 data types. This is particularly important where operation over low bandwidth channels (for example, radio) is still required. PER scores much better than BER on this dimension, without too many penalties on other dimensions.

CPU cycles: Minimization of the CPU costs of encoding and decoding is always a useful property. The LWER set of encoding rules score much better than BER on this dimension, admittedly at some cost on the 'open' dimension described below, but still with a very useful score overall.

Openness: Encoding rules specific to a single implementation are encouraged for optimizing CPU cycles, but clearly score poorly on openness, and are not appropriate for international standardization. None the less, it is possible to identify a number of machine architectures such that vendor-independent standardization of exchanges designed to minimize CPU cycles on such architectures provides very useful standards with an acceptable level of openness, although not as much as BER or PER, but with much less CPU cycle cost. This is the positioning of the LWER set.

Extensibility: Support for extensions to the ASN.1 specification of a protocol without this resulting in changes to the encoding of values that were present in the earlier version of the protocol is sometimes a requirement. BER scores very highly on this dimension, and it is unlikely that any other encoding rule standard will be able to score as well. There are some additional extensibility rules that are informally invoked by some application standards (for example: 'If there are elements at the end of a SEQUENCE that are not in the type definition, ignore them'). If these were added to BER, it would score even better on this dimension, although this is not currently planned, and would probably further worsen BER's score on the CPU dimension.

Implementation effort: This dimension relates to the complexity of the encoding rules. PER scores worse than BER on this dimension, and LWER probably considerably better.

Security: There are a number of security-related features that could give rise to requirements for additional encoding rules. Some of them, such as selective field encryption, may even require additions to the notation to identify fields to be encrypted. Up to the time of writing (1995) there were no plans for any security-related encoding rules, other than the work on canonical versions of BER and PER.

Structure in the encoding: This dimension relates to the ability to identify parts of the encoding with parts of the (structured) abstract value, making it possible to provide a receiving application with detailed information on what fields are not what was expected while still providing values for other fields. A high score on this dimension generally goes with a high score on the extensibility dimension, but usually carries penalties on the bandwidth and CPU dimensions. BER is strong on this dimension, and PER and LWER much weaker.

Processing without knowledge: This dimension relates to the ability to carry out a number of processing tasks on a received encoding without knowledge of the ASN.1 type from which it was derived. BER, using only `EXPLICIT TAGS`, scores very highly, enabling a line monitor to display the structure of the encoding, with characters fields as characters, integers as integers, booleans as true and false, and so on. With `IMPLICIT` tags BER is much weaker, but it is still possible to identify structures and to parse the encoding into primitive elements. Both PER and LWER can do very little with an encoding unless the ASN.1 type is available (and the same as the encoder used). Again, a high score on this dimension tends to correlate with a high score on the extensibility dimension.

To quote from an ISO output document produced in early 1992: 'A judicious population of the transfer syntax dimensional framework will considerably enhance the capability of OSI applications and other specifications using ASN.1 to operate in a range of environments, without causing an undue proliferation of options that could prejudice interworking.'

8.3   Other candidates for abstract syntax definition

To conclude this chapter, we look at two other notations used to define data structures to be used for computer communications.

The first notation to consider is the EDIFACT graphical notation. EDIFACT (Electronic Data Interchange for Finance, Administration, Commerce and Transport) is a development of a number of EDI (Electronic Data Interchange) and TDI (Trade Data Interchange) standardization efforts. The work on standards for the transfer of documents related to trade (and particularly to international trade) proceeded in parallel with OSI development, with both groups relatively unaware of what the other group was doing. EDIFACT was produced starting in the late 1970s and through the 1980s by the United Nations Working Party on Facilitation of International Trade Procedures, and is the result of merging earlier work, notably the ANSI X12 Standard and earlier UN work within the UN Economic Commission for Europe, called Guidelines for Trade Data Interchange (TDI). Unfortunately the result at this time has not been to produce a single standard, but rather a third standard, and when the X.400 (electronic mail) Recommendation was extended in 1991 to handle the transmission of EDIFACT documents, it provided an ASN.1 OCTET STRING to carry encodings of the documents, together with a flag (an OBJECT IDENTIFIER) saying whether it was the ANSI X12 version, or the TDI version, or the EDIFACT version that was being carried.

Some parts, but by no means all, of the documentation of EDIFACT have been submitted to ISO and are an ISO standard. In particular, the encoding rules for EDIFACT documents are ISO 9735. The encodings use text characters throughout, and were originally designed to enable EDIFACT documents to be transferred over the telex system.

The interesting part of EDIFACT for the purposes of this chapter is the notation for defining message structures at the abstract level. This is the **graphical syntax** of EDIFACT. Figure 8.19 shows an example of a simple data structure defined using the EDIFACT notation, and Figure 8.20 shows the equivalent ASN.1 type definition. Some work has been done comparing the power of this notation with ASN.1, and it is clear that a formal mapping could be defined from the EDIFACT graphical syntax to ASN.1 (but not the reverse – ASN.1 is

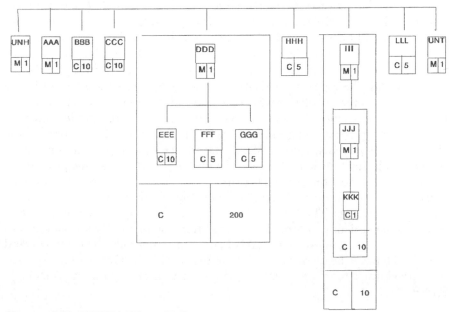

Figure 8.19 *EDIFACT graphical syntax.*

```
SEQUENCE
 {UNH,
  AAA,
  SEQUENCE (1..10) OF
      BBB OPTIONAL,
  SEQUENCE (1..10) OF
      CCC OPTIONAL,
  SEQUENCE (1..200) OF
   SEQUENCE
    {DDD,
     SEQUENCE (1..10) OF
         EEE OPTIONAL,
     SEQUENCE (1..5) OF
         FFF OPTIONAL,
     SEQUENCE (1..5) OF
         GGG OPTIONAL} OPTIONAL,
etc
```

Figure 8.20 *Equivalent ASN.1.*

more powerful). Those who are not computer programmers generally find the EDIFACT graphical notation more usable than ASN.1, and it remains the case for the present and perhaps foreseeable future (in the mid-1990s) that EDIFACT will remain as an abstract syntax notation and encoding rules for transfer syntax alongside ASN.1. Its use is likely to be (as the name implies) largely restricted to the definition of trade-related documents and perhaps personnel record systems, rather than for general-purpose Application Layer protocols. It would not be totally unreasonable to equate ASN.1 with Fortran and EDIFACT with Cobol.

The second notation that is worth a brief mention is the RPC (Remote Procedure Call) Interface Definition Notation (IDN). The RPC standard (and its relationship to ROSE) is discussed in more detail in section 9.5, but its main technical content is the definition of a language for defining the parameters of a procedure call, and the results it returns. Thus it is directly replacing the use of ASN.1 with the ROSE OPERATION and ERROR macros. The aim in the IDN was to produce a notation which was somewhat closer to the data type definition syntax of traditional programming languages, with the explicit intent of trying to get programming language standards to write in support for the IDN. After some discussion, ASN.1 was rejected as too communication-oriented to be acceptable in this role. Having said that, at least one provider of ASN.1 tools has now produced a C compiler and run-time system that directly accepts ASN.1 as a means of defining data structures that can be accessed by C language statements. The IDN standard does not define its own transfer syntaxes. Rather it defines a formal mapping from use of the IDN notation into an ASN.1 data type, allowing the ASN.1 encoding rules then to be applied (and the ASN.1 types to be carried in ROSE messages). Thus RPC can be seen primarily as providing a more programming-language-friendly interface to ASN.1 and ROSE.

9

And yet more tools

This chapter and the next are concerned with the application layer. The concern, however, is with the layer as a whole, and individual applications are in the main treated only where they illustrate more general points about application design. For a detailed treatment of any one application other books exist and should be consulted.

9.1 Application Layer Structure

Before reading this chapter, the reader is invited to review the discussion in Chapter 2 on the OSI architecture. Moreover, it will be hard to grasp and remember abstract model concepts before the practical examples have been presented. On the other hand, it is easier to show how the examples relate to and make use of the model concepts if the model has been presented first! The reader may wish to return to and re-read this chapter after the later chapters have been read.

There has been a lot of change (from 1978 to 1995) in the theory of how to define computer protocols and appropriate terminology and model concepts.

First let us introduce the term **application association**, or just **an association**. In the lower layers we talk about a network connection, or a presentation connection. The definition of connection in the Basic Reference Model is based on the idea of layer (N) providing a service to entities in layer (N+1), and an (N)-connection is defined (Figure 9.1) as 'an association between two entities in layer (N+1) provided by the entities in layer (N)'. Thus a network connection is an association between a pair of transport entities provided by the entities in

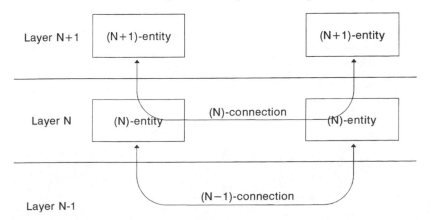

Figure 9.1 *Definition of an N-connection.*

the network layer. This clearly fits with normal usage. But now consider what an **application connection** would mean: this would be an association between entities above the application layer (and there are no such things) provided by the application layer. Thus the term application connection is an inappropriate one, and is not used. Applying the definition again, however, we see that a presentation connection is 'an association between two application entities' provided by the presentation layer. Thus we can use the term application association as a synonym for **presentation connection** if we want to focus on the interaction between the applications, rather than on the underlying communications (which we do).

There have been attempts to use the term application association in a somewhat broader fashion. If two application entities are communicating interactively using connectionless communication, with some sort of state information shared between them for the duration of the communication, then one might wish to speak of an application association between them, even though there is no presentation connection. Similarly, if two applications have recovery procedures in place to re-establish their operation from a checkpoint following loss of a presentation connection, one might again wish to say that their application association had not been lost. At the present time, however, application association equates with presentation connection, with the ACSE (Association Control Service Element) Standard providing an A-ASSOCIATE service primitive to 'establish an application association' (which it does by issuing a P-CONNECT), and a corresponding A-RELEASE and A-U-ABORT and A-P-ABORT which marry together loss of the application association with loss of the presentation connection. (ACSE is discussed in more detail below, but Figure 9.2 is worth a moment's inspection. It shows an application

Resulting services available to an application designer

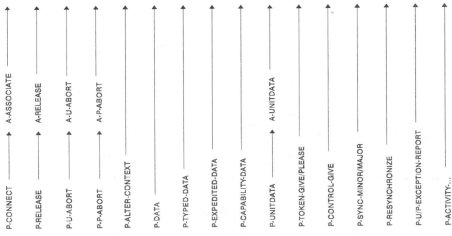

Figure 9.2 *Services from Presentation + ACSE.*

layer designer choosing to use the ACSE tool as having available to him a set of service primitives consisting of the P-service primitives *less* those 'stolen' by ACSE, *plus* the A-service primitives provided by ACSE.) With that introduction of the term association, and a brief mention of ACSE, we now return to the problem of modelling the application layer, and the terminology introduced.

In the earliest work, people were expecting simple (and probably large) monolithic specifications for an application on top of the Presentation Service. All necessary common tools were provided by the middle layers, and all that remained was to produce the real application standards. In the late 1970s, work was started on three application standards: FTAM – File Transfer, Access and Management; VT – Virtual Terminals; and JTM – Job Transfer and Manipulation. Work was well advanced on these by the time other ideas of application layer structure emerged, and these three standards (now full international standards) remained largely monolithic standards, covering in one standard all the necessary details of the protocol exchanges for these three applications.

The original ISO model terminology talked about entities in each layer that communicated, using the services of the layer below. Thus we had network entities, transport entities, session entities, presentation entities and application entities. These entities were the abstraction of a protocol handler, and were broadly in one-to-one correspondence with protocol standards.

The beginnings of the idea that this was not the right approach came from the CCITT OSI Reference Model, with the idea that, in the application layer, there would not be a single monolithic Standard specifying the behaviour of the application entity, but rather a collection of standards used together. Thus while for some aspects of the behaviour of the application entity we can still regard it as atomic (it is still a useful model term), we can peer inside it and find it is made up of Common Application Service Elements (CASEs) and Specific Application Service Elements (SASEs), rather as a physical atom is made up of neutrons and protons. See Figure 9.3 for the view of application layer structure taken in the earliest Reference Model Standard. The CASE standards provide additional infrastructure in the application layer and the SASE standards provide for real applications using that infrastructure. Thus ACSE was a CASE Standard. (In fact, the Reference Model, as shown in Figure 9.3, also included a **User Element**, which was supposed to provide the top-level use of the standardized services. This term was dropped in later work.)

It was in the middle to late 1980s that this was seen to be a move in slightly the wrong direction, and the terms CASE and SASE were abandoned, describing the basic building blocks (main standards) of the application layer simply as ASEs (Application Service Elements), with a collection of ASEs used to support some application (forming an application entity). The distinction, blurred as it may be, is none the less useful for tutorial purposes, and roughly speaking the standards discussed in this chapter are infrastructure or CASE standards, and those in the next chapter are real applications or SASE standards.

The concept of ASEs was present in the first Basic Reference Model Standard, but there was still a lot of work needed to make the concept usable. The most important question was: 'What glue is needed to put a set of ASEs together?'

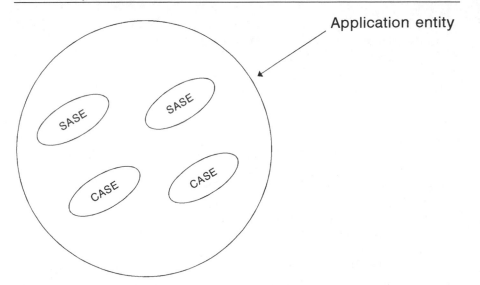

Figure 9.3 *Earliest approach to ALS.*

The immediately obvious answer is the service primitive concept, designed in the lower layers to enable one protocol standard to invoke the procedures of some adjacent layer protocol standard. This notation, however, was designed primarily to pass parameters to fill in holes in parameterized messages, and assumed a strict hierarchy of layers, with one layer completely hiding the services of the layers beneath. None the less, an attempt was made to use this approach. Every Application Layer Standard defined not merely its protocol, but a set of service primitives by which some other ASE could reference it and cause its procedures to be invoked. The concept from the lower layers was slightly modified for use in the application layer to reflect the idea that the lowest ASEs (like ACSE) will 'steal' some P-service primitives, providing a total service consisting of the rest of the P-service primitives and the new services of these ASEs. At first sight, any of these ASEs can be used in any combination (provided they don't 'steal' the same P-service primitives) to provide a total service which can be used by other application designers to build yet more ASEs. This model of **nested service primitives** is illustrated in Figure 9.4. Unfortunately, there are some problems with this simple approach.

The reader might, for example, like to consider that layering and service primitives are all about filling in 'holes'. How then does this nested service primitive model relate to the use of ASN.1 macros or information objects to fill in holes? There was, in the early 1990s, no clear answer to this and to many other similar questions.

Part of the general problem of combining ASEs through the nested service primitive model comes in clearly defining what is the total service available to someone writing a new application when there are a lot of ASE specifications (building blocks) available. For example, suppose one ASE (providing a set of

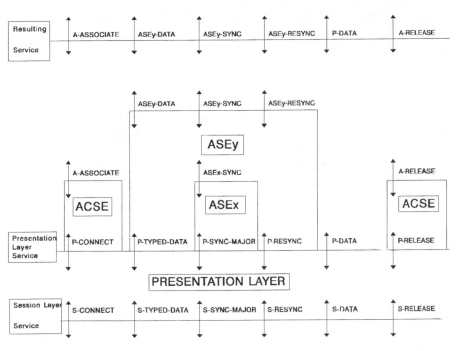

Figure 9.4 *Nested service primitives model.*

X-service primitives, say) has been written using the Session Service activity functional unit, and another ASE (providing a set of Y-service primitives, say) has been written using the major synchronization functional unit. Rules concerning the order in which the X-service and Y-service primitives can be issued (by some third application layer designer who wishes to use these two ASEs as building blocks) can be deduced from the Session Layer rules, but are not necessarily obvious from the definition of the X-service and Y-service, which may not even specify what Session Service primitives they are mapped onto. An even bigger problem arises if the X-ASE uses the TWA Session Service and the Y-ASE uses the TWS Session Service! What we really want is two independent sets of Session Service primitives and messages, one for each ASE, but operating in a coordinated fashion so that messages from the different ASEs do not get out of order. We also have to worry about the effects of resynchronization invoked by one ASE on the messages of the other ASE. Even if both ASEs use similar Session Services, there can still be problems in combining them. Suppose they both define messages that need to be carried on a major synchronization primitive. What is probably required is to combine them in such a way that both their messages are carried on a single major synchronization primitive, not to issue two separate primitives.

Finally, let us consider the use of ACSE. It is the issuing of an A-ASSOCIATE request that establishes a presentation connection to support an application association. With the simple model of nested service primitives described above, there can be precisely one ASE that issues the A-ASSOCIATE primitives. But the broad characteristics of the association are determined when it is first established (and in particular the functional units) by parameters of the A-ASSOCIATE primitives. Thus if the model of flexible re-use of ASEs is to work, we cannot have the A-ASSOCIATE primitives 'stolen' by any one ASE.

Again a small digression: the FTAM and JTM standards specify completely the use of A-ASSOCIATE, and follow very much the 'nested service primitives' approach. The VT Standard, produced slightly later, merely makes clear the characteristics of the application association that it requires, and makes no pretence of 'stealing' A-ASSOCIATE. TP, produced later still, talks about 'managing a pool of associations', with no concern about how or when they were established.

These, then, are some of the issues to be addressed in making the ASE concept work.

An attempt was made to produce the beginnings of a solution in the late 1980s with the development of a new Application Layer Standard (ISO 9545) called 'Application Layer Structure' (ALS). Much of the work leading up to this was dominated by concerns over whether an application entity could be described as handling only a single connection, with things dealing with more than one connection not part of OSI, but part of something else. There were at that time two standards at a late stage of development that were indeed concerned with coordinated activity on more than one connection, CCR (Commitment, Concurrency and Recovery) and JTM (Job Transfer and Manipulation), and it was apparent that coordinating activity over more than one connection was an important part of the specification for some applications. The resulting ALS structure therefore recognized two levels in the building up of a complete application entity (Figure 9.5). First, there were ASEs that operated over a single

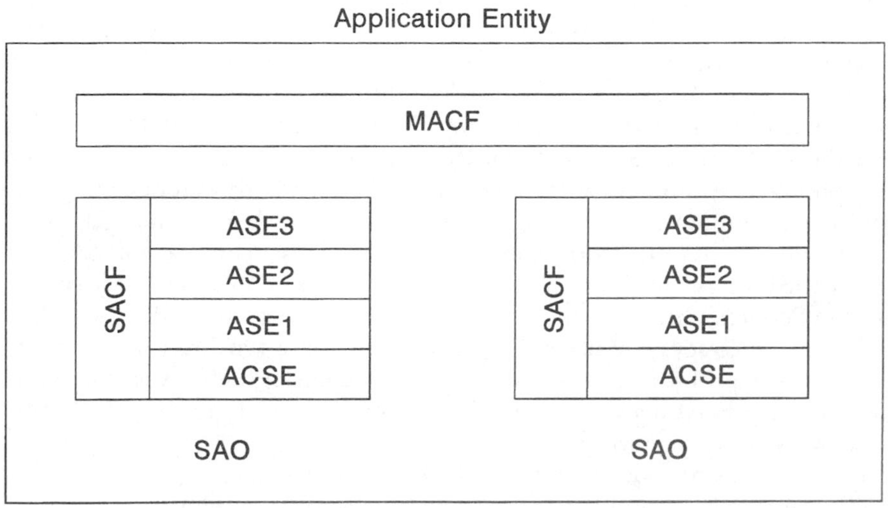

Application Entity

Figure 9.5 *Application Layer structure* circa *1989.*

application association, forming a **Single Association Object** (SAO). These were shown as a vertical stack with ACSE at the bottom, implying something of the nested service model, and alongside them there was shown a **Single Association Control Function** (SACF). The SACF was the necessary specification of how those ASEs were to be used together on the single association, but no SACF standards as such were ever produced: the idea was that this picture modelled the sorts of specification that were needed, but the SACF would in fact be text distributed through the main ASE standards relating to their use of or use by other ASEs. The Single Association Objects might then be combined into a **Multiple Association Object** by some **Multiple Association Control Function** (MACF) text that said how activity on the different associations was to be related.

This was a reasonable starting point, but again it proved to be a slightly off-track development. The picture really implies there is an ASE operating for each association. While this may be appropriate for ACSE, which is only concerned with a single association, it is highly inappropriate for CCR and TP (described in section 9.4) or JTM, which are very much concerned with the coordinated handling of many associations. The next step in the thinking involved work in the early 1990s on what was called 'The Extended Application Layer Structure' (the XALS), which became an International Standard in 1992. This work was published as Amendment 1 to ISO 9545, but the amendment actually struck out virtually all but the introductory text and replaced it with completely new text! It is effectively a new Application Layer Structure Standard.

What are the new concepts this amendment introduced? First, the concepts of Single Association Objects and Multiple Association Objects, and the related concepts of SACF and MACF, were deleted from the main text and relegated to an informative annexe: the concepts and distinctions they implied were not considered useful in the practical job of combining ASE specifications into complete applications.

The new concepts introduced recognized (like the nested service primitives model) an arbitrarily deep hierarchy of nested specifications, but placed much more emphasis on the concept of a specification of a **Control Function** that would relate component parts together. The major new term introduced was the **Application Service Object** (ASO). (Everybody started talking about objects in the late 1980s and early 1990s, and to be fair there was a real attempt to apply the information-hiding concepts of object orientation. The class concept and inheritance was less frequently introduced, and was not present in the XALS.) The other 'actors' in the model were **Control Functions** (CFs) and **Application Service Elements** (ASEs), with **Application Entities** (AEs) as still the outermost structure. How do these relate together?

An Application Service Element is a basic building block, and has no component parts. An ASO, by contrast, has a recognized structure involving precisely one CF (Control Function) together with a collection (one or more) of either ASOs or ASEs. The CF within the ASO determines how the component parts are to be combined to form the ASO. An AE (Application Entity) is now defined as the outermost ASO operating on an association. The focus, then, is on the structured combining of objects in a hierarchy of specifications, each of which must contain CF text.

Note that an ASE (in the thinking of the 1990s) does not make use of other ASEs. In service primitive terms, it is self-contained and interacts with other ASEs (or ASOs) through the specification of a CF. Note also that an Application Entity (AE) is never just an ASE. It is defined as an ASO – that is, it has a CF and one or more ASE and ASO components. This can be interpreted as meaning that some standards previously called ASEs, particularly those originally termed SASEs, are no longer ASEs with the new definition. In particular, those that reference and use A-ASSOCIATE (like FTAM and JTM), or the CCR service primitives (like TP), are strictly speaking now ASOs. In some cases, and particularly that of FTAM, there is a view that it should indeed be an ASE, making no use of ACSE, and that a number of ASOs should be defined as actual international standards for the combination of an FTAM ASE with other ASEs (particularly with CCR).

There is one final important aspect to the XALS work: the ASE specifications are no longer expected to identify the presentation layer service that the application's messages are to be carried by. That is a piece of specification that should appear only in the outermost CF (the one that specifies the complete Application Entity). The advantages of this for combining specifications that currently appear wholly incompatible, such as ones that use session activities with ones that do not, will be obvious, but it will take some time before there is a clear separation in the documentation of the syntax and semantics of application messages from the actual service primitives carrying these messages.

The ramifications of the XALS specification were not clear in the early 1990s (most of the Standards experts who were not directly concerned with the work had little knowledge of it), but its importance for obtaining full reusability of specifications was recognized. There were, however, serious doubts about whether the concepts had arrived too late, most of initial set of OSI standards being complete, and there being little enthusiasm to revise them to produce the separation of text identified above. Work has, however, been undertaken to:

- modify ACSE to take account of the new model (the model not only changed terminology, it also introduced some new naming concepts for identifying ASOs within ASOs);
- get a consistent treatment of references or non-references to ACSE in other standards;
- investigate the problems of splitting some standards into an ASE component and a CF component.

In the latter case, the ASE component would consist of the messages they defined (with their semantics and the properties needed for their carriage – major sync or resync like, etc.), while the ASO component would contain the CF that would specify how those messages were carried in P-service primitives and how ACSE was used. These could be separate standards, or separate parts of one Standard. This would pave the way for other ASO specifications that could use the same ASE part, perhaps with ASEs from some other Standard, to define a different ASO. Unfortunately, this book has been written too soon to describe the outcome (or even the likely outcome) of this work. Look out for the second edition!

There is one further point to consider, and this relates to the entire upper layer architecture (Session, Presentation and Application). We have already made some mention of the way in which the contents of 'holes' need their syntaxes identifying in much the same way as the Presentation Layer identifies the outer level. If we are to have relay-safe encodings, this identification must not be by reference to a real outer-level presentation concept. Thus we begin to get the concept of mini presentation layers inside each hole (and, of course, holes recursively nest, and maybe more or less correspond to ASE/ASO structuring). Further, we have spoken of the problems of combining one ASE/ASO that uses the session activity concept with one that uses major sync. These problems might be addressed by divorcing their messages and semantics from the P-service primitives carrying them, but there is an alternative: could we, in some way to be determined, provide each ASE/ASO with its own independent session functionality, where any session purging purges only the messages of that ASE/ASO, and not those of any other ASE/ASO with which it might be combined? What we would end up with if this approach is followed would be a five-layer model, with the bottom four layers (up to the Transport Layer) as now, and with the top layer being a recursively nested structure of ASOs, each ASO containing its own session and presentation functionality (layer would now be the wrong term). A simple unstructured application would still have a session, presentation, and Application Layer as now, so existing standards would not necessarily be disrupted. A paper from a US expert advocating the adoption of this 'five plus a three-layer recursion' model was informally circulated round the world early in 1992, but was considered by many to be too radical a change for introduction so late in the development of OSI. None the less, in mid-1995 drafts are in preparation for amendments to the session, presentation and ACSE Standards that will support 'nested session connections', allowing the establishment of session connections (with presentation and ACSE and other ASEs on top) within an existing connection. This nested connection can be used to support an ASO (defined earlier perhaps as a complete specification) which is now being embedded within a newly defined ASO. The inner connection has its own set of session primitives, and any purging on this nested connection does not affect its parent (but purging of the parent does affect the nested connection).

Unless the reader is getting alarmed, however, it is important to note that we are here discussing 'architecture', that is, the way we structure the documentation of what has to be implemented. Changing this documentation structure need not, and indeed will not, affect the actual 'bits on the line'.

At this stage the discussion has to be drawn to a close. The text has moved into very uncertain waters, and the reader is cautioned that the later parts of the above discussion are still somewhat speculative. The ideas presented may provide dramatic changes in the modelling and architecture of OSI, or they may quietly die.

9.2 ACSE and addressing issues

We have already said quite a lot about ACSE. Let us try to complete the picture. First, we need to discuss briefly the addressing provision in the OSI layers, then we will look at the added value provided by ACSE beyond that available from the Presentation Service.

The OSI architecture has the concept of a Network Service Access Point (NSAP) address, discussed earlier, which is world-wide unambiguous, which is carried in the Network Layer protocol, and which is used by routers to establish a connection (or transfer connectionless traffic) to the remote end-system. NSAP addresses are passed in the N-CONNECT primitives. The Transport Layer carries in its connect message additional addressing information that can be used to 'fan-out' within the end- system. This information is called the **Transport Selector**, and the combination of an NSAP address and a Transport Selector forms a Transport Service Access Point (TSAP) address. It is TSAP addresses that are passed in T-CONNECT service primitives. Similarly, in the Session Layer there is a Session Selector, and in the Presentation Layer a Presentation Selector. We have (see also Figure 9.6):

> PSAP address = SSAP address + Presentation Selector
> SSAP address = TSAP address + Session Selector
> TSAP address = NSAP address + Transport Selector

Why do we need to provide for fan-out in all three layers? There are two reasons. The first relates to the lack of a protocol identifier in the OSI layers. The selectors provide the ultimate fall-back for identifying, using addressing

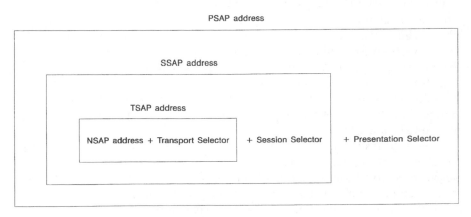

Figure 9.6 *Structure of layer addresses.*

information, the protocol in the layer above. The second relates to recognition that there will be many varying implementation architectures. Suppose, for example, that in one implementation the whole of the Network and Transport Layers are implemented behind the operating system fire-walls by the main computer vendor, but the applications are each implemented by a third-party vendor as separate monolithic implementations of session, presentation and application, running as processes on that operating system. It would be natural to use the transport selector to determine which of these applications is to receive an incoming call. On the other hand, change the implementation architecture so that all layers up to and including the Presentation Layer are provided by the computer vendor, with third-party products being processes implementing only the application layer, and fan-out using information carried in the presentation layer, while not essential, is natural. Thus we are led to expect that, in any real system, all selectors except one might be null, but the non-null one might vary with implementation architecture. This is still a bit too simplistic, however. Suppose the computer vendor provides, perhaps for historical reasons, direct interfaces to both the transport and the presentation layer functions, allowing implementations by third-party vendors of both the above sorts to co-exist as processes on the vendor's system. In this case, fan out might be used in the transport layer (with one value of the transport selector saying 'stay inside'), and also (for that value of the transport selector) fan-out in the presentation layer. Clearly in the general case we might have non-null selectors in all the layers.

This addressing structure is clearly not very human-friendly, and may also be subject to change as implementation architectures and the positioning of applications within one of a set of systems changes due to software or system upgrades. As with many protocol architectures (compare the Domain Name of TCP/IP), there is a separate level of world-wide unambiguous, implementation-structure-independent naming provided in the application layer to identify application entities. This is the **Application Entity title** (AE-title), and its precise form is defined as an ASN.1 data type in the ACSE Standard (from where it is imported by FTAM and other standards). The first ACSE Standard had a raw ASN.1 ANY as the definition of the AE-title, because of lack of agreement on its form. This was later replaced (using the defect report mechanism!) by a definition of the AE-title as either an ASN.1 OBJECT IDENTIFIER (not very human-friendly, but certainly not dependent on the structure of the implementation or the positioning of the application in some particular system) or a **Directory Distinguished Name**. This latter is defined by importation from the X.500 standards, and provides an organizationally structured human-friendly name. In the strict addressing architecture of OSI (Part 3 of the Basic Reference Model), the AE-title is made up of an **Application Process title** (AP-title) with an **AE-qualifier**. This in principle means that one can identify a number of application entities as associated with the same application process. However, the concept of application process is ill-defined, and no OSI application to date makes any use of this structure. To all intents and purposes, the AE-title can be regarded as an atomic entity.

Both forms of name can, in principle, be passed to the X.500 Directory Service and will result in a world-wide search which maps the name into the PSAP address needed to access the named application entity. In early 1992, however, the use of X.500 to perform searches using an ASN.1 OBJECT IDENTIFIER was still not sufficiently well specified in standards, nor were X.500 implementations yet widely deployed. Thus in the early 1990s, the distribution of information about the mapping from application entity titles to PSAP addresses had to be manual.

Let us now turn to the functionality of the ACSE Standard. It has two main pieces of added value compared with direct use of the Presentation Service: the transfer between the communicating partners of their AE-titles and the negotiation of an **application context**. An application context is identified by an ASN.1 OBJECT IDENTIFIER. Standards which expect to be used as complete applications (hitherto called SASEs, now called ASOs that can – on their own – form application entities), such as FTAM, X.400, X.500, VT and JTM, all allocate a value for their application context within the base Standard. It is effectively a protocol identifier for that Standard. The negotiation is very simple: an OBJECT IDENTIFIER goes across in the request/indication, and another one returns in the response/confirm. The relationship between these (if any!) is a matter for the application Standard, but they can, for example, be used to negotiate a **basic class** operation or a **full class** operation by use of two object identifiers, with the rule that if basic is offered basic has to be accepted and if full is offered either basic or full can be accepted. JTM (Job Transfer and Manipulation) uses them in this way. In the XALS terminology, this specification would be part of the CF of the outer-level ASO.

The value of exchanging application contexts will be clear: where a single implementation can handle a number of protocols, a single address can be used and the protocol to be used can be dynamically selected. This is probably of more value where the protocols are closely related (as in the JTM full/basic case) than if they are totally unrelated (like FTAM or VT), but it is clearly a useful provision. The value of exchanging the application entity titles is less clear, but consider the situation where the mapping from AE-titles to addresses has got knotted, for whatever reason. It is desirable at an early stage to discover that you are, in fact, knocking on the wrong door! A perhaps more important reason is that a recipient who knows only the PSAP address of a caller (passed up in the P-CONNECT indication) cannot use that to find out anything further about him from the X.500 Directory Service. On the other hand, if you have his AE-title, you can go to the Directory (at least in principle, once X.500 is fully deployed) and get his public key to check authentication information, to find out what abstract and transfer syntaxes he might support, or even what machine the call is from. In other words, you have a usable identification of your peer. With the AE-title, ACSE also carries an AE-invocation-identifier. The use of this is usually left as implementation-dependent, and no OSI Application Layer standards currently make any use of it. Notionally, it identifies this particular invocation of this application entity, and could be useful for logging and diagnostic purposes, or for an application Standard specifying some form of recovery mechanism.

ACSE also provides an A-service to replace use of P-U-ABORT, P-P-ABORT and P-RELEASE because as it is used to set up an association it should sensibly be used to tear one down. There is, however, only very minor added value on these primitives (slightly changed error codes and reasons). The complete set of parameters on the A-ASSOCIATE request/indication (apart from those which are part of the P-CONNECT and are transparently passed through ACSE) are:

- Application Context Name
- Called and calling AE-title and AE-invocation-identifier
- Implementation Information (an ASN.1 `GraphicString` – unlimited length, any characters registered in the International Register of Character Sets).

On the response/confirm we get the same set, except that the called and calling AE-title and AE-invocation-identifier are replaced by a single responding AE-title and AE-invocation-identifier.

In one respect ACSE is negative. The P-CONNECT has a list of Presentation Data Values in its user data parameter. ACSE uses just one of these to carry the ACSE-defined ASN.1 data type, but does not provide any access to the others, providing for a list of presentation data values as a parameter of the A-ASSOCI-ATE but mapping these into embedded pdvs using `SEQUENCE OF EXTERNAL`, with the problems that were discussed earlier for an `EXTER-NAL` carried in the P-CONNECT when contexts have not yet been established and multiple encodings may be needed. (It may be that with the maturing of the ASE/ASO concept, ACSE should increasingly be seen to steal only the first presentation data value of the P-CONNECT, with the others available directly to other ASE/ASOs that are sharing the application association.)

It would in principle have been possible to put the whole of the ACSE parameters as additional fields in the P-CONNECT. This would not have noticeably have increased the size of the Presentation Layer standards, but would have been regarded as a violation of the layering principles: the Presentation Layer is about negotiation of representations, and these parameters have nothing to do with that.

There are two final points on addenda to ACSE that have been produced. One permits the carriage of authentication information with the A-ASSOCIATE exchange. It is nothing more than an `OBJECT IDENTIFIER` which identifies the authentication algorithm, and a 'hole' for information or parameters associated with that algorithm. There is as yet no International Standard for such algorithms (see the discussion on security in section 11.3). The second addendum provides an A-UNITDATA (not yet used by any International Standard in 1995) primitive, carrying the same parameters as the A-ASSOCIATE, thus completing the provision for connectionless services right up to the Application Layer. This, of course, 'steals' the P-UNITDATA.

9.3   ROSE and RTSE

The reader may be wondering what else is coming. We have surely got enough tools now to build our real applications without more infrastructure? Well, not quite. ROSE and RTSE were developed specifically (both originally with CCITT Recommendation X.410) to ease the task of developing the X.400 electronic mail application. They were later seen as an important part of the OSI infrastructure, equivalent ISO standards were produced, and they were moved into the X.200 series.

ROSE (Remote Operations Service Element) has been repeatedly discussed earlier in the text. It is again quite a short Standard. It defines an ASN.1 type that is a CHOICE of four types – its messages. Protocol messages are often called **Protocol Data Units** (PDUs), a term introduced in the Basic Reference Model. The first is the RO-Invoke PDU, the second the RO-Result PDU, the third the RO-Error PDU, and the fourth the RO-Reject PDU. All except the last have 'holes' in them.

These messages are used to support the concept of sending a message that invokes some operation or processing on a remote system, and to tie together the invocation message with the eventual reply carrying the result of the operation or processing.

ROSE defines neither an abstract syntax nor an application context. It merely provides these data types with rules for their use. Once the holes are filled, an abstract syntax and an application context can be defined by the using application. Originally ROSE was ROS (Service, no Element), then it was considered to be an application service element (ASE), and we got ROSE. But with the new XALS (ASOs, CFs, etc.) how do we view ROSE? Pass!

The RO-Invoke PDU carries an OPERATION identifier, an ASN.1 data type for the arguments of that operation, and an **invocation identifier**. Invocation identifiers are used sequentially to identify the invocation of an operation within an association (ROSE messages are carried as P-DATA with an application association, although recent proposed changes are discussing use of A-UNITDATA). An operation can be invoked, then another and another and another (of the same or a different operation) before the first has completed (Figure 9.7). Results do not necessarily come back in the order of the invokes. The invocation identifier is thus used to tie together the RO-Invoke PDU and the later RO-Result PDU that carries only the invocation identifier and an ASN.1 data type carrying the results of the operation.

The ROSE model is of a complete set of operations that are related through having common error returns. Thus as well as defining a set of operations, the user defines a set of error codes (and an ASN.1 data type for each one which

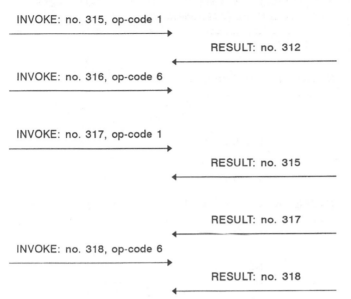

INVOKE: no. 315, op-code 1

RESULT: no. 312

INVOKE: no. 316, op-code 6

INVOKE: no. 317, op-code 1

RESULT: no. 315

RESULT: no. 317

INVOKE: no. 318, op-code 6

RESULT: no. 318

Figure 9.7 *Pattern of ROSE invokes and results.*

carries parameter information associated with it). Each operation has associated with it one or more of these errors. When an operation is invoked, there is either an RO-Reject PDU returned (which has no holes – this is used when the invocation fails for reasons independent of the operation, such as overload, or unknown operation), or an RO-Result carrying a successful completion, or an RO-Error carrying an error code and parameters. Operations can also be defined that do not report results or do not report errors.

An additional feature is the provision for **call-back**. This is quite an important feature in supporting invocation across a network. If we consider procedure calls in a programming language, it is common to have parameters passed 'by value' or 'by reference'. In the former case the value is copied into the procedure on entry, and copied out on return. In the latter case, an address is passed which can be used from within the procedure to access the parameter. Clearly only the former mechanism is directly available when the calling and called parties are separated by a network. But the 'call by reference' mechanism is an important optimization where the value is a large array and its copying would be expensive in CPU cycles or in memory. There is equally a problem if such a large array were to be transferred across the network when the called procedure is actually only going to look at and/or change a small part of it. The call-back mechanism is designed to address this problem. When the called procedure needs to make an access that would previously have been handled by a 'call by reference', it invokes a linked operation on the system from which the call came in order to perform the necessary actions. It is clearly important that such invocations identify the original invocation to which they are linked, as well as the operation they are now invoking, and ROSE makes provision for this in

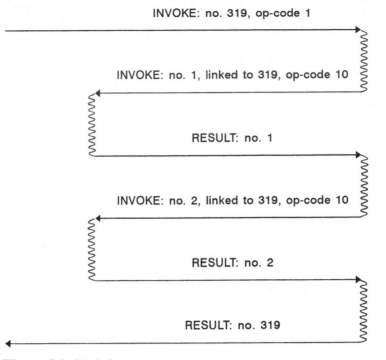

Figure 9.8 *Linked operations.*

the protocol, as well as for defining which operations are linked to which in the notation for defining operations (originally the ASN.1 OPERATION macro, now the ASN.1 OPERATION Information Object Class, described earlier). Figure 9.8 shows a possible flow of control with a set of linked operations.

ROSE provides a useful and simple piece of infrastructure, supported by a well-defined notation, for the application designer with a set of requirements that can easily be mapped into the ROSE model of invoking operations on a remote system. In fact, this is a very convenient model for a great deal of protocol design, and the combination of ROSE for the invocation model and ASN.1 for defining the data types for the arguments, results and error parameters of the operations makes specifying an application protocol in this way a relatively easy task.

Turning now to RTSE, this is also quite small and simple, and provides for the other main feature that an application designer might need to consider: how to transfer a series of documents, typically stacked up on disk, between a pair of systems with checkpointing and restart to cope with failures. This is the requirement for relaying X.400 mail, and this is the part of X.400 that has to be compatible with Teletex. Almost any reader who has managed to read this far, and has fully understood the Session Layer, could make a good attempt at writing the RTSE Standard, and would come up with the same result: there are no surprises. It uses activities in the expected way, a TWA session service,

P-TOKEN-PLEASE and P-CONTROL-GIVE to determine which end is transmitting the documents, and P-SYNC-MINOR to support checkpointing. The added value over the session service is in precisely specifying the primitives to be used and the application of checkpointing. The process is to get control, start an activity, transmit the document, issue minor syncs, end, discard or inter-rupt the activity. If crashes occur, the association can be re-established and an activity restart enables continuation from the last checkpoint.

Originally written to sit directly on top of the Session Service, it can use X.410-1984-mode or normal-mode Presentation Service. In fact A-ASSOCI-ATE formally also has an X.410-1984-mode which makes A-ASSOCIATE completely transparent (no transfer of AE-titles, etc.). This allows the fiction to be presented that RTSE works with ACSE, but in reality it is direct Presentation Layer access.

A rather more interesting point arises from the data transfer. In X.410-1984 mode, the P-DATA request/indication primitive carries what is described in ISO 8822 as 'a single presentation data value which is the value of an ASN.1 octet string'. This value is mapped transparently (in X.410-1984 mode) onto the octet string of the S-DATA user data parameter, making the Presentation Layer completely null after connection establishment in X.410-1984 mode. Con-tinuing the modelling of RTSE operation, the document to be transferred is an abstract value (typically the value of a large and complex ASN.1 data type). RTSE specifies the encoding of this value using a **syntax matching service**, which is a local implementation way of determining the negotiated transfer syntax and performing the encoding. This produces an OCTET STRING value (at least that is what RTSE assumes!), which is then fragmented to allow the issue of minor syncs at suitable points, and each fragment is passed as the octet string value for a P-DATA, with interspersed minor syncs. This same approach is continued in normal mode: RTSE encodes (using 'local magic' to determine the transfer syntax) into an OCTET STRING, which is fragmented to produce values that go into an ASN.1 OCTET STRING. This is the dreaded OCTET STRING hole, with some local magic to ensure that the end result can still make use of negotiation.

To be fair to the RTSE workers, there is a very real problem here. How do you place checkpoints in the transfer of pure information (an abstract value)? Or to put it another way, how can an abstract value, even if defined as the value of an ASN.1 type, be fragmented into smaller values so that each fragment can be sent on a separate P-DATA with a P-SYNC-MINOR between them? There is no easy answer to this question. The FTAM Standard addressed the problem by requiring the definer of a document for checkpointed transfer to specify it as a series of (small) abstract values, between any pair of which a checkpoint (minor sync) can be placed during transfer. This then allows the full power of the Presentation Layer to operate, with check-points at what are called **semant-ically meaningful points** – in other words, at points that are not dependent on the encoding – thus allowing negotiation of a different transfer syntax (because the back-up line has different QOS characteristics) when recovering from a crash. But the resulting complexity in defining the form of a document is a high price. RTSE wanted to be able to handle any (large and structured) document that can be defined using ASN.1, and in the days when BER was the only encoding rule available, the approach taken was not wholly unreasonable, but the penalty is not being able to use a different transfer syntax on the back-up line, and some slightly dubious model additions (the **syntax matching service**).

Work was proposed in early 1992 to specify once and for all an algorithm which would map any arbitrary ASN.1 type into a list of semantically meaning-ful (component parts of the ASN.1 structure) presentation data values. The pro-posal was actually made in the context of FTAM support, but it could be equally applicable to a revised RTSE, but at the time of writing this text it was not clear whether that work would proceed or not.

Thus we see that RTSE provides another important tool for application layer designers, but its use of TWA session, of activities, and the lack of real support for Presentation Layer concepts make it unattractive to many experts. Broadly, use of RTSE in new work is supported by CCITT/ITU-T workers, and opposed by ISO workers reflecting the broad nature of the views of many of those in the two groups on session activities, TWA and the Presentation Layer.

9.4   CCR and TP

A book could be written (and no doubt soon will be!) solely about CCR (Com-mitment, Concurrency and Recovery) and TP (Transaction Processing). (TP is sometimes called DTP: Distributed Transaction Processing.)

It is not therefore possible or appropriate in this text to undertake a detailed technical coverage of these standards. But in order to understand the way they fit into the architecture, the problems the architecture has to address in order to accommodate them, and the tools they provide for application designers, it is necessary to give a brief introduction to what these standards are about.

We have got the Session Layer tools. We have got the Presentation Layer and ASN.1. We have got ROSE and RTSE. What other problem is there that could sensibly be solved by another ASE Standard?

What we are addressing in this section is an application that needs to operate with more than two systems. Consider Figure 9.9. You as the application designer have to specify a financial services application protocol that will enable system A which is accessing a bank B to debit an account on B with a million dol-lars, and at the same time to credit an account on bank C with the million dollars. You design a simple protocol where you simultaneously open up a pair of as-sociations, and send on each one a ROS-Invoke (or design an exchange of ASN.1-defined messages, whichever you prefer), on the association to B request-ing a debit and on that to C requesting a credit. B replies saying: 'OK, done', and C replies saying: 'Sorry, the account does not exist with this bank'. And a

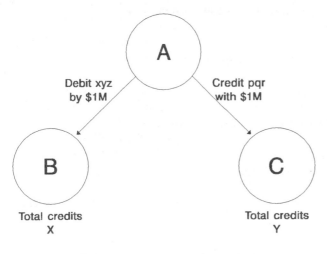

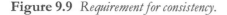

Constraint: X + Y remains constant

Figure 9.9 *Requirement for consistency.*

bulldozer goes through your communications lines to the outside world. The banking system is now short of a million dollars, and nobody is getting any interest on it! This is almost but not quite as bad as the situation where C did the credit but B refused the debit, and before your line was repaired somebody drew out the million dollars from C!

This is just one of many possible applications where there is an implicit or explicit **consistency condition** to be met which goes across the systems involved. In this case, the condition is that the amount of money in the banking system as a whole should not change as a result of this transfer operation. Database designers on stand-alone systems are used to this problem. A database is nothing more than a large structured file except for one thing: the software supporting it maintains **integrity constraints** (consistency conditions) across the entire database. In the better systems, these are explicitly specified to the database management system as part of the definition of the database, and application programs (perhaps written in Cobol) cannot cause the conditions to be violated, at least as seen by an outside observer. In practice, the Cobol program may need to change many parts of the database to perform its functions and leave the database in a consistent state, and it can only do one operation at a time, just as our application A can only really do one operation at a time. If only one operation is performed, the consistency is violated. Database systems introduced the concept of **atomic actions**: a set of operations by the Cobol program, with a known beginning and a known end, which (to an outside observer) were either all performed (leaving the database in a consistent state), or none were performed.

In order to achieve this, we have the following requirements.

- The atomic action has to be delimited (the reader will recognize that in communication this looks like a candidate for a major sync or an activity exchange).
- The database management software has to be concerned with commitment (will it commit itself to accepting the changes the Cobol program has made, or will it rollback to the start of the atomic action?)
- There also has to be concern for concurrency (some form of lock had better be applied to prevent other users from accessing those parts of the database affected by changes not yet committed, or from changing data that was used in developing the changes being made).
- Finally, we have to consider recovery (if the complete computer system crashes, then on restarting it, the atomic action had better be rolled back).

These key points – Commitment, Concurrency and Recover – give us the title of the Standard, usually known simply as **CCR**.

How would the basic CCR exchange between A and B and A and C work? CCR is concerned with a tree of activity, originated by A. It may have one, two or more subordinates (two – B and C – in our example), and these may in turn have further subordinates. Using CCR, A issues C-BEGIN (carried on P-SYNC-MAJOR) to B and to C to indicate that what is to follow is not actually to be done (committed, made visible) yet. It signals the start of an atomic action. A then conducts an application-specific exchange with B and C. The details of this exchange are quite outside the CCR Standard, possibly invoking ROSE operations, possibly using P-DATA, possibly using RTSE ... Whoops! Not RTSE: RTSE uses activities, and we can't put major syncs round activities, only inside them, remember? Once A has told B and C what it would like done, it then asks B and C if they are prepared to commit to the changes by issuing a C-PREPARE (mapped to P-TYPED-DATA). At this stage, A has not lost control. It has not itself committed to the actions, it is merely seeking to determine if the actions can be committed at all sites. If all subordinates, having used CCR in a similar way with any subordinates they might have, reply saying: 'Yes, I am prepared to COMMIT the changes' (the C-READY primitive, carried on P-TYPED-DATA again – the data token might be at the wrong end in TWA), then A will issue the CCR C-COMMIT to all subordinates, which maps to P-SYNC-MAJOR, is a confirmed service, and both orders commitment and obtains confirmation that commitment has indeed occurred. Alternatively, if one or more subordinates said: 'No, we want to ROLLBACK this action' (the C-ROLLBACK primitive, mapped onto P-RESYNCHRONIZE), then either the atomic action being attempted must be modified by using another subordinate, or by some further exchange (if it is not too late) with other subordinates, or else a C-ROLLBACK must be issued to all subordinates. This latter is an example of an MACF (Multiple Association Control Function) rule. TP, discussed below, imposes the MACF rule that a rollback on one association has to result in a rollback on all others up and down the tree. CCR is not quite so strict, and imposes the minimum necessary MACF rules to ensure that the atomicity is not lost.

This is often called **two-phase commitment**, and involves a minimum of two confirmed exchanges: in Phase I, there is a 'start atomic action' message followed by an exchange of messages defining the action precisely. These conclude with a reply saying 'OK, I am prepared to commit' or 'Won't'. In Phase II (assuming an 'OK' was received in Phase I) there is a 'Do it now' with a 'Done response'.

Notice that while we cannot prevent bulldozers from going through lines when commitment (or rollback) commands have got through to some but not all systems, this will not leave the universe in an inconsistent state. It will merely (!) mean that concurrency controls (locks) will be present on some systems while released on others until the recovery procedures have been applied and the atomic action can be correctly completed. Unfortunately, for some (but not all) applications, it can be more damaging to keep concurrency controls in place for long periods of time (for example, while waiting 48 hours for a spare part to be flown from the USA to repair a broken system A). It can also happen that systems not only fall over, but their disks can be wiped clean, in which case the CCR protocol will not be honoured and recovery will never be instituted. (The whole CCR concept is based on the updating of what is called **atomic action data** – data that survives a crash: in other words, data stored on disk – at critical points in the protocol exchange. Possible loss of such data is recognized, but represents a complete breakdown of CCR.) In these circumstances it is necessary to allow systems that have locks in place (have offered commitment but not yet received any order to commit or rollback) to either commit or to rollback and release the locks. This is called a **heuristic decision** because it requires some (possibly human) intelligence to determine whether, for this application, rollback or commitment is most likely to be ordered, and which wrong guess would be the most damaging, or whether locks should be kept in place anyway!

The history of CCR was very chequered. It was originally developed to support JTM (Job Transfer and Manipulation), the work starting in about 1980 and maturing in about 1984. The initial work was done in the management group of OSI, because CCR was thought to be about managing multiple associations. As soon as it was registered as a Draft Proposal (the very first Draft Proposal from the management group!) it was taken away from them and given to the group looking after ACSE, as CCR was seen to be another CASE.

Shortly thereafter, IBM announced the LU6.2 sync point verb as part of SNA. This rather curiously sounding term is actually more or less synonymous with CCR in terms of functionality of the exchange and what it is trying to do. This resulted in a comparison between LU6.2 sync point and CCR, a greater concern with heuristic commitment, and a slight destabilization of what was very nearly a full Standard. This, however, was nothing compared with later developments.

A New Work Item Proposal was made and accepted that ISO should develop a Standard for Distributed Transaction Processing (DTP or TP). At the time the precise relationship to CCR was unclear, but whereas CCR had been developed with a group whose attendance rarely exceed a dozen people, the TP group had an attendance of close to 100, most of them with a good knowledge of LU6.2!

The TP Standard provides a gloss or interface to CCR. It 'steals' the CCR primitives, and provides some added value with user data on the CCR primitives and by direct exchanges. For example, CCR is concerned solely with a single atomic action. TP allows notification that, following commitment to the current action, another will immediately begin (a chained transaction), or not (unchained). TP provides a single set of service primitives that allow an application to control an atomic action through a single service access point, mapping each one onto as many C-service primitives as are needed (one for each association). TP steals all primitives, and provides a complete service, including a TP-DATA primitive. TP also allows exchanges within a tree structure without using CCR (no guarantees of atomicity), and supports TWA and TWS exchanges explicitly. The TP work resulted in a serious destabilization of CCR, with a major change to the recovery procedures (introduction of something called the **presumed abort paradigm**), and a request for the introduction of a new synchronization service from Session (acceded to) to replace the use of major sync to start an atomic action – the TP group was powerful!

The end result is a TP Standard that has enabled a prominent computer vendor to offer a product that allows a Cobol program to use an operating system interface providing the functionality of the TP service primitives to communicate with other systems. One branch of the atomic action tree can be using TP over CCR over the OSI stack, and another the vendor's own protocol, and the Cobol program does not know the difference. Neat?

It is worth talking a little about TP-DATA. The TP group recognized the Presentation Layer concepts, and the value of the separation of abstract and transfer syntax, but were concerned that small groups (or even individuals) wanting to write Cobol programs to use TP would not have access to object identifiers, nor perhaps to tools supporting the use of ASN.1. They are therefore included as part of the TP work Part 6: Unstructured Data Transfer. This was designed for those who were content for the COBOL programs to exchange (using TP-DATA) information that was simply the value of an arbitrary length octet string (with any syntax conversion performed by the application). It defined this as the (only) parameter of the TP-DATA, and therefore formally closed all the 'holes', making this no longer an ASE/ASO, but a fully defined SASE-like Standard. This Part allocates an abstract syntax object identifier for the values of this octet string, a transfer syntax object identifier for the transfer syntax that contains an identical bit-pattern for the transfer syntax, and an application context object identifier for the resulting complete protocol.

Putting aside the Unstructured Data Transfer Part, there is a lot of interest in combining the use of CCR/TP with other ASE specifications, particularly ROSE/RPC, FTAM, and so on, giving practical reality to many of the XALS considerations.

9.5   Remote Procedure Call (RPC)

RPC has already been briefly mentioned. In some ways it bears the same relationship to ROSE that TP bears to CCR. It adds little to the underlying model and exchanges, but puts a big gloss on the interface and access to the services.

At the beginning of 1992, RPC was still at the Committee Draft level (the first stage of balloting). Its major technical content was the RPC Interface Definition Notation (IDN). This provided a notation broadly equivalent to (a subset of) ASN.1, but somewhat closer to the sort of notations used in programming languages. The main hope and intent of the effort was to encourage the provision, within programming languages, of support for the invocation of RPC calls to support the calling of procedures in one machine from programs in another, possibly written in different programming languages.

The Standard specifies that when an interface is defined, an object identifier is specified for it. The interface definition maps into ASN.1 data structures and ROSE operations in a defined way, and the object identifier maps into the necessary abstract syntax object identifier. An application context object identifier is defined for Basic RPC within the Standard. RPC was the first ASN.1 user group to take a serious interest in the ASN.1 Packed Encoding Rules, seeing them as perhaps as the encoding rules to be made mandatory for implementations of RPC.

9.6   Management standards framework

The work on management in OSI was again one of the areas that were begun at about the same time as the reference model, and has now grown to an extensive and still growing set of standards.

A detailed treatment of OSI management standards is outside the scope of this text, but the architecture and overall approach is covered here.

The earliest versions of the Reference Model spoke about Application Management, Systems Management, and Layer Management, but there was a very limited amount of text discussing their differences, and for many years the management working group tried to put some flesh on the bones. What exactly was OSI management trying to manage? What was the difference between these forms of management? There, was, in the beginning, the view among some parties that anything that was not a simple interchange between two systems was 'management'. There was also the view that OSI management was about developing management protocols for anything that might need managing over a network. This was a very broad brief!

We have already noted that the CCR work was originally considered 'management', and was progressed to a Draft Proposal (the original name for Committee Drafts) by the management working group. Even today, the management working group is actually two almost independent groups, with little overlap of membership; the first is concerned with real management standards, and the second with the X.500 Directory standards. We are discussing only the former work here.

It was as late as 1984 that significant progress started to be made in OSI management, and this stemmed directly from agreement in two important areas: the Management Framework (eventually published as Part 4 of the Basic Reference Model), and Common Management Information Service and Protocol (CMIS/CMIP).

The Management Framework delineated the scope of OSI management with the very important piece of text: 'OSI management is concerned with the standards needed to manage the OSI resource.' In other words, the protocols to be developed were to be concerned only with the management of those parts of a computer system concerned with the implementation of OSI functionality and standards, not with such things as registering users on systems, access to and transfer of student records, distribution of general operating system or applications software, or anything else that might be described as a 'management' activity. Of course, it has turned out that the protocols developed for managing the OSI resource (for example, for controlling the operation of a network layer router) are actually pretty good at controlling the operation of things like a modern computer-controlled radar dish or a telescope, but requirements specific to such applications were excluded from consideration.

The Management Framework also introduced the very important concept of the **Management Information Base** (the MIB), and put to rest once and for all the distinction between layer management and systems management. (All this in a six-page document!)

So ... what is the MIB? The idea is that an implementation of a layer protocol will have a variety of pieces of information associated with it, both dynamic and static, both controlling its actions and reflecting its state. For example, the handler of a connection-oriented protocol will probably have some limit on the number of simultaneous connections it can handle. Moreover, there may be an absolute limit based on memory size, but there may also be a more flexible limit which could sensibly be large at night and low in the day time. It will probably have a number of states, for example 'running normally', 'closing down' (not accepting new connections) and 'closed down'. There may be variables that affect the way it behaves, for example accept connections from any source, or accept connections only from a priority list. There may be events occurring within it, for example failure of an outgoing connection attempt (perhaps subdivided by defined failure reasons). These events maybe could be logged, or at least counted, if the implementation supports this. The concept of the MIB, then, is of a model of the total information that reflects or results from the operation of the OSI implementation on a system, or controls that implementation. It is specifically not the prescription of a real database on disk. The way the MIB information is held, modified and obtained (when it is being read) is a local implementation matter, and may involve direct interaction with layer implementation code and in-core state, or may involve indirect communication via a real database. Finally, the MIB will potentially contain information that

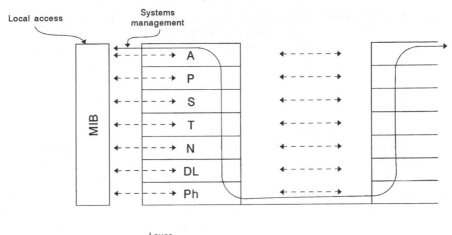

Figure 9.10 *The Management Information Base (MIB).*

would relate to almost any conceivable implementation of an OSI protocol, together with information that is very specific to a particular implementation. The precise definition of MIB information, either standardized or vendor-specific, was a growing trade in the late 1980s and early 1990s.

Once the MIB concept is in place, we can now make what at first sight seems to be an almost arbitrary answer to the questions: 'What is layer management? What is system management?' (Figure 9.10). We define them as follows.

- Access to MIB information by management protocol in a particular layer is restricted to those parts of the MIB that relate to the implementation of protocols defined for that layer, and is called **layer management**, and the necessary protocols have to be defined by the Working Group responsible for that layer.
- A protocol operating through the full OSI stack (involving a Systems Management Application Entity), to be defined by the management working group, can access any part of the MIB, and is called **systems management**.

This was probably the most controversial part of the Management Framework, but it stuck. Interestingly, in the early 1980s there was a lot of concern that Network Layer 'boxes' (routers, X.25 switches, and the like) should not have to implement protocol layers above those needed for their main function (the Network Layer down) in order to be managed. In the 1990s, with the possible exception of link layer protocols to manage bridges on local area networks, there is almost universal acceptance in OSI that management control of almost everything will be by systems management (layer 7 protocols), and there is very little interest within the layer groups in defining Layer Management protocols. Efforts were rather concentrated on defining those parts of the MIB that were amenable to international standardization. After all, if the separation out of Transport and Session and Presentation functions was relevant and important for general application standardization, why should it be less important for exchanges related to management?

Where, then, does that leave **application management**? There was only one real piece of work started that could be described as 'application management', and that was abandoned (formally, merely suspended) in the mid-1980s. This was called **Control of Application Process Groups**. The main interest in progressing it came from Japan, and there was generally a fairly widespread lack of interest in and/or understanding of the work. The idea is roughly as follows: suppose you are the implementor (a mere user, not a computer vendor) of a new (OSI) (application) protocol that involves exchanges between four (say) systems. How do you test it? Or maybe later run it? The answer in the early 1980s was that you would line up four dumb terminals on your desk, login to your four systems, invoke the necessary code in the foreground, and monitor them to see what status messages they generated, and whether they 'fell over'. Actually, apart from using one intelligent workstation with four windows, you couldn't do much better in the early 1990s! Now suppose the resources this application process group needed prohibited running in the foreground, and required scheduling as background tasks by the operating system. What then? This was the problem being addressed.

The approach was to postulate that each Open System would contain an **Application Management Application Entity** (AMAE), and that the implementor would first define (through his/her local system and protocol exchanges between the AMAEs) an **application process group**: the set of his/her programs that needed to be run simultaneously. He/she would then request from his/her local system that his/her application process group be activated. After appropriate scheduling negotiation between the AMAEs, the relevant programs would start to run, and would be monitored by the local AMAE, with status messages and 'it's fallen over' messages returned to the AMAE where the activation was initiated, and hence to the implementor. That is about as far as it got. The work was abandoned for lack of international interest, and there has been no other OSI management work in the application management area.

Let us now turn to CMIS/CMIP. Given the concept of the MIB, and of systems management, we clearly need a protocol to enable remote systems to read and write elements of the MIB. This work, in the late 1980s, adopted the **object orientation** paradigm. We talk about **classes of managed objects** (for example, the class of all connection-oriented layer protocol handlers), and subclasses (for example, the network layer connection-oriented protocol handlers). The object-oriented concept of class inheritance can now be applied: there are some properties that the subclass inherits from the definition of the superclass, and there are some that are specific to the subclass. What sort of things do we want to define about a class of managed objects? Well, there will be specific instances of objects of that class. And perhaps we can talk about creating and destroying such instances as a way of modelling the switching on and off of a communications capability in some system. A managed object will have attributes that can be read (to determine its current state) or set (to affect its operation). Reading or setting these attributes will require the transfer of a value of some ASN.1 type specific to that attribute of that object. From time to time certain events might occur related to that managed object, and such events might be logged or counted in various ways. Such logs and counters might need to be created and destroyed. Finally, the occurrence of certain events, or a counter passing a certain threshold, might require that an alarm be generated and sent to some nominated system that was managing the system where the alarm occurred.

With this model, we clearly need a protocol to create and destroy instances of managed object classes, to read and set attributes, to create, read, reset and destroy logs and counters, and to handle the reporting of alarms. Moreover, we can start to define attribute classes (for example, those concerned with starting up, running and shutting down) that are likely to be relevant and useful for a number of classes of managed objects. Thus begins a whole range of Standardization activity, initially with the relatively simple CMIS/CMIP.

How are we going to identify managed object classes, instances of them, their attributes, etc? I hope the reader will by now have learnt to answer 'With ASN.1 OBJECT IDENTIFIERs, of course!' When the first draft of CMIP was produced in the mid-1980s, it was about half-a-dozen pages long, most of it an ASN.1 definition, and just about every other line was an OBJECT IDENTIFIER data type (identifying an object or an attribute) and an ANY (to hold the data type for writing to or reading an attribute, or associated with an event). It was full of 'holes'! And at this time not a single actual object or attribute had been defined! Note also that CMIP's use of communications is through a ROSE OPERATIONs macro: CMIS (sometimes now called CMISE – SE for Service Element) is an ASE that uses the ROSE ASE.

An awful lot has happened since the early work. With this model, there is clearly a need for a notation to aid the definition of managed object classes and their attributes (what is to fill the 'holes' in CMIS/CMIP). Other protocols would have used the ASN.1 macro to provide this notation, but by then this was in disrepute, and English language was used to specify **GDMO** (Generic Definition of Managed Objects), the notation to be used. When the Information Object Class concept was introduced into ASN.1, work by the Japanese demonstrated that it was 'man enough' to take over from GMDO, but of course by then GMDO was firmly established in this role, and take-over did not occur.

There is now a very large amount of text in a series of OSI standards concerned with extensions and specializations and additional functions broadly building on this model, and on the structure and definition of MIB information. There is also a growing body of MIB definitions, particularly related to the management of Network Layer functionality (Network Management), but the reader should note the remark made earlier: CMIS/CMIP can be used to remotely control any piece of computer-controlled equipment, provided only that the control procedure can be adequately described as the reading and setting of attributes, the recording of events, the generation of alarms, and so on.

In the early 1990s, after previously ignoring the management work, ITU-T as it then was became seriously interested and the work has now been included in ITU-T Recommendations as the X.700 series. (The X.600 series is used for the many Recommendations that specify how to provide the OSI Network Service over the many different real-world communications links.)

A final comment is needed in this section on **CMOT** and **SNMP**. The TCP/IP suite had little by way of management functionality before the ISO work began, and it imported OSI concepts and definitions at an early stage. CMOT is **CM**IS **O**ver **T**CP/IP. It is the specification of how to carry the CMIP protocol over TCP/IP for the purposes of managing TCP/IP network boxes. There was little implementation interest in it up to the early 1990s. SNMP is **Simple Network Management Protocol**, and is a simple ASN.1-defined protocol using the OSI Managed Object and MIB concepts. There are also a lot of MIB definitions within the TCP/IP suite. In the early 1990s, there was probably more use of SNMP than CMIS/CMIP to control network boxes, but the ongoing standardization effort related to OSI, and particularly the inclusion of work related to security and to management domains, and the introduction of the X.700 series are expected to change this situation.

10
Real applications – at last!

10.1   Message Handling Systems

The X.400 series of Recommendations (also ISO/IEC 10021) is a large and complex piece of work. The collected set of ASN.1 definitions stretches to some 5000 lines. There are a number of separate protocols within the suite. The basic provision is for the exchange between **Message Handling Systems** (electronic mail systems) of electronic mail in a Standard form, but these X.400 'messages' can be not only messages from a human to another human (so-called **interpersonal messages**), but also formatted messages from one computer to another to support exchange of trade-related messages (generally called **electronic data interchange** or EDI). Even for the interpersonal messaging system (IPMS), the messages go rather beyond old-fashioned electronic mail (which was in the 1980s and for much of the 1990s confined to ASCII text), being capable of carrying a very wide variety of so-called **body parts**, paving the way for multi-media messages. There are complete books on X.400 alone, and we shall be covering here only aspects that are of general architectural interest.

The model contains a **User Agent** (UA) (think of it as an implementation on a personal computer or workstation) that prepares a piece of mail for sending. The mail is an ASN.1 data type which defines the form of header fields corresponding roughly to the letter heading on a normal letter, but also including (optionally) things like references to other letters that this one obsoletes, expiry dates, and so on. This so-called inter-personal message contains holes that can carry one or more Body Parts. In the earliest version, a small number of Body Parts of different types were hard-wired into the Standard, but with the maturing of the ASN.1 Object Identifier concept, a so-called **Extended Body Part** can be defined (with an ASN.1 macro in the late 1980s). The macro collects an object identifier and an ASN.1 data type, but these holes are really presentation data value holes, capable of holding spreadsheets or wordprocessor files, as has been discussed earlier (section 8.2.1), and the definition of Extended Body Parts would actually have been better cast as the definition of an abstract and transfer syntax for such objects. The set of header fields in the IPMS were again hard-wired in the original Standard, but later became ASN.1 data type holes, using EXTERNAL and a macro to define new object identifiers and data types to support additional headers.

Early in 1992 implementations of User Agents were beginning to appear, but there was still a lack of international agreement on object identifiers for Extended Body Parts that were vendor specific, particularly image formats that were *de facto* standards, spreadsheets from popular packages and common word processing formats. One would expect such object identifiers to be allocated by the third-party vendor of these image, spreadsheet or word processing packages, and distributed with the documentation of those packages, but at the start of the 1990s this had not yet begun to happen.

Once the Interpersonal Message (IPM) has been constructed (with any necessary body parts), it needs to be submitted to a **Message Transfer Agent** (MTA) for delivery to a remote MTA. MTAs are simple relay systems that use the so-called P1 protocol to transfer mail between them. The P1 protocol involves the definition (as an ASN.1 data type) of fields that correspond to envelope information in normal mail (although again with a great deal more richness and power). It is only the fields of the P1 protocol that are used by MTA implementations for relaying between MTAs to transfer the mail to a destination MTA. The relaying of these data structures is a simple and direct use of RTSE, which was originally developed for precisely this purpose). This P1 data structure has one major 'hole' which carries the contents of the message. In the original work the contents were either an interpersonal message, or various notifications of receipt or non-receipt coming back after a message had reached its destination. (The envelope itself contained provision for notification of delivery or non-delivery to the intended destination.) In 1990 the role of X.400 was considerably extended with provision to carry in this hole not just Interpersonal Messages intended for human beings, but also EDIFACT, X.12 and TDI (see earlier discussion of EDIFACT in section 8.3) messages intended to be generated and processed by computers. Thus the electronic mail facility was extended from human–human communication to computer–computer communication. These extensions were published as F.435 and X.435.

How does the IPMS get from a UA implementation to an MTA? In the 1984 version there was a ROSE-based protocol (P3) that allowed mail to be submitted or collected, but this was never implemented, and a UA was typically part of some MTA implementation, and used local interfaces to embed the IPMS protocol as a P1 contents. In 1988 (further extended from 1988 to 1992), the concept of a message store was introduced. With this concept, an MTA may be implemented alone on a system, may have collocated UAs in the old way, or may (and this is the direction implementations are taking) have supported on the same system a **message store**. When messages are to be sent, a UA uses another ROSE-based protocol (a set of ROSE operations, called the P7 protocol) to deposit the message in a local message store and to request its transmission. At the receiving end, the message goes into the message store. It is here that the value of the IPM headers becomes apparent. The message store is a very rich and active structure. The P7 protocol allows a UA to browse the messages that are waiting for him/her, making selections based on any of the header fields of the IPM definition. Moreover, the message store can be requested, through P7, to selectively (based on header fields) forward messages, delete messages, put messages in particular folders (group them together for easier inspection), and so on. Actions can be set up that are automatically applied when a new message arrives at the message store, as well as being performed by direct interaction from the UA.

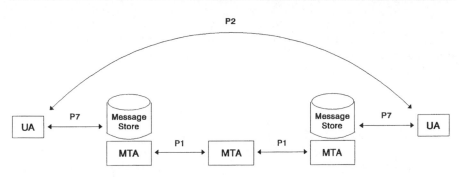

Figure 10.1 *Message Handling System (MHS) components and interactions.*

Figure 10.1 shows the model of interactions within X.400. There are still a lot of features that have not even been touched on in the above discussion. Two are worth a brief mention here.

The first is interaction between X.400 and other services. In the 1984 work, there was a lot of effort put in to define the ability for a piece of X.400 mail to be sent to a suitable MTA and then sent out over either Teletex or Telex. This did not appear as a PTT service generally. More interestingly, in 1988, text was added to introduce the concept of **physical delivery**: once implemented, I could send from my office or home PC in the UK a piece of X.400 mail to my aged grandmother living at the top of a mountain in the USA, and have it printed out at the local post office at the bottom of the mountain. The local postman will then trudge up the mountain, deliver the mail, trudge down, and trigger the sending of a **delivery notification**. The specification carefully states that the printing of the mail is to be upside down, the letter automatically folded and placed in a 'window envelope', so that the postman cannot see the confidential information that I am on my death-bed. Unfortunately my aged grandmother can only reply by an ordinary mail letter, and by the time I receive that, I am dead! In fact a very similar system (using vendor-specific protocols, not X.400) allowed parents in the USA with home PCs attached to E-mail systems to send mail electronically to their sons serving in the Gulf War. On arrival in the Gulf, it was printed off and then physically delivered.

The second area to discuss is security features. X.400 was one of the first standards to introduce (in 1988) a very strong level of support for security features. These were largely based on the use of so-called **public key encryption** techniques, and the X.500 series (published for the first time in 1988) provided substantial support for the distribution of the necessary encryption keys. The X.400 features broadly covered three areas: confidentiality (preventing unauthorized reading of part or all of a message), authentication (being able to guarantee who had sent it), and a variety of 'proof of' exchanges. In particular, the UA can request from the message store/MTA a **proof of submission**, which is a package of (encrypted) information provided by the message store/MTA that the UA could take to a third-party judge (and which the UA cannot forge) to prove that a particular message was indeed submitted. Similarly, there are **proofs** of delivery exchanges. In the early 1990s, there was a lot of implementation interest in the security features of X.400, but significant implementations had not been widely deployed, and X.500 support for the distribution of public keys had not yet been implemented.

10.2   Directories (X.500)

While X.500 (ISO/IEC 9594) is not as big as X.400 (it is four years behind: the first Recommendation was 1988, while for X.400 it was 1984; it may be that by 1996, they will be equally large!), it is still a substantial specification, and there are again complete books written about this alone.

From a protocol and conceptual point of view, X.500 is a very simple set of Recommendations. It is nothing more than a series of ROSE OPERATION definitions, with a number of ASN.1 data type 'holes' in the operations. The most significant set of 'holes' are those used in the X.500 name, the so-called Distinguished Name, which is used for looking up information.

The X.500 system is essentially a single world-wide distributed database in which a bundle of information (an **object entry**) resides as a master copy on some computer system somewhere in the world. The object entry is nothing more than an unordered collection of ASN.1 data type holes: a set of ASN.1 data types, each of which has an object identifier to identify its type and a data type to hold its value. Again, there are ASN.1 macros defined to support the definition of the set of attributes of an object entry. A small number of attributes (like telephone number) have been defined, and object identifiers allocated, within the base Standard, but a particular object entry is neither required to contain these attributes, nor prevented from containing any other arbitrary attributes.

How does a remote system get information from an object entry? A key part of an object entry is a set of attributes which must be present called the **distinguished name** of the object entry. Thus an X.500 name is actual just a list of ASN.1 data type holes! However, the attributes used to form the distinguished name are required to conform to a more specific structure, and a typical X.500 name would look like that shown in Figure 10.2. Here the parts before the equals sign are identifying the type of the attribute, and in transfer are represented by an ASN.1 OBJECT IDENTIFIER, while the parts after the equals sign are the **value**, and are carried in the corresponding ASN.1 data type (frequently an ASN.1 PrintableString data type). Much concern has been expressed about the character set to be used for attribute values in X.500 (remembering that it is providing a world-wide service), which had not been finally resolved

@C = GB@O = Salford University@OU = Information Technology Institute
@CN = John larmouth@

Figure 10.2 *A typical X.500 name.*

by the mid-1990s. This name structure is used to navigate the so-called **Directory Information Tree** or **Directory Information Base** (the terms are interchangeable). For an artist's impression (a fictitious but possible example), see Figures 10.3 and 10.4. I receive the name shown in Figure 10.3 on the back of someone's business card, and go to my local friendly X.500 implementation, type in the name, and say 'Find dog, find!'. The system at Salford gives a gulp, and says 'Never heard of France, or of IBM, but I will ask a computer I know about that looks after a lot of object entries which contain information about the UK academic community, and knows about the location of others.' It formulates an X.500 message (ROSE operation) and makes the enquiry ([1] in the figure). Still no luck, but that system knows about another system run by our friendly PTT (British Telecom (BT)), and **chains** the request to the BT system ([2] in the figure). And now we are beginning to hit pay dirt: BT will not make

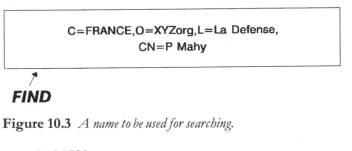

Figure 10.3 *A name to be used for searching.*

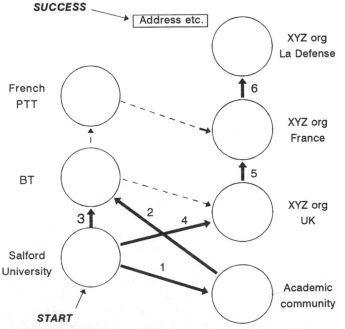

Figure 10.4 *The search process.*

calls on our behalf, but information has been lodged with it that the French PTT is a good place to go to find out about the location of object entries beginning with 'C=FRANCE'. Moreover, 'OU=IBM' has been registered in almost all countries, and the BT system has also been told that enquiries about 'C=XXX, OU=IBM' should be referred to a particular computer system in Sale, a town near Salford, for a wide range of XXX. The academic community machine thinks it has now done enough for Salford, and returns the information gleaned so far, together with the address of the system it got it from, so Salford has gained further **knowledge** about Directory Systems and the names they can handle and can cache that to speed future searches. The Salford system could now **multi-cast** to the French PTT and to Sale, but has enough sense to try the local call first ([3] in Figure 10.4). And now we have hit pay dirt. Sale has a leased line to La Defense, the IBM headquarters in Paris, where a PC on the top floor contains the master copy of the entry I am trying to reach. Whoops: I mistyped the name – it should have been Ma*u*hy, not Mahy. Never mind, fuzzy match, the hackers' paradise! (In fact, X.500 does include use of fuzzy matching, but not in relation to specific enquiries quoting a distinguished name, so a little bit of artistic licence was used in the above!)

That little scenario has tried to illustrate in very broad terms the navigation of X.500 using the name. In fact, the master copies of object entries will normally be grouped together in groupings broadly related to name structure, but this is not a requirement. In principle, every single object entry could be located on a different computer system, and X.500 would still successfully navigate to it. Following the work in the early 1990s, **shadowing arrangements** can be set up for an object entry such that whenever it is changed, the changes are automatically distributed to a tree structure of **shadows**. Thus if system A frequently needs to refer to some object entry, it will attempt to position itself on the shadow tree for that entry. If it infrequently refers to it, it will navigate to the entry (perhaps caching the location of the entry) on each reference to the information.

There are two sorts of OSI-related information that X.500 might support. The first is the mapping from application-entity-titles to presentation service access point addresses, and the second is the (secure) distribution of **certificates** containing public keys that can be used to support security features in other applications, such as those present in X.400. In fact, the early prototype implementations of X.500 that were deployed in the early 1990s were used for anything but these purposes, storage and distribution of telephone directories being one common use.

The whole question of the eventual role of X.500 was not resolved by 1995, with a number of things it could be used for remaining contentious and being handled by other mechanisms. One area of discussion was the extent to which the holes in object entries should become presentation data value holes to support the storage and retrieval of more general material (images, video, voice, and so on) as attributes of object entries. This potentially brings X.500 into the area of a general wide-area information service, bringing it into potential conflict with the TCP/IP protocol of that name: Wide Area Information Service

(WAIS), whose use developed during the 1990s. It is important to note here, however, that WAIS is oriented to retrieval of documents using natural language and full-text indexing of the documents to be retrieved, while X.500 is based on providing a very formalized name for the object entry that is being retrieved. Thus for many purposes X.500 will be unable to compete with WAIS, while WAIS is already used for purposes such as access to telephone directories that X.500 experts consider to be a potential application for X.500.

Another question which arose in the early 1990s (and was not resolved when this text was written) was concerned with the trader for ODP (Open Distributed Processing). One of the concepts of ODP is that of **location independence**: access to some piece of functionality does not require knowledge of where in the network that functionality is being provided. To support this, the **trader** concept envisages a protocol which will enable a package to **export** its interface (announcing the availability of its services and their location), and a potential user then to request and to **import** that interface prior to connecting to and using those services. There were some experts that contended that X.500 could be used as the basis for building trader support.

10.3   Remote Database Access (RDA)

The work on RDA has a somewhat different focus from X.500. Here we are not talking about a globally distributed database, but rather about the somewhat simpler concept of remote access to a single computer system database.

The primary interest here is the infrastructure on which RDA is built. In particular, it uses ROSE for its operations and TP to provide atomicity. The Standard defines a Generic RDA which again is full of holes, and an SQL Specialization to produce an implementable Standard. (SQL – Structured Query Language – is the name for the ISO Standard for relational databases.) In early drafts, an ASN.1 macro was defined to fill the Generic RDA hole to produce the specializations, but when ASN.1 macros found disfavour, this was replaced by use of ordinary English.

10.4   File Transfer, Access and Management (FTAM)

FTAM was one of the earliest standards to be developed, and was mature long before ROSE and RTSE were discussed. Its development really dated back to the original thinking of monolithic specifications in the Application Layer, with no ASE concept. It almost became an International Standard without using A-ASSOCIATE (direct use of P-CONNECT), but at a relatively late date it was modified to use A-ASSOCIATE as the sole user of A-ASSOCIATE, using the nested service primitives model. It introduces a complete range of service primitives, including F-INITIALIZE (mapped on to A-ASSOCIATE), F-DATA (mapped on to P-DATA), and F-P-ABORT (to reflect an upcoming

A-P-ABORT) as well as FTAM-specific service primitives to open and close files for access (F-OPEN, F-READ, F-CLOSE) or (added much later) to transfer complete files (F-GET-FILE and F-PUT-FILE).

It was built on use of P-SYNC-MINOR and P-RESYNCHRONIZE for bulk data transfer, integrated into the main FTAM specification. There was an attempt made late in the development of FTAM to extract the data transfer text and to establish a New Work Item to develop a Standard for Bulk Data Transfer which FTAM could then be re-written to use, and which could be used by other standards, but by then work on RTSE was in progress, and the New Work Item proposal was turned down. Still later, there was a major controversy to try to get FTAM to modify its bulk data transfer phase to use the activity functional unit, and hence to align itself with (and/or to use) RTSE. This attempt also failed, so FTAM remains with FTAM-specific text, which is not usable by any one else, providing more or less the same functionality as RTSE. Many observers attribute the failure of this attempt to get FTAM to adopt the use of activities as the reason why CCITT/ITU-T has never (to this day) published the FTAM specification as a CCITT/ITU-T Recommendation, but has rather developed the DTAM (Document Transfer, Access and Management) and DFR (Document Filing and Retrieval) Standards, both of which use activities, and both of which have functionality strongly overlapping that of FTAM. None the less, in the early 1990s there was much more implementation interest and deployment of systems for FTAM than for both DTAM and DFR taken together.

The development of FTAM raised the big question: 'What is a file?' In the file transfer protocols developed in the 1970s (prior to OSI), the answer was relatively clear: it was either a string of binary octets or a series of lines of text which were transferable either as ASCII or as EBCDIC. In the 1980s, particularly with the focus on file access, the model of a file was more difficult to agree. In particular, the ability to read and write (using FTAM) parts of the picture represented by a Computer Graphics Metafile (a standard for storing computer generated pictures) or of similarly structured files was one of the aims. Moreover, reading and writing parts of files when the material was written to a server by one system (with one form of representation of structures and characters) but read back by another with a different representation was considered important. This is broadly covered by the Presentation Layer concepts of abstract and transfer syntax, but meant that specifying the part of a file to be read or written had to be done in terms of the abstract structure, not in terms of the string of octets in some particular encoding of that structure. This is a similar (but not quite the same) issue to that of positioning checkpoints in the transfer of a file discussed in the section on RTSE (section 9.3).

In order to progress the FTAM protocol, then, there needed to be agreement on what constitutes a filestore, in terms of the nature of a file's contents, any other associated attributes (such as the form of a filename, the date it was created and last read, access controls, and so on), and the nature of the directory structure. There was no International Standard available in this area, nor was it likely that if one was produced it would be accepted: filing systems are well established, and are very varied in these areas. The FTAM approach was to define a **Virtual Filestore**, not as an attempt to standardize filing systems, but as a model on which protocol exchanges were designed to operate. An implementor would identify features of real systems that the implementation would map to the virtual filestore. If the virtual filestore was not rich enough, then vendor-specific protocols would remain, for there would be features of real systems that could not be mapped, and hence could not be reached by the FTAM protocol. On the other hand, if it was too rich, it would be impossible for any implementor to implement more than a subset of FTAM unless either the real filing system was modified to fit the FTAM Virtual Filestore model, or a complete new sub-filing system was built within an existing binary file, accessed only by the FTAM protocol handler. The latter is a possible option for a dedicated LAN file server, but is otherwise unattractive as local utilities, editors, compiler run-time systems, etc. would all need to be modified to access files in the real Virtual Filestore. In fact, the attempt was made (particularly in relation to file attributes) to make FTAM as rich as possible, but to give good support for implementors that could only implement a subset. The reader should bear this in mind as the following text is read.

One of the most important parts of the FTAM Virtual Filestore model is the model of the contents of a file, illustrated in Figure 10.5. The file is based on a tree structure (and we do mean the file contents here, not some directory structure), with a root node, nodes beneath that, and so on, to any depth. Each node is potentially named (we will ask later what is the form of the name), and each node has associated with it a possibly empty **Data Unit** (DU) (absence of a Data Unit and an empty Data Unit are the same thing). Again, we will see later what a Data Unit is. The unit for access is the **FADU** (File Access Data Unit), which should not be confused with a Data Unit. There is an outer-level

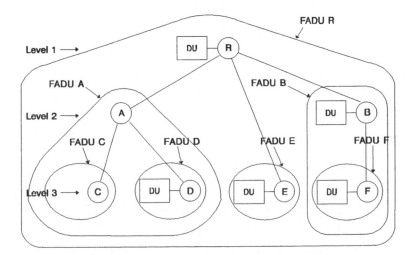

Figure 10.5 *FTAM contents.*

FADU that consists of the entire file's contents, and nested FADUs for every possible subtree of the tree structure. Thus, using FTAM, any subtree (FADU) can be read individually, deleted, replaced, or a new complete subtree added anywhere in the structure. (FTAM also allows any Data Unit to be extended.)

Let us address the node names and the Data Units. What are these? Perhaps the reader can guess. They are holes! The node name is a presentation data value from some abstract syntax. Each Data Unit is an ordered list of presentation data values from one or more abstract syntaxes. How is all this mapped to what we conventionally think of as a file, and in particular to the fairly simple sequential structures (perhaps with random access) that we are used to for lines of text files and so on? There are two important steps. The first is to restrict the general hierarchical model in useful ways to fit particular actual file structures and access requirements, and the second is to fill in the holes by specifying actual abstract syntaxes.

FTAM defines in the Standard, and identifies with ASN.1 OBJECT IDENTIFIERs, a number of **constraint sets** to restrict the hierarchical model. The simplest **constraint set** is the **unstructured constraint set**. In this case, there is a root node only, with no name, and no child nodes. Thus the only operations possible are to read or write the whole file, or to append more presentation data values to this root Data Unit. This is illustrated in Figure 10.6. If an implementation supports only the unstructured constraint set, then FTAM file access becomes particularly simple, and in particular there would be no support in the implementation for any form of random access to files. Another constraint set is the **flat constraint set**, where there is a root node with no name and no Data Unit, and child nodes all of which are required to have (non-empty) Data Units. In the simplest possible definition of an FTAM file, a constraint set is specified plus a single abstract syntax that contains the values that can be used for node names and elements of Data Units. In practice, however, this is rarely used. FTAM goes further and introduces the concept of

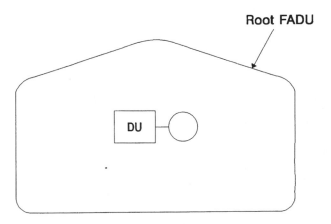

Figure 10.6 *File contents (unstructured).*

a **Document Type**, which is identified by a single object identifier, and consists of fairly stylized English text specifying precisely the constraint set in use, the abstract syntaxes used (more than one is possible), and any additional restrictions. Thus, for example, if we specify the flat constraint set, require each Data Unit to contain precisely one presentation data value of ASN.1 type Visible-String, and have node names that are numbers and serially number the nodes that are children of the root, we have straightforwardly (!) got an ASCII text file with random access to the lines of text, allowing reading of any individual line or series of lines, and insertion of a new line of text or series of lines of text at any point (Figure 10.7). On the other hand, if we specified the unstructured constraint set and the same set of presentation data values (with the single Data Unit now containing arbitrarily many presentation data values), we have the same ASCII text file, but with only the ability to read it as a whole or to append new lines of text at its end (Figure 10.8). Clearly, a file which is actually supported for random access could be made to look like the simpler form for access by some systems. This is called a **simplification** of the Document Type into another Document Type. All permitted simplifications are defined when the Document Type is defined, and FTAM supports reading (but not writing) a file using a defined simplification of its actual form. The above Document Types would be different again if the presentation data values were restricted to a single character from a character set that includes an encoding of carriage return as well as printing characters (Figure 10.9). We now have a file modelled as a simple sequence of these characters with, in the one case, random access to each character, and in the other only the ability to append new characters to the end of the file. By contrast, the full power of the hierarchical structure is needed to represent the Computer Graphics Metafile abstract syntax.

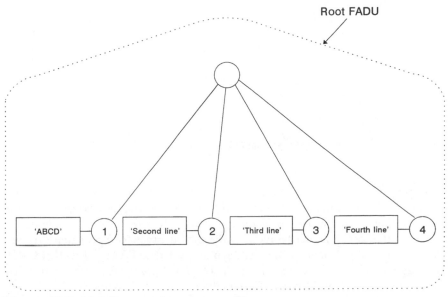

Figure 10.7 *Modelling a random access text file.*

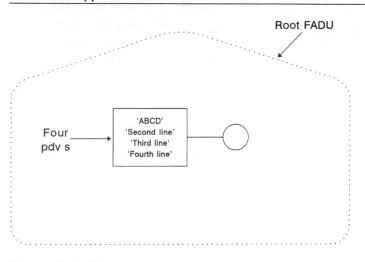

Figure 10.8 *The same text without random access.*

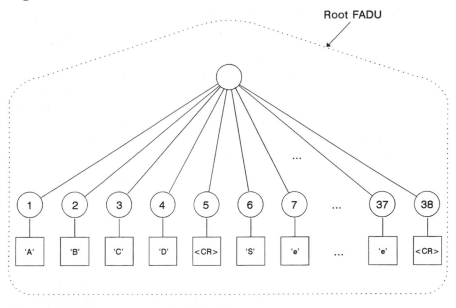

Figure 10.9 *Random access to individual characters.*

Suppose we want to transfer an FADU (the whole file or some part of it), either to read an FADU, to add a new FADU somewhere in the tree, or to replace an FADU; how do we transfer a tree structure? FTAM defines a flattening of the file for transfer. The transfer requires the establishment of a presentation context for an FTAM-defined abstract syntax called **FTAM STRUCTURE** which is the values of the ASN.1 type shown in Figure 10.10. This provides values 'up', 'down', and 'node-info' which carries a node name (the EXTER-NAL), a boolean flag specifying the presence or absence of a Data Unit at that

```
FTAM-Structure-Data-Element  ::= CHOICE
   {enter-sub-tree-data-element   [APPLICATION 1] NULL,
    exit-sub-tree-data-element    [APPLICATION 2] NULL,
    node-descriptor-data-element [APPLICATION 0] SEQUENCE
        {name          CHOICE
            {GraphicString,
             EXTERNAL      }
         arc-length  INTEGER DEFAULT 1,
         data-exists BOOLEAN DEFAULT TRUE}                        }
```

Figure 10.10 *Type for FTAM STRUCTURE abstract syntax.*

node, and an integer containing an **arc length**. (FTAM has the concept of a child node sitting at some particular level beneath its parent – the arc length – not necessarily immediately beneath it; this is the **long-arc** concept discussed later.) It is also necessary to have presentation contexts for node names, for any presentation data values appearing in Data Units, and for those needed for node names. (FTAM uses only the presentation context identifier form of the EXTERNAL.)

The transfer of an FADU consists of a simple list of presentation data values which can (unless checkpointing is needed) be carried as the list of presentation data values in the user data parameter of a single P-DATA. If checkpointing is needed, the list of presentation data values can be split between one or more P-DATA primitives, and P-SYNC-MINORs inserted. The first presentation data value in the list is 'down' to enter the FADU, then a value of 'node-info', giving the node name of the root node, its arc length from its parent (zero in this case) and flagging the presence or absence of a Data Unit at the root node. If a Data Unit is present, the presentation data values in that Data Unit are next in the list. Then there is a 'down', transmission in a similar way of the FADU of the child (recursive application of this description), then an 'up', then another 'down' to the next child, or an 'up' if no more children, to complete the transfer of the FADU. Thus we see that the end of the list of presentation data values in the Data Unit is determined by the presence of an 'up' or a 'down' from the FTAM abstract syntax. It can, however, happen that a presentation data value in the file may be a value from the FTAM-defined abstract syntax used for 'up', 'down', etc. This could, for example, occur if the file was a log file that had been logging the values transferred in an FTAM transfer. To prevent any danger of confusion of data contents with a real 'up', 'down', etc., a presentation data value being transferred is only interpreted as an 'up', 'down', etc. for this transfer if the presentation context is the first defined presentation context for the FTAM-STRUCTURE abstract syntax, preventing any ambiguity. Thus it can be seen that FTAM fully embraces the Presentation Layer concepts of abstract and transfer syntax, and indeed uses them heavily to provide transparent transfer of file contents.

There is only one other major issue to discuss in relation to FTAM, and that is the question of **file attributes**. Many operating systems keep additional information (typically notionally part of some directory entry) with a file. As well as the file name, there is often the size of the file, the date (and time) it was created, perhaps (for a multi-user system) the identity of the creator, and an access control list. Operating systems differ very much in the nature of the file attributes they support, and it is not easy to see what should be supported by the FTAM standards. The reader will recall a similar problem for the header fields of an Interpersonal Message in X.400. In the first version a limited set of headers were hard-wired into the protocol: later, ASN.1 data type holes were added to allow easy addition of new headers. FTAM in fact has not (as of 1995) progressed beyond the hard-wired stage for file attributes. There is a set provided that is believed to be sufficient for most systems, with significant support for implementations to handle only a subset. They can agree, via nego-tiation on F-INITIALIZE, that 'We are not going to talk about values of this group of attributes', and a responder, when asked for the value of an attri-bute in a group that they have agreed to talk about, can say 'Sorry, no value available'.

Finally, we will mention briefly some of the extensions to FTAM that occurred in the early 1990s. We discuss below directory structure, service enhancement, overlapped access, and security.

The initial FTAM Standard contained no text related to the directory struc-ture of the Virtual Filestore. This was deliberate in order to progress the Stand-ard quickly (it still took close to ten years!). An addendum in the early 1990s added support for directory structure, and in the process changed the notation for file. We now talk not about files, but about **file objects**! We also have **direc-tory objects** and **reference objects**. The structure will be fairly familiar: direc-tory objects contain file objects, other directory objects, or reference objects. Reference objects point to directory or file objects anywhere in the Virtual File-store. All objects have most of the attributes previously associated with files, in particular date created, creating user, and access control lists. One of the interest-ing side-effects is that the ability to access a file can depend on the route through the directory structure that is taken (using reference objects) to reach the file.

In the original FTAM Standard, to transfer a file it was necessary to issue a number of primitives to select it, open it, position at the desired FADU, transfer the data, end the transfer, close the file, deselect the file. (This does not imply a lot of round trips: some of these primitives are unconfirmed, and some of the resulting messages can be carried in the same P-DATA, but the service descrip-tion looks complicated, and can be messy for any Standard using FTAM to spe-cify.) Moreover, where implementors take service primitives as a model for implementation interfaces (which they shouldn't, but ...) this can make FTAM appear very complex. The **service enhancement** addendum made no change to bits on the line, but merely added two additional service primitive interactions that invoked everything necessary to read and write a single file: F-GET and F-PUT.

The **overlapped access** addendum is particularly interesting, in that the pri-mary specification is written in the LOTOS FDT language (see Chapter 3), with the English language text being mainly descriptive. While FTAM in prin-ciple uses an association in a two-way simultaneous manner, in practice a lot of the time it is a one-way flow, particularly when a file is being transferred. This addendum enables requests for any FTAM operation, possibly involving the reading and the writing of data, to be stacked up, with each request processed only when that particular direction of flow becomes free and permits the request to be satisfied. The reader will recognize the complexity of the resulting State Table, and hence the reason for using an FDT to specify this annexe. The service enhancement providing F-GET and F-PUT helps in visualizing what is going on. A system accessing a file server using FTAM can stack up a number of F-GET requests and a number of F-PUT requests, and they will be serviced in turn, ensuring a continuous flow of data in both directions simultaneously. The complications of this arise mainly from the problems of checkpointing and recovery after crashes! Opinions differ on the importance of driving an application association in a two-way manner. It would clearly be possible in theory to set up two separate session connections multiplexed onto a single transport connection (classes 2, 3 or 4), and to use one for F-GET requests and one for F-PUT requests, thus achieving two-way flow over the actual medium, but keeping FTAM simple. But you could not do that over classes 0 or 1! Readers must form their own views.

We have not discussed the FTAM Access Control List in detail, but it is a very rich structure. It allows access controls to be based on the location (application-entity-title, authenticated by the addendum to ACSE) from which the access is being requested, the identity of the accessing user (based on a password carried in F-INITIALIZE), or on a set of eight passwords, one each for the different sorts of actions that might be attempted (reading the file, deleting the file, changing attributes, and so on). The granularity of control is also at the level of these eight possible actions, so permission to read attributes can be given without giving any other access to the file. There are a number of flaws: first, apart from the ACSE authentication of the AE-title, the authentication is all by a simple password, vulnerable to a line monitor, not an encrypted exchange; second, there is no ability to give blanket access permissions, then to exclude particular users, and finally, despite the eight actions that can be separately controlled, it was not possible to separately control the ability to change the access control attribute from the ability to change other attributes. In the late 1980s, a short study showed that these flaws, particularly the last two, would prevent a file-access implementation based on FTAM from getting any sort of security classification under a very common test based on something colloquially called the DoD Orange Book (more formally 'Department of Defense Trusted Computer System Evaluation Criteria'). This resulted in a New Work Item to look more closely at the security features of FTAM, and resulted in the early 1990s in a more substantial report on what was needed, what could be regarded as FTAM-specific, and what was better progressed in a way which would be applicable to all applications. The final outcome of this work was not clear by 1995.

10.5 Virtual Terminals (VT)

The work to produce standards supporting terminal access to remote computers was again one of the earliest OSI standards to be commenced, and started in the days of dumb terminals. The work made little progress for several years, as a result of differing views of an appropriate model of terminal communication.

The first model stems from the CCITT X.3, X.28 and X.29 specifications (often called **triple-X**), originally produced at about the same time as X.25, and supporting dumb terminal access over X.25 to remote machines as if they had been directly connected. In its day it was a very important set of standards, providing the bulk of early X.25 use. The triple-X protocols are not OSI protocols: X.29 sits directly on top of X.25, and uses the **Q-bit** feature of X.25 which is absent from the Network Service definition. (The Q-bit is a one-bit field present in every X.25 data message, but whose use is not defined in X.25: rather, it is left for the application using X.25 to specify its use — in the case discussed here, X.29.) The triple-X model is shown in Figure 10.11. Here we have an X.25 connection between a host and a **PAD** (Packet Assembler Disassembler), used in accordance with X.29. The PAD has an asynchronous line connection to a dumb terminal (often dial-up over a modem), and receives characters from the keyboard typed by the human hand, and sends characters to the screen, seen by the human eyeball shown in the figure. The PAD's main function is to stack up characters received from the keyboard until it is appropriate to forward the packet across the network (usually as the result of the arrival of a carriage return character, but it could be time-out or various other rules), and to receive packets across the network and send them as a series of characters to the screen. This gives rise to its name. A number of parameters (specified in X.3) control the operation of the PAD. In particular the **echo** parameter determines whether the PAD also copies all characters received from the keyboard back to the screen. Other parameters relate to forwarding conditions and to the insertion of carriage returns in output to provide line-folding of long lines (very necessary on the oldest dumb terminals called **teletypes**). The X.29

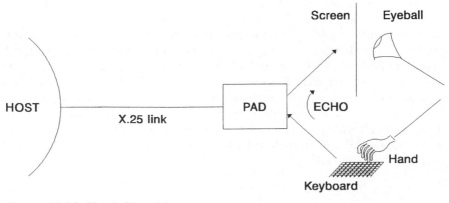

Figure 10.11 *Triple-X model.*

protocol uses the Q-bit to identify an X.25 message either as material for the screen or from the keyboard, or as messages allowing the host to read and write the X.3 parameters in the PAD. The X.28 Recommendation was essentially a user interface specifying how a user could read and write the X.3 parameters in the PAD from the terminal. Anybody accessing a remote database over an X.25 network in the 1980s and early 1990s is likely to have been using triple-X. This, then, was one possible model on which to build the Virtual Terminal protocol. Note that in this model there is a two-way simultaneous use of X.25, one direction taking keyboard data, the other data going to the screen.

The second model proposed was rather more abstract (Figure 10.12). In this model, the terminal end and host end are simply two pieces of intelligence, and are indeed symmetric. In the middle of the communications line there is a glass screen, and each piece of intelligence has both a paintbrush that can be used to paint the screen and an eyeball that can be used to view it. The main thing to worry about is that both sides should not be allowed to paint the same part of the screen at the same time, so we need some sort of token control. The simplest approach would be to control the Session Layer token (TWA use of session), at the level of the whole use to provide the control.

How can these rather different models be combined/reconciled? Suppose we move the PAD into the centre of the communications line, and recognize that it provides essentially two independent one-way flows, with the 'echo' capability cross-connecting them. We will worry about other parameters later, but very many of the X.3 parameters are concerned with line-folding and similar matters that are irrelevant once we accept intelligence at the terminal end, rather than a dumb terminal. We can redraw the PAD model as shown in Figure 10.13. Now we have two glass screens in the middle of the communication line, and

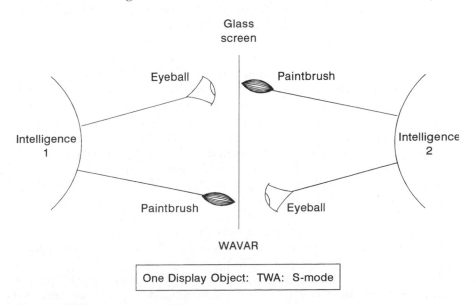

Figure 10.12 *Symmetric model.*

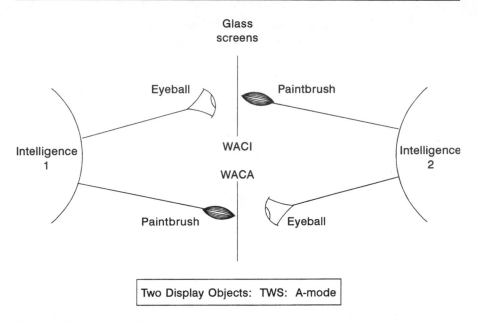

Figure 10.13 *Revised PAD model.*

one end is restricted to painting on one (and viewing the other), while the other end does the opposite. Apart from the echo path, this is a simple two-way flow. Of course, the Standard does not talk about glass screens, it talks about **Display Objects**. These two models now look a lot more similar to each other than was the case when we used the original PAD model, and perhaps we can now reconcile them in a single Standard. Remember the adage 'If you can't agree, make it optional ...'. And so we get, in the VT Standards, two **modes** of operation, either or both of which can be implemented by implementors, and which form effectively two non-interworking VT Standards packaged in the same text. In **A-mode** (A for asynchronous), we have TWS operation of session, two Display Objects, and what it calls an **Echo Object** that can be written to by either end to determine whether echoing takes place or not. The access to the two display objects does not vary – one is writable by the initiator of the as-sociation, one by the acceptor of the association. We have WACI/WACA (pro-nounced 'wacky wacka', a lovely phrase!) access control (Write Access Controlled by Initiator/Write Access Controlled by Acceptor). In **S-mode** (S for synchronous), we have TWA operation of session, a single Display Object, and no Echo Object. Access control is WAVAR (pronounced 'wave-ah') (Write Access Variable), and is controlled by the positioning of the session token. (The reader may find it easier to remember all this if it is noted that the A-mode is TWS and the S-mode is TWA!)

Readers who have used (dumb) terminals connected to a host, will be aware of two styles of operation: one major computer manufacturer locks the keyboard when the system has control of the screen, and unlocks it only when you are able to type. This is essentially S-mode. Another major computer manufacturer leaves the keyboard unlocked at all times, and what is typed gets mixed up with any output currently going to the screen in a fairly random way. This is A-mode. Interestingly, early in the 1990s there seemed to be more implementation interest in A-mode than in S-mode.

So much for the model. But what exactly was the nature of a Display Object (the glass screen)? It was a simple character box device, with foreground and background colours, with one, two or three dimensions of cells containing characters. The precise number of dimensions and size, the number of foreground and background colours (and the actual colours), the number of levels of emphasis (and whether these were flashing or double intensity) were all matters that were negotiated between the two ends. Most of the complexity of the initial VT Standards was in the negotiation of the mode, parameters of the display object(s), and the existence of control objects (as well as Echo, there can be control objects called 'function key n', or 'on/off', or 'beep' – in other words, facilities for out-of-band signalling). In order to ease this negotiation task (and to give it some chance of succeeding!), the VT Standards introduce the concept of **Terminal Profiles** (collections of these parameters) which are identified (you must have guessed!) by an ASN.1 object identifier. In fact, a machine-readable language has been defined to specify terminal profiles, and a glint in the eye of the VT group is that implementations could be made quite flexible by looking up (using the X.500 Directory service) the meaning of any Terminal Profile object identifier value that they were offered, without having to have it hard-wired into the implementation.

Let us finish this brief overview with a short scenario. An intelligent terminal connects to a host. There is negotiation of the terminal profile to be used (establishment of the **Virtual Terminal Environment** (VTE)), and the screen comes to life as a very basic black and white screen for the login dialogue. Once logged in, a profile associated with the user name in the host is used to negotiate a new (scrolling) terminal environment with a single foreground and a single background colour, but no longer black and white, forming a new VTE. The user then invokes a graphics package, and suddenly the screen comes to life in many colours – a new VTE has been negotiated. When the use of the graphics package is completed, that VTE is destroyed, and the scrolling VTE of the command processor is reinstated, with the screen in the state it was left in when the graphics package was entered. A new package can now be entered, and another VTE negotiated. Notice finally that if an application wants a very large screen, it is a local matter for an intelligent terminal end to provide local controls to window onto that: it is not necessary to refuse a VTE if the screen the application desires is larger than the actual physical screen on the terminal.

This brings in the whole question of windows, and indeed of raster and geometric graphics rather than simply character cells. In the early 1980s, the work described above was called **Basic Class Virtual Terminals**, and more advanced support was planned. Such work was never progressed, and VT remains a character-box-only protocol. As a character box protocol, however, a number of support features have been added as addenda that make it quite powerful for form-filling applications. In particular, a forms (screen) design (with protected fields and stated forwarding conditions when certain keys are pressed) can be invoked at the terminal end, either by sending it down the line or by sending an ASN.1 object identifier to invoke one already known at the terminal end. Thus all the work of handling the completion of the form is exported to the terminal end, with only the characters eventually filling the form being sent up the line to the application. This can enable an application to handle a large number of terminals for this sort of application, compared with, for example, the use of X-windows for the same purpose.

In the late 1980s, work on **Terminal Management** was introduced to begin to address the question of multiple windows, each potentially associated with a different server. This work never progressed, was overtaken in the early 1990s by work intended to lead to the standardization of X-windows over the OSI stack, and was subjected in 1992 to a formal review process designed to abandon the Terminal Management work. Thus in the early 1990s, it looked as if the choice for terminal handling in OSI would for some time remain either the efficient character-box-oriented VT Standard, or the X-windows over the OSI stack Standard for more general activity.

The VT Standard, as might be expected from the date the work was started (late 1970s), is a monolithic Standard, making no use of ROSE or of RTSE. (RTSE is probably not relevant to VT, and ROSE would probably have introduced too many overheads on the individual character transfers that tend to be characteristic of advanced terminal handling, so this is probably a good thing!) In contrast to FTAM, it does not 'steal' A-ASSOCIATE, but rather assumes that an association with the right properties has been established for its use. Thus it fits a little more easily into the XALS structure. VT makes use of many session services, including major synchronization, resynchronization, expedited data and orderly release.

11
What has not been covered

OSI is now a very large subject, and inevitably in any text of reasonable length there is a large amount left uncovered. This text has aimed to cover the basic work and principles, together with more recent work that affects principles, or infrastructure facilities that affect what is available to the application designer. Its treatment of specific applications has, of necessity, been somewhat sketchy. The reader who has persevered this far should be well placed to understand discussions of specific standards, or to read the ISO or ITU-T texts themselves.

It only remains in this last brief chapter to at least provide some pointers to other work that has not been discussed at all or only very briefly in the earlier text.

11.1   Functional Profiles

The problem of options remaining in base standards was originally addressed by implementors groups in the USA, Europe and the Pacific Basin, and latterly by regional standards bodies in these regions. These bodies produce **Functional Profiles** that are intended to specify merely the selection of options and the combination of base standards to support specific applications or specific environments. They now feed into further ISO activity involved with **International Standardized Profiles** (ISPs), which is a new form of ISO publication that is neither an International Standard nor a Technical Report. Thus there are now beginning to emerge international specifications that can be referenced in procurement and provide 'standards' with few options (but often lacking a lot of the functionality of the base standards). The eventual importance of the ISP work is unclear. We may see base Standard features not included in ISPs never implemented, and effectively lost, or we may see base standards fully implemented, in which case ISPs will be irrelevant. It is at least arguable that ISPs are important in the short term of partial implementation to ensure interworking, but that they will become increasingly less important as vendors implement the complete contents of standards.

11.2   Conformance testing

Another major area of work (closely linked to formal description techniques, but separate from it) is that of conformance testing. Concern has always been present about the problem inherent in OSI of potential non-interworking of systems from different vendors, all of which claim conformance to the same Standard. This is not just an option question, it also relates to errors in interpreting the standards or in implementation. In order to try to address these problems, standards specifying a series of tests to be carried out (in themselves a further protocol, exercising all the options – and some error cases – of the base Standard) have been produced. A lot of work has also been done on the architecture of testing conformance to some layer Standard, such as the Session Layer. The reader will remember that conformance to OSI relates mainly to the bits on the line. Interfaces in implementations are not specified, nor is there any requirement for an interface of any sort corresponding to a layer service boundary. Moreover, the mapping of top-level service primitives, such as those of FTAM, onto real events in real systems is a matter for implementation design, not something laid down by standards. Despite these problems, a lot of progress has been made on conformance testing, with a number of centres in all parts of the world providing OSI conformance testing services.

11.3   Security

We have touched on security issues from time to time throughout this text. In the early days of OSI there was little attention to security. One of the interesting snippets in the early OSI documents lodged in the UK Archives of the History of Computing was a proposal in 1978 that a series of meetings should take place to discuss security issues in OSI; this proposal was blocked by the BSI Secretariat on the grounds that 'It is not clear what standard it will produce.' In fact security issues were not seriously addressed in a general way in OSI until the late 1980s (about ten years later), with the first reference model and most early standards paying little attention to security issues. Indeed, there were people that argued that 'security' (usually implying some degree of closed operation) and 'Open' Systems Interconnection were a logical contradiction of terms. The turning point came with the publication in 1989 of Part 2 of the Basic Reference Model: Security Architecture, and with the almost simultaneous maturing of the 1988 X.400 and X.500 specifications with significant security-related features.

Work in the late 1980s and early 1990s has been guided by the rather complex approach shown in Figure 11.1. This recognizes the two main strands of standards work, Open Systems Interconnection on the left, and Open Distributed Processing on the right. Central to the approach is a series of 'Framework' documents that would identify the options and techniques for providing certain security features, an Upper and Lower Layers security architecture document to supplement Part 3 of the Basic Reference Model, and a variety of models specific to particular application areas, leading finally to actual security features in OSI Service and Protocol Standards. While this outline has not been completely adhered to, most of the documents shown in the Figure were at some stage of draft in 1995, although few could be said to be really mature.

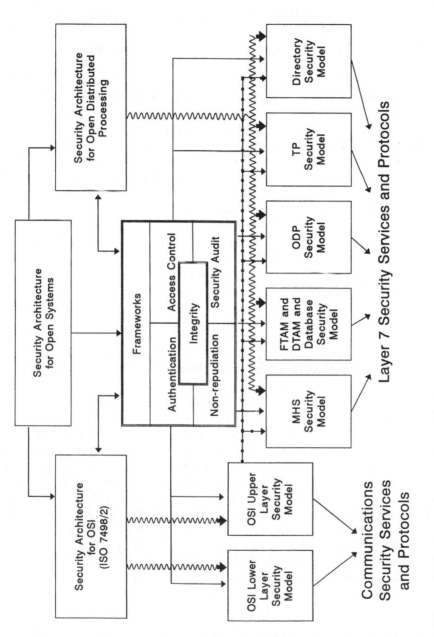

Figure 11.1 *Approach to security specification.*

Specific security features in FTAM and X.400 and X.500 have already been briefly discussed, but the reader should also be aware of four other pieces of ongoing work in the early 1990s whose detailed treatment is beyond this text.

- In the lower layers, work was maturing rapidly for major security additions to services and protocols at the transport/network boundary.
- Work was in progress in the Application Layer on specifying interfaces to locally provided security features that could then be referenced in protocol standards.
- Work was in progress defining a **Security ASE** that would perform a number of security-related functions (particularly authentication and initialization for secure exchanges) that were not application-specific.
- A **Generic Transfer Syntax** for security had been drafted. This recognized that secure transfer syntaxes could be developed by applying a series of transformations to an abstract value, starting with the application of a normal encoding rule (such as BER), and followed by encryption or signature transformations. The generic transfer syntax effectively applied the transformations, and carried in the head of the first encoding an ASN.1 data structure identifying the transformations (and any applicable parameters) that had been applied.

11.4   Changes resulting from high bandwidth requirements

Developments for high-bandwidth networks and applications have already been touched on at the end of the Network Layer discussions. If followed through appropriately, these could give rise to networking where round-trip times, buffers in the network, and flow control (and hence the need for expedited data and perhaps for resynchronization) become an irrelevance, with consequent knock-on effects on the Session Layer. By 1995, however, the only specific proposal that had been made was for a 'graceful termination' feature to be added to the OSI Transport Layer, bringing it nearer to TCP in functionality, and perhaps making S-RELEASE unnecessary (or at least, provided without Session Layer protocol). At the time of writing this text, it is only possible to say that the outcomes of this new work could be fundamental and far-reaching, but could also prove to be a damp squib with little real impact. It is hard to tell.

11.5   Other application standards

There are a number of other standards that are loosely related to OSI. Here we merely list them (and there will be others that we have missed – there is no list of what is an OSI Standard).

- Office Document Architecture (ODA) and Standard Generalized Markup Language (SGML) are both standards which are intended to assist in the production, maintenance and transfer of highly structured documents. ODA is ASN.1-based, and can be expected to extend to multi-media documents, but the extent to which it can replace or encompass a real multi-media authoring system is very unclear. SGML is more text-based on the surface, but does have the capability to include other material. Major implementations supporting local production and editing of ODA documents, with transfer to other systems using ODIF (ODA Interchange Format), are expected to become commonplace in the late 1990s.

- Manufacturing Message Specification was a standard originally produced by General Motors as the main application standard in their MAP (Manufacturing Automation Protocol). The protocol in MAP 1 was hand-crafted, but it was later rewritten using ASN.1 and eventually standardized by ISO.

- CASE (Computer Aided Software Engineering) Data Interchange Format (CDIF) was a further application-specific standard developed in the early 1990s. The group developing it were largely unaware of ASN.1, and it took its own model and approach to syntax definition and the equivalent of the ASN.1 object identifier. The importance of this work will only become clear in the late 1990s.

- Job Transfer and Manipulation (JTM) became an International Standard in the late 1980s. It was one of the initial three (VT, FTAM and JTM) begun in the late 1970s. It has a number of interesting features, but suffers from being monolithic (no use of ROSE or RTSE), large, and complex to implement. The scope implied by the title, submission of background jobs to a number cruncher queue and (much) later distribution of output, while not the only thing it can be used for, has largely become a requirement of the past. There have been no major implementations of the Standard, and it is largely seen in the early 1990s as an irrelevance.

- Open Distributed Processing has been mentioned very briefly earlier in this text. While not really an application standard, its impact is generally expected to be mainly in the application area. In the early 1990s the ODP Reference Model was beginning to mature, but with the exception of the trader concept discussed in the X.500 section, it was still unclear precisely what sort of standards would emerge and what its impact would be. Watch this space!

11.6   Postscript

It is hoped that the reader has at least enjoyed this text, and now has an improved perception of what OSI is about. This book has attempted to present the more interesting and/or difficult concepts and approaches introduced by OSI, and to answer wherever possible and appropriate the 'Why?' questions.

OSI standardization is not a static subject. It is highly dynamic, with new proposals arising all the time, and with areas hitherto considered stable and 'finished' (such as the Transport Protocol, and maybe even the most basic concept of seven layers) suddenly becoming highly unstable through the acceptance of New Work Item proposals. It should also be remembered that all ISO standards are required to be formally reviewed and modified, withdrawn, or reaffirmed every five years. Thus any knowledge of OSI inevitably becomes dated and requires frequent updating, but it is hoped and expected that the reader will continue to benefit from the understandings that have been gained from this text, and will not find it difficult to read and discuss any primary OSI material that might be encountered in the future, or even to contribute to the ongoing OSI standardization process. If so, this book will have served its purpose.

Appendix Glossary

ACK	acknowledge
ACSE	Association Control Service Element
AE	Application Entity
AFNOR	Association Française de Normalisation
ALS	Application Layer Structure
AMAE	Application Management Application Entity
ANSI	American National Standards Institute
ASCII	American Standard Code for Information Interchange
ASE	Application Service Element
ASN.1	Abstract Syntax Notation One
ASO	Application Service Object
ATM	Asynchronous Transfer Mode
BER	Basic Encoding Rules
B-ISDN	Broadband Integrated Services Digital Network
BNF	Backus-Naur Form
BSI	British Standards Institute
BT	British Telecom
CASE	Common Application Service Element; Computer Aided Software Engineering
CCIR	International Radio Consultative Committee
CCITT	International Telegraph and Telephone Consultative Committee
CCR	Commitment, Concurrency and Recovery
CD	Committee Draft
CDIF	CASE (Computer Aided Software Engineering). Data Interchange Format
CF	Control Function
CLIP	Connectionless Internet Protocol
CLNP	Connectionless-mode Network Protocol
CMIS/CMIP	Common Management Information Service and Protocol
CMISE	Common Management Information Service Element
CMOT	CMIS over TCP/IP
CPU	Central Processing Unit
CRC	Cyclic Redundancy Check
DARPA	Department of Defense Advanced Research Projects Agency
DCE	Data Circuit Equipment
DCS	defined context set
DFR	Document Filing and Retrieval

DIN	Deutsches Institut für Normung
DIS	Draft International Standard
DLE	data link escape
DoD	Department of Defense
DP	Draft Proposal
DTAM	Document Transfer, Access and Management
DTE	Data Terminating Equipment
DTP	Distributed Transaction Processing
DU	Data Unit
EBCDIC	Extended Binary Coded Decimal Interchange Code
ECMA	European Computer Manufacturers Association
EDI	Electronic Data Interchange
EDIFACT	Electronic Data Interchange for Finance, Administration, Commerce and Transport
ETC	end of text
FADU	File Access Data Unit
FDT	Formal Description Technique
FTAM	File Transfer, Access and Management
GDMO	Generic Definition of Managed Objects
GOSIP	Government OSI Profile
HDLC	High Level Data Link Control
HTML	Hyper-Text Markup Language
ICD	International Code Designator
IDN	Interface Definition Notation
IEC	International Electrotechnical Commission
IONL	Internal Organization of the Network Layer
IP	Internet Protocol
IPM	Interpersonal Message
IPMS	Interpersonal Messaging System
IS	International Standard
ISDN	Integrated Services Digital Network
ISP	International Standardized Profile
ITU	International Telecommunications Union
ITU-T	Telecommunications Standardization Sector of the ITU
JISC	Japanese Industrial Standards Committee
JTC1	Joint Technical Committee 1
JTM	Job Transfer and Manipulation
LAN	Local Area Network
LOTOS	Language of Temporal Ordering Specification
LWER	Lightweight Encoding Rules
MAC	Medium Access Control
MACF	Multiple Association Control Function
MAP	Manufacturing Automation Protocol
MHS	Message Handling System
MIB	Management Information Base
MTA	Message Transfer Agent

NFS	network file server
NNI	Nederands Normalisatie-Institut
NSAP	Network Service Access Point
NWI	New Work Item
ODA	Office Document Architecture
ODIF	ODA Interchange Format
ODP	Open Distributed Processing
OSI	Open Systems Interconnection
PAD	Packet Assembler Disassembler
PC	Personal Computer
PDAM	Proposed Draft Amendment
PDU	Protocol Data Unit
pdv	presentation data value
PER	Packed Encoding Rules
PICS	Protocol Implementation Conformance Statement
PSAP	Presentation Service Access Point
PTT	Postal, telephone and telegraph administration
QOS	Quality of Service
RDA	Remote Database Access
RFC	Request for Comment
ROSE	Remote Operations Service Element
RPC	Remote Procedure Call
RPDA	Registered Private Operating Authorities
RTSE	Reliable Transfer Service Element
SACF	Single Association Control Function
SAO	Single Association Object
SASE	Specific Application Service Element
SC	Sub-Committee
SDH	Synchronous Digital Hierarchy
SDL	System Description Language
SGML	Standard Generalized Markup Language
SNMP	Simple Network Management Protocol
SOH	start of header
SQL	Structured Query Language
SSAP	Session Service Access Point
STX	start of text
TC	Technical Committee
TCP	Transmission Control Protocol
TDI	Trade Data Interchange
TLV	Type, Length, Value
TP	Transaction Processing
TSAP	Transport Service Access Point
TWA	two-way alternate
TWS	two-way simultaneous
UDP	User Datagram Protocol
UA	User Agent

UN	United Nations
VT	Virtual Terminals
VTE	Virtual Terminal Environment
WACA	Write Access Controlled by Acceptor
WACI	Write Access Controlled by Initiator
WAIS	Wide Area Information Service
WAVAR	Write Access Variable
XNS	Xerox Network Services

Index